TILL JESUS COMES

TILL JESUS COMES

*Origins of Christian
Apocalyptic Expectation*

CHARLES L. HOLMAN

HENDRICKSON
PUBLISHERS

© 1996 by Hendrickson Publishers, Inc.
P. O. Box 3473
Peabody, Massachusetts 01961–3473
All rights reserved
Printed in the United States of America

ISBN 0–943575–74–5

First Printing — October 1996

Library of Congress Cataloging-in-Publication Data

Holman, Charles L.
    Till Jesus comes: origins of Christian apocalyptic expectation   /
Charles L. Holman
    Includes bibliographical references and index.
    ISBN 0–943575–74–5 (pbk.)
        1. Apocalyptic literature.   2. Eschatology—Biblical teaching.
3. Second Advent—Biblical teaching.   I. Title
BS646.H65   1996
236′.09′015—dc20   96–10722
                                                                                    CIP

Affectionately dedicated to my beloved wife Rose

TABLE OF CONTENTS

Part Three:
Expectation in New Testament
Apocalyptic Writings

Part Four:
Conclusion and Challenge for Today

PREFACE

THIS VOLUME IS AT ONCE A REDUCTION AND AN EXPANSION of my Ph.D. thesis, which was submitted to the University of Nottingham, England, in 1982 under the supervision of my mentor, James D. G. Dunn. The dissertation was entitled "Eschatological Delay in Jewish and Early Christian Apocalyptic Literature."

In the interest of attracting a broader readership than only those who are interested in Ph.D. theses, I have expanded the theme to focus on eschatological expectation more generally. The Introduction and Part One are for the most part entirely new. Hermeneutical implications and a challenge for Christian praxis in Part Four are likewise new. On the other hand, I have greatly reduced discussion in Parts Two and Three, but hopefully have retained enough data pertaining to my thesis to merit serious consideration of my conclusions. Also, I have sought to interact with works published since my thesis was completed.

I am aware that my subject is a difficult one, with a wide variety of opinion represented by biblical scholars. Since it is impossible to engage in exegesis without betraying one's presuppositions, I readily confess that my theological orientation is what is commonly known as "Evangelical." At the same time, I have made an effort to let textual evidence in critical matters direct my conclusions, rather than simply subscribing to a particular party line.

As will be evident from Part Four, my objective is to relate findings concerning end time expectation to the life of the church today. According to those who gather such data, interest in the "end times," the "second coming" of Christ, etc. has accelerated toward the end of this century. Of particular note is Hal Lindsay's *The Late Great Planet Earth,* first published in 1970, which has now sold well into the millions. Further evidence of the popular interest in eschatology is given in my Introduction. My purpose is to look carefully at the theological foundations of biblical expectation and to discuss its relevance for today.

This is a subject that has attracted my interest for a great many years. I am indebted to Ralph P. Martin for his encouragement in an early essay I did at Fuller Theological Seminary: "The Idea of an Imminent Parousia in the Synoptic Gospels," subsequently published in *Studia Biblica et Theologica* 3 (1973). I am indeed indebted to Professor Dunn for successfully directing my thesis project. I am very grateful for the patience and wise guidance rendered by him as both mentor and friend during my days in the "cloister" of the library at the University of Nottingham. I owe thanks to the library staff for the friendly cooperation I received there.

It is impossible for me to say how much I owe my wife Rose for her interest and support in so many ways from the earliest days of doctoral study to this present work. It is to her I affectionately dedicate this book.

I wish also to acknowledge the assistance I have received from dear friends and colleagues here at Regent University. John Rea (now retired) read an early draft of chapters one and two. J. Rodman Williams has read practically the entire draft. John Goldingay of St. John's College in Nottingham read an early version of chapters one and two and wisely redirected me in a significant way. (My own expertise is more in New Testament than Old Testament.) I very much appreciate the efforts of these my colleagues. Any weaknesses in the monograph are of course my sole responsibility.

My thanks also to Mary McFadden, my secretary, and to Chris Malamisuro, Tom Tree, and Doug Veenstra, who all assisted in various phases in production of the manuscript.

If this volume will inspire serious minded students of the Bible to think further of the relevance of a biblical hope for our day, I shall be sufficiently rewarded.

ABBREVIATIONS OF BIBLICAL BOOKS AND RELATED TEXTS

Old Testament

Gen	Genesis
Exod	Exodus
Lev	Leviticus
Num	Numbers
Deut	Deuteronomy
Josh	Joshua
Judg	Judges
1 Sam	1 Samuel
2 Sam	2 Samuel
1 Kgs	1 Kings
2 Kgs	2 Kings
1 Chron	1 Chronicles
2 Chron	2 Chronicles
Neh	Nehemiah
Ps(s)	Psalm(s)
Isa	Isaiah
Jer	Jeremiah
Ezek	Ezekiel
Dan	Daniel
Hos	Hosea
Obad	Obadiah
Mic	Micah
Hab	Habakkuk
Zeph	Zephaniah
Hag	Haggai
Zech	Zechariah
Mal	Malachi

New Testament

Matt	Matthew
Rom	Romans
1–2 Cor	1–2 Corinthians
Gal	Galatians
Eph	Ephesians
Phil	Philippians
Col	Colossians
1–2 Thess	1–2 Thessalonians
Phlm	Philemon
1–2 Pet	1–2 Peter
Rev	Revelation

Apocrypha, Pseudepigrapha, Qumran Texts, Talmudic Material, and Early Patristic Writings

Apoc. Ab.	*Apocalypse of Abraham*
Apoc. Mos.	*Apocalypse of Moses*
As. Mos.	*Assumption of Moses*
Bar	Baruch
2 Bar.	*Syriac Baruch*
CD	*Damascus Document*
Did.	*Didache* (Teaching of the Apostles)
1 Enoch	*Ethiopic Enoch* (unless Greek text is indicated)
Jub.	*Jubilees*
1 Macc	1 Maccabees
2 Macc	2 Maccabees
Mart. Isa.	*Martyrdom of Isaiah*
Pss. Sol.	*Psalms of Solomon*
Q	Qumran (Number preceding Q indicates which cave)
4QEng	Qumran Greek portion of *1 Enoch*
1QH	*Hodayot (Thanksgiving Hymns)*
1QM	*War Scroll (Milhamah)*
1QpHab	*Pesher on Habakkuk*
1QS	*Manual of Discipline*
1QSa	Appendix A to 1QS
Sanh.	*Sanhedrin* (tractate of Mishnah and Talmud)
Sib. Or.	*Sibylline Oracles*
T. Dan	*Testament of Dan*
T. Iss.	*Testament of Issachar*
T. Jud.	*Testament of Judah*
T. Levi	*Testament of Levi*
T. Mos.	*Testament of Moses*
T. Naph.	*Testament of Naphtali*

T. 12 Patr.	*Testaments of the Twelve Patriarchs*
T. Zeb.	*Testament of Zebulun*
Tob	Tobit

Eusebius

Hist. eccl.	*Ecclesiastical History*

Josephus

Ag. Ap.	*Against Apion*
Ant.	*Antiquities of the Jews*
Life	*The Life*
J.W.	*The Jewish War*

Other Abbreviations

A.D.	Anno Domini
B.C.	Before Christ
ch(s).	chapter(s)
esp.	especially
KJV	King James Version
ln.	line
LXX	Septuagint
MSS	manuscripts
MT	Masoretic (Hebrew) Text
n.	note
NASB	New American Standard Bible
NIV	New International Version
NRSV	New Revised Standard Version
NT	New Testament
OT	Old Testament
Pt.	Part
RSV	Revised Standard Version
v(v).	verse(s)
vol.	volume

SHORT TITLES

Aalders, *Genesis*
> Aalders, G. Ch. *Genesis*. Translated by W. Heynen. 2 vols. BSC. Grand Rapids: Zondervan, 1981.

AB
> Anchor Bible

ABD
> *The Anchor Bible Dictionary*. 6 vols. Edited by D. N. Freedman, et al. New York: Doubleday, 1992.

ABRL
> The Anchor Bible Reference Library

Albrektson, *History*
> Albrektson, B. *History and the Gods: An Essay on the Idea of Historical Events as Divine Manifestations in the Ancient Near East and in Israel*. CBOTS 1. Lund: C.W.K. Gleerup, 1967.

Albright, "Oracles"
> Albright, W. F. "The Oracles of Balaam." *JBL* 63 (1944) 207–33.

Allen, *Joel*
> Allen, L. C. *The Books of Joel, Obadiah, Jonah and Micah*. NICOT. Grand Rapids: Eerdmans, 1976.

AMWNE
> *Apocalypticism in the Mediterranean World and the Near East*. Proceedings of the International Colloquium on Apocalypticism, Uppsala, August 12–17, 1979. Ed. D. Hellholm. 2d ed. Tübingen, Mohr, 1989.

AnBib
> Analecta Biblica

Aune, *Literary Environment*
> Aune, D. E. *The New Testament in Its Literary Environment*. Philadelphia: Westminster, 1987.

AOT
> *The Apocryphal Old Testament*. Ed. H. F. D. Sparks. Oxford: Clarendon, 1984.

APAT
>   *Die Apokryphen und Pseudepigraphen des Alten Testaments.* 2 vols.
>   Translated and edited by E. Kautzsch. Tübingen: Mohr, 1900.

APOT
>   *The Apocrypha and Pseudepigrapha of the Old Testament.* 2 vols. Edited
>   by R. H. Charles. 1913. Reprint. Oxford: Clarendon, 1963.

BAGD
>   *A Greek-English Lexicon of the New Testament and Other Early Christian
>   Literature.* 3d ed. Translated and adapted from the German work of
>   W. Bauer by W. Arndt and F. W. Gingrich, later revised by F. W.
>   Danker. Chicago: University of Chicago, 1979.

Bahnson, *Theonomy*
>   Bahnson, G. L. *Theonomy in Christian Ethics.* 2d ed. Phillipsburg,
>   N.J.: Presbyterian and Reformed, 1984.

Baldwin, *Haggai*
>   Baldwin, J. G. *Haggai, Zechariah, Malachi.* TOTC. Downers Grove,
>   Ill.: InterVarsity, 1972.

BAR
>   *Biblical Archeology Review*

Barr, "Apocalyptic"
>   Barr, J. "Jewish Apocalyptic in Recent Scholarly Study." *BJRL* 58
>   (1975–76) 9–35.

Barrett, "Eschatology"
>   Barrett, C. K. "New Testament Eschatology." *SJT* 6 (1953) 136–55.

Barron, *Heaven on Earth?*
>   Barron, B. *Heaven on Earth?: The Social and Political Agendas of
>   Dominion Theology.* Grand Rapids: Zondervan, 1992.

BASOR
>   *Bulletin of the American Schools of Oriental Research*

Bauckham, "Delay"
>   Bauckham, R. J. "The Delay of the Parousia." *TB* 31 (1980) 3–36.

Bauckham, *Jude*
>   Bauckham, R. J. *Jude, 2 Peter.* WBC 20. Waco, Tex.: Word, 1983.

Bauckham, "Martyrdom"
>   Bauckham, R. J. "The Martyrdom of Enoch and Elijah: Jewish or
>   Christian?" *JBL* 95 (1976) 447–58.

Bauckham, *Revelation*
>   Bauckham, R. *The Theology of the Book of Revelation.* Cambridge
>   University, 1993.

Baumgarten, *Paulus*
>   Baumgarten, J. *Paulus und die Apokalyptic: Die Auslegung apokalyptischer
>   Überlieferungen in den echten Paulusbriefen.* Düsseldorf: Neukirchener,
>   1975.

Beale, *Use of Daniel*
>   Beale, G. K. *The Use of Daniel in Jewish Apocalyptic Literature and in the
>   Revelation of St. John.* Lanham, Md.: University Press of America, 1984.

Beasley-Murray, *Last Days*
> Beasley-Murray, G. R. *Jesus and the Last Days*. Peabody, Mass.:
> Hendrickson, 1993.

Beasley-Murray, *Jesus and the Kingdom*
> Beasley-Murray, G. R. *Jesus and the Kingdom of God*. Grand Rapids:
> Eerdmans, 1986.

Becker, *Untersuchungen*
> Becker, J. *Untersuchungen zur Entstehungsgeschichte der Testament der
> zwölf Patriarchen*. Leiden: Brill, 1970.

Beckwith, Apocalypse
> Beckwith, I. T. *The Apocalypse of John*. 1919 Reprint. Grand Rapids:
> Baker, 1979.

Beckwith, "Dan 9"
> Beckwith, R. T. "Daniel 9 and the Date of Messiah's Coming in
> Essene, Hellenistic, Pharisaic, Zealot and Early Christian
> Computation." *RevQ* 10 (1981) 521–42.

Beker, *Apocalyptic*
> Beker, J. C. *Paul's Apocalyptic Gospel: The Coming Triumph of God*.
> Philadelphia: Fortress, 1982.

Berkouwer, *Return*
> Berkouwer, G. C. *The Return of Christ*. Translated by J. Van
> Oosterom and edited by M. J. Van Elderen. Grand Rapids:
> Eerdmans, 1972.

Best, *Thessalonians*
> Best, E. *A Commentary on the First and Second Epistles to the
> Thessalonians*. Peabody, Mass.: Hendrickson, 1972, 1986.

Betz, "Der Katechon"
> Betz, O. "Der Katechon." *NTS* 9 (1962–63) 276–91.

BSC
> Bible Student's Commentary

BJRL
> *Bulletin of the John Rylands Library*

Black, "Bibliography"
> Black, M. "A Bibliography on 1 Enoch in the Eighties." *JSP* 5 (1989)
> 3–16.

Blaising, *Progressive Dispensationalism*
> Blaising, C. A., and D. L. Bock. *Progressive Dispensationalism*.
> Wheaton: BridgePoint, 1993.

Bloch, *Apocalyptic*
> Bloch, J. *On The Apocalyptic in Judaism*. Philadelphia: Dropsie
> College for Hebrew and Cognate Learning, 1952.

Boak, *History*
> Boak, A. E. R. *A History of Rome to 565 A. D.* New York: Macmillan,
> 1921.

Borg, "Temperate Case"
    Borg, M. J. "A Temperate Case for a Non-Eschatological Jesus."
    Foundations & Facets Forum. 2 (3, 1986) 81–101.
Boring, *Revelation*
    Boring, M. E. *Revelation.* Interpretation. Louisville: John Knox, 1989.
Bornkamm, "End-Expectation"
    Bornkamm, G. "End-Expectation and Church in Matthew." Pages
    15–51. In *Tradition and Interpretation in Matthew.* Edited by
    G. Bornkamm, G. Barth, and H. J. Held. Translated by Percy Scott.
    London: SCM, 1963.
Bornkamm, "Verzögerung"
    Bornkamm, G. "Die Verzögerung der Parusie." Pages 116–26. In
    In Memoriam: E. Lohmeyer. Edited by W. Schmauch. Stuttgart:
    Evangelisches Verlagswerk, 1951.
Bousset, *Apokalyptik*
    Bousett, W. *Die jüdische Apokalyptik: Ihre religionsgeschichtliche
    Herkunft und ihre Bedeutung für das Neue Testament.* Berlin: Reuther &
    Reichard, 1903.
Bousset, *Legend*
    Bousset, W. *The Antichrist Legend.* ET: London: Hutchinson, 1896.
Bousset, *Religion*
    Bousset, W. *Die Religion des Judentums im Späthellenistischen Zeitalter.*
    Edited by H. Gressmann. Tübingen: Mohr, 1966.
Bovon, *Luke the Theologian*
    Bovon, F. *Luke the Theologian: Thirty-three Years of Research
    (1950–1983).* Translated by K. McKinney. PTMS 12. Allison Park,
    Pa.: Pickwick Publications, 1987.
Box, *Apocalypse of Abraham*
    Box, G. H. (ed.) with J. I. Landsman. *The Apocalypse of Abraham.*
    Translated from the Slavonic text. London: SPCK, 1918.
Bright, *Covenant*
    Bright, J. *Covenant and Promise.* Philadelphia: Westminster, 1976.
Bright, *History*
    Bright, J. *A History of Israel.* 2d ed. Philadelphia: Westminster, 1972.
Bright, *Jeremiah*
    Bright, J. *Jeremiah.* AB 21. 2d ed. Garden City, N.Y.: Doubleday,
    1985.
Brock, "Psalms of Solomon"
    Brock, S. P. "The Psalms of Solomon." *AOT,* 649–82.
Brownlee, *Ezekiel 1–19.*
    Brownlee, *Ezekiel 1–19.* WBC 28. Waco, Tex.: Word, 1986.
Brownlee, *Habakkuk*
    Brownlee, W. H. *The Midrash Pesher of Habakkuk.* Missoula:
    Scholars, 1979.

Bruce, *Biblical Exegesis*
> Bruce, F. F. *Biblical Exegesis in the Qumran Texts*. Grand Rapids: Eerdmans, 1959.

Bruce, "Daniel"
> Bruce, F. F. "The Book of Daniel and the Qumran Community." Pages 221–35. In *Neotestamentica et Semitica: Studies in Honour of Matthew Black*. Edited by E. E. Ellis and M. Wilcox. Edinburgh: T. & T. Clark, 1969.

Bruce, *Thessalonians*
> Bruce, F. F. *1 and 2 Thessalonians*. Waco, Tex.: Word, 1982.

Büchsel, γενεά
> Büchsel, F. γενεά, γενεαλογία, γενεαλογέω, ἀγενεαλόγητος. *TDNT*. 1.662–65.

Budd, *Numbers*
> Budd, P. J. *Numbers*. WBC 5. Waco, Tex.: Word, 1984.

Bultmann, *History*
> Bultmann, R. K. *History and Eschatology*. Gifford Lectures. Edinburgh: Edinburgh University Press, 1975.

Bultmann, *Theology*
> Bultmann, R. K. *Theology of the New Testament*. 2 vols. Translated by K. Grobel. New York: Scribners, 1951, 1955.

Caird, *Language*
> Caird, G. B. *The Language and Imagery of the Bible*. Philadelphia: Westminster, 1980.

Carroll, *Jeremiah*
> Carroll, *Jeremiah*. OTL. Philadelphia: Westminster, 1986.

Carroll, *Prophecy*
> Carroll, R. P. *When Prophecy Fails: Reactions and Responses to Failure in the Old Testament Prophetic Traditions*. London: SCM, 1979.

Casey, *Son of Man*
> Casey, M. *Son of Man: The Interpretation and Influence of Daniel 7*. London: SPCK, 1979.

CBC
> Cambridge Bible Commentary

CBOT
> Coniectanea Biblica, Old Testament

CBQ
> *Catholic Biblical Quarterly*

CBQMS
> Catholic Biblical Quarterly Monograph Series

Chance, *Jerusalem*
> Chance, J. B. *Jerusalem, the Temple, and the New Age in Luke–Acts*. Macon, Ga.: Mercer, 1988.

Charles, *Assumption*
> Charles, R. H. *The Assumption of Moses*. London: A. & C. Black, 1897.

Charles, "Assumption of Moses"
Charles, R. H. "Assumption of Moses." *APOT.* 2.407–24.
Charles, "Enoch"
Charles, R. H. "Book of Enoch." *APOT.* 2.163–281.
Charles, "Jubilees"
Charles, R. H. "Jubilees." *APOT.* 2.1–82.
Charles, *Revelation*
Charles, R. H. *A Critical and Exegetical Commentary on the Revelation of St. John.* 2 vols. ICC. Edinburgh: T. & T. Clark, 1920.
Charles, "II Baruch"
Charles, R. H. "II Baruch." *APOT.* 2.470–526.
Charlesworth, *OTP*
Charlesworth, J. H., ed. *The Old Testament Pseudepigrapha.* 2 vols. Garden City, N.Y.: Doubleday, 1983, 1985.
Charlesworth, "Books of Enoch"
Charlesworth, J. H. "The SNTS Pseudepigrapha Seminars at Tübingen and Paris on the Books of Enoch." *NTS* 25 (1978–79) 315–23.
Charlesworth, *Jesus within Judaism*
Charlesworth, J. H. *Jesus within Judaism: New Light from Exciting Archaeological Discoveries.* New York: Doubleday, 1988.
Charlesworth, *Modern Research.*
Charlesworth, J. H. *The Pseudepigrapha and Modern Research with a Supplement.* Missoula: Scholars, 1981.
Charlesworth, "Scrolls"
Charlesworth, J. H. "The Origin and Subsequent History of the Authors of the Dead Sea Scrolls: Four Transitional Phases among the Qumran Essenes." *RevQ* 38 (1980) 213–33.
Childs, *Introd.*
Childs, B. S. *Introduction to the Old Testament as Scripture.* London: SCM, 1979.
Chilton, *Paradise Restored*
Chilton, D. *Paradise Restored: A Biblical Theology of Dominion.* Tyler, Tex.: Reconstruction, 1985.
Clements, *Abraham*
Clements, R. E. *Abraham and David: Genesis XV and its Meaning for Israelite Tradition.* SBT, 2d series, 5. London: SCM, 1967.
Clements, *Isaiah 1–39*
Clements, R. E. *Isaiah 1–39.* NCB. Grand Rapids: Eerdmans, 1980.
Clements, "Messianic Hope"
Clements, R. E. "The Messianic Hope in the Old Testament." *JSOT* 43 (1989) 3–19.
Clements, *Prophecy*
Clements, *Prophecy and Covenant.* SBT 43. London: SCM, 1965.

Clines, *Theme*
> Clines, D. J. A. *The Theme of the Pentateuch*. JSOT Suppl. 10. Sheffield: JSOT, 1978.

Cohn, *Pursuit*
> Cohn, N. *The Pursuit of the Millennium*. Revised and expanded. New York: Oxford University Press, 1970.

Collins, *Apocalypse*
> Collins, A. Y. *The Apocalypse*. Wilmington: Glazier, 1979.

Collins, *Crisis*
> Collins, A. Y. *Crisis and Catharsis: The Power of the Apocalypse*. Philadelphia: Westminster, 1984.

Collins, *Apocalyptic*
> Collins, J. J. *The Apocalyptic Imagination: An Introduction to the Jewish Matrix of Christianity*. New York: Crossroad, 1984.

Collins, "Date and Provenance"
> Collins, J. J. "The Date and Provenance of the Testament of Moses." *STM*, 15–32.

Collins, *Oracles*
> Collins, J. J. *Sibylline Oracles of Egyptian Judaism*. Missoula: Scholars, 1974.

Collins, "Provenance"
> Collins, J. J. "The Provenance of the Third Sibylline Oracle." Bulletin of the Institute of Jewish Studies 2 (1974) 1–18.

Collins, "Sibylline Oracles"
> Collins, J. J. "Sibylline Oracles." *OTP*. 1.317–472.

Collins, "Transcendence"
> Collins, J. J. "Apocalyptic Eschatology as the Transcendence of Death." *CBQ* 36 (1974) 21–43.

Conzelmann, *Outline*
> Conzelmann, H. *An Outline of the Theology of the New Testament*. Translated by J. Bowden. London: SCM, 1969.

Conzelmann, *Theology of St. Luke*
> Conzelmann, H. *The Theology of St. Luke*. Translated by G. Buswell. New York: Harper & Row, 1961.

Court, *Myth*
> Court, J. M. *Myth and History in the Book of Revelation*. London: SPCK, 1979.

CQR
> *Church Quarterly Review*

CRINT
> Compendia Rerum Iudaicarum ad Novum Testamentum

Craigie, *Old Testament*
> Craigie, P. C. *The Old Testament: Its Background, Growth, and Content*. Nashville: Abingdon, 1986.

Cranfield, *Mark*
> Cranfield, C. E. B. *The Gospel According to Mark*. Cambridge: Cambridge University Press, 1959, 1977.

Cross, *Ancient Library*
> Cross, F. M. Jr. *The Ancient Library of Qumran & Modern Biblical Studies*. Rev. ed. Grand Rapids: Baker, 1961.

Cross, *Canaanite Myth*
> Cross, F. M. *Canaanite Myth and Hebrew Epic*. Cambridge, Mass.: Harvard, 1973.

Crossan, *Historical Jesus*
> Crossan, J. D. *The Historical Jesus: The Life of a Mediterranean Jewish Peasant*. San Francisco: Harper, 1991.

Cullmann, *Christ*
> Cullmann, O. *Christ and Time: A Primitive Christian Conception of Time and History*. Translated by F. V. Filson. Rev. ed. Philadelphia: Westminster, 1964.

Cullmann, *Salvation*
> Cullmann, O. *Salvation in History*. Translated by S. G. Sowers. New York: Harper, 1967.

Davenport, *Eschatology*
> Davenport, G. L. *The Eschatology of the Book of Jubilees*. Leiden: Brill, 1971.

Davies, *Damascus Covenant*
> Davies, P. R. *The Damascus Covenant: An Interpretation of the "Damascus Document."* JSOT Suppl 25. Sheffield: JSOT, 1983.

Davies, "Eschatology at Qumran"
> Davies, P. R. "Eschatology at Qumran." *JBL* 104 (1985) 39–55.

Davies, *1QM*
> Davies, P. R. *1QM, the War Scroll from Qumran: Its Structure and History*. Rome: Biblical Institute, 1977.

Delling, τέλος
> Delling, G. τέλος, κτλ. *TDNT*. 8.49–87.

Denis, *Introduction*
> Denis, A.-M. *Introduction aux pseudépigraphes grecs d'Ancien Testament*. Leiden: Brill, 1970.

Denton, *Knowledge of God*
> Denton, R. C. *The Knowledge of God in Ancient Israel*. New York: Seabury, 1968.

Dexinger, *Henochs*
> Dexinger, F. *Henochs Zehnwochenapokalypse und offene Probleme der Apokalyptik-Forschung*. Leiden: Brill, 1977.

Dibelius, *Thessalonicher*
> Dibelius, M. *An die Thessalonicher I–II, An die Philipper*. Tübingen: Mohr, 1925.

Dimant, "Qumran"
> Dimant, D. "Qumran Sectarian Literature." *JWSTP*, 483–550.

DNEB
> Die neue Echter Bibel

Driver, *Deuteronomy*
>Driver, S. R. *A Critical and Exegetical Commentary on Deuteronomy* ICC. New York: Scribners, 1906.

Dupont, "Discours"
>Dupont, J. "La Ruine du Temple et la fin des temps dans le discours de Marc 13." Pages 207–69. In *Apocalypses et théologie de l'espérance.* Edited by the Association catholique française pour l'étude de la Bible. Paris: Cerf, 1977.

Dunn, *Christology*
>Dunn, J. D. G. *Christology in the Making: An Inquiry into the Origins of the Doctrine of the Incarnation.* London: SCM, 1980.

Dunn, "Demythologizing"
>Dunn, J. D. G. "Demythologizing—The Problem of Myth in the New Testament." Pages 285–307. In *New Testament Interpretation.* Edited by I. H. Marshall. Grand Rapids: Eerdmans, 1977.

Dunn, *Jesus*
>Dunn, J. D. G. *Jesus and the Spirit: A Study of the Religious and Charismatic Experience of Jesus and the First Christians as Reflected in the New Testament.* London: SCM, 1975.

Dunn, *Unity*
>Dunn, J. D. G. *Unity and Diversity in the New Testament: An Inquiry into the Character of Earliest Christianity.* London: SCM, 1977.

Dupont-Sommer, *Essene Writings*
>Dupont-Sommer, A. *The Essene Writings from Qumran.* Translated by G. Vermes. Oxford: Blackwell, 1961.

Eichrodt, *Theology*
>Eichrodt, W. *Theology of the Old Testament.* 2 vols. Translated by J. A. Baker. Philadelphia: Westminster, 1961.

Eissfeldt, *Old Testament*
>Eissfeldt, O. *The Old Testament: An Introduction.* Translated by P. Ackroyd. Oxford: Blackwell, 1965.

EJ
>*Encyclopedia Judaica.* 17 vols. Jerusalem: Keter, 1971–72.

Elliger, *Studien*
>Elliger, K. *Studien um Habakuk—Kommentar vom Toten Meer mit 1 Beilage.* Tübingen: Mohr, 1953.

Ellis, "OT Canon"
>Ellis, E. E. "The Old Testament Canon in the Early Church." Pages 653–90. In *Mikra: Text, Translation, Reading, and Interpretation of the Hebrew Bible in Ancient Judaism and Early Christianity.* Edited by M. J. Mulder and H. Sysling. CRINT 2.1. Philadelphia: Fortress, 1988.

Ellis, *Eschatology*
>Ellis, E. E. *Eschatology in Luke.* Philadelphia: Fortress, 1972.

ET
>English translation

Fitzmyer, *Essays*
 Fitzmyer, J. A. *Essays on the Semitic Background of the New Testament.*
 London: Chapman, 1971.

Ford, *Abomination*
 Ford, D. *The Abomination of Desolation in Biblical Eschatology.*
 Washington, D.C.: University Press of America, 1979.

France, *Matthew*
 France, R. T. *The Gospel According to Matthew.* TNTC. Grand
 Rapids: Eerdmans, 1985.

Frend, "Persecutions"
 Frend, W. H. C. "The Persecutions: Some Links between Judaism
 and the Early Church." In *Religion Popular and Unpopular in the Early
 Christian Centuries.* London: Variorum Reprints, 1976.

Friesen, "Ephesus"
 Friesen, S. "Ephesus: Key to a Vision in Revelation." *BAR* 19 (3,
 1993) 24–37.

Frost, *Apocalyptic*
 Frost, S. B. *Old Testament Apocalyptic: Its Origins and Growth.* London:
 Epworth, 1952.

Gaston, *No Stone*
 Gaston, L. *No Stone on Another: Studies in the Significance of the Fall of
 Jerusalem in the Synoptic Gospels.* Leiden: Brill, 1970.

Geddert, *Watchwords*
 Geddert, T. J. *Watchwords: Mark 13 in Markan Eschatology.* JSNT
 Suppl 25. Sheffield: JSOT, 1989.

Geffcken, *Oracula*
 Geffcken, J. *Die Oracula Sibyllina.* Leipzig: Hinrichs'sche, 1902.

Giblin, *Threat*
 Giblin, C. H. *The Threat to Faith: An Exegetical and Theological
 Reexamination of 2 Thessalonians 2.* Rome: Pontifical Biblical
 Institute, 1967.

Gnilka, *Markus*
 Gnilka, J. *Das Evangelium nach Markus.* 2 vols. Zürich: Benziger, 1979.

Goldingay, *Daniel*
 Goldingay, J. E. *Daniel.* WBC. 30. Dallas: Word, 1989.

Goldingay, *Theological Diversity*
 Goldingay, J. *Theological Diversity and the Authority of the Old
 Testament.* Grand Rapids: Eerdmans, 1987.

Grässer, *Problem*
 Grässer, E. *Das Problem der Parusieverzögerung in den synoptischen
 Evangelien in der Apostelgeschichte.* Berlin: de Gruyter, 1977.

Gray, *Numbers*
 Gray, G. B. *A Critical and Exegetical Commentary on Numbers.* ICC.
 New York: Scribners, 1903.

Gray, "Psalms of Solomon"
    Gray, G. B. "The Psalms of Solomon." *APOT*. 2.625–52.
Gundry, *Matthew*
    Gundry, R. H. *Matthew: A Commentary on His Literary and Theological Art*. Grand Rapids: Eerdmans, 1982.
Gunkel, "Esra"
    Gunkel, H. "Das vierte Buch Esra." *APAT*. 2.331–401.
Haenchen, *Acts*
    Haenchen, E. *The Acts of the Apostles: A Commentary*. Translated by B. Noble, G. Shinn, with H. Anderson and R. McL. Wilson. Philadelphia: Westminster, 1971.
Hanson, "Apocalypticism"
    Hanson, P. D. "Apocalypticism." *IDBSup*, 28–34.
Hanson, *Dawn*
    Hanson, P. D. *The Dawn of Apocalyptic: The Historical and Sociological Roots of Jewish Apocalyptic Eschatology*. Philadelphia: Fortress, 1979.
Hanson, *People Called*
    Hanson, P. D. *The People Called: The Growth of Community in the Bible*. San Francisco: Harper & Row, 1986.
Hanson, "Apocalyptic Re-examined"
    Hanson, P. D. "Old Testament Apocalyptic Re-examined." *Int* 25 (1971) 454–79.
Harnisch, *Verhängnis*
    Harnisch, W. *Verhängnis und Verheissung der Geschichte: Untersuchungen zum Zeit- und Geschichtsverständnis im 4. Buch Esra und in der syr. Baruchapokalypse*. Göttingen: Vandenhoeck & Ruprecht, 1969.
Harrison, *Introduction*
    Harrison, R. K. *Introduction to the Old Testament*. Grand Rapids: Eerdmans, 1969.
Hartman, *Prophecy*
    Hartman, L. *Prophecy Interpreted: The Formation of Some Jewish Apocalyptic Texts and of the Eschatological Discourse: Mark 13 Par*. Translated by N. Tomkinson. Lund: C.W.K. Gleerup, 1966.
Hartman, "Survey"
    Hartman, L. "Survey of the Problem of Apocalyptic Genre." *AMWNE*, 329–43.
Hemer, *Letters*
    Hemer, C. J. *The Letters to the Seven Churches of Asia in Their Local Setting*. JSNT Suppl 11. Sheffield: JSOT, 1986.
Henderson, *Civil War*
    Henderson, B. W. *Civil War and Rebellion in the Roman Empire: A. D. 69–70: A Companion to the "Histories" of Tacitus*. London: Macmillan, 1908.

Hengel, *Judaism*
> Hengel, M. *Judaism and Hellenism: Studies in Their Encounter in Palestine during the Early Hellenistic Period*. 2 vols. Translated by J. Bowden. London: SCM, 1974.

Hennecke-Schneemelcher, *NT Apocrypha*
> Hennecke, E. W., and Schneemelcher, W. *New Testament Apocrypha*. 2 vols. Translated and edited by R. McL. Wilson. Philadelphia: Westminster, 1963.

Hillers, *Micah*
> Hillers, D. R. *Micah*. Hermeneia. Philadelphia: Fortress, 1984.

HNT
> Handbuch zum Neuen Testament

Holm-Nielsen, *Hodayot*
> Holm-Nielsen, S. *Hodayot: Psalms from Qumran*. Acta Theologica Danica 2. Aarhus: Universitetsforlaget, 1960.

Holman, "Eschatological Delay"
> Holman, C. L. "Eschatological Delay in Jewish and Early Christian Literature." Ph.D. thesis presented to the University of Nottingham (England), 1982.

Holman, "Imminent Parousia"
> Holman, C. L. "The Idea of an Imminent Parousia in the Synoptic Gospels." *Studia Biblica et Theologica* 3 (1973) 15–31.

Holman, "A Lesson"
> Holman, C. L. "A Lesson from Matthew's Gospel for Charismatic Renewal." Pages 48–63. In *Faces of Renewal: Studies in Honor of Stanley M. Horton*. Edited by P. Elbert. Peabody, Mass.: Hendrickson, 1988.

Hooker, *Son of Man*
> Hooker, M. *The Son of Man in Mark*. London: SPCK, 1967.

HTKNT
> Herders theologischer Kommentar zum Neuen Testament

Hubbard, "Hope"
> Hubbard, D. A. "Hope in the Old Testament." *TB* 34 (1983) 33–59.

Hubbard, *Joel and Amos*
> Hubbard, D. A. *Joel and Amos: An Introduction and Commentary*. TOTC. Downers Grove, Ill.: Inter-Varsity, 1989.

ICC
> International Critical Commentary

IDBSup
> Supplementary volume to *The Interpreter's Dictionary of the Bible*

Int
> *Interpretation*

Interpretation
> Interpretation. A Bible Commentary for Teaching and Preaching.

James, "Recovery"
> James, M. R. "The Recovery of the Apocalypse of Peter." *CQR* 80 (1915) 1–36.

Isaac, "1 Enoch"
> Isaac, E. "1 Enoch." *OTP.* 1.5–89.

Janssen, *Das Gottesvolk*
> Janssen, E. *Das Gottesvolk und seine Geschichte: Geschichtsbild und Selbstverständnis im palästinensischen Schrifttum von Jesus Sirach bis Jehuda ha-Nasi.* Neukirchen-Vluyn: Neukirchener, 1971.

JBL
> *Journal of Biblical Literature*

Jeremias, *Parables*
> Jeremias, J. *The Parables of Jesus.* Translated by S. H. Hooke from the 6th edition, 1962, with revisions; 2d rev. ed. New York: Scribners, 1972.

Jeremias, *Theology*
> Jeremias, J. *New Testament Theology.* Vol. 1, *The Proclamation of Jesus.* London: SCM, 1971.

Jewett, *Correspondence*
> Jewett, R. *The Thessalonian Correspondence: Pauline Rhetoric and Millenarian Piety.* Philadelphia: Fortress, 1986.

JJS
> *Journal of Jewish Studies*

JLCRS
> Jordan Lectures in Comparative Religion Series

JNES
> *Journal of Near Eastern Studies*

JSJ
> *Journal for the Study of Judaism*

JSNT Suppl
> Journal for the Study of the New Testament Supplement Series

JSOT Suppl
> Journal for the Study of the Old Testament Supplement Series

JSP
> *Journal for the Study of the Pseudepigrapha*

JTS
> *Journal of Theological Studies*

JWSTP
> *Jewish Writings of the Second Temple Period: Apocrypha, Pseudepigrapha, Qumran Sectarian Writings, Philo, Josephus.* Ed. M. E. Stone. CRINT 2.2. Assen: Van Gorcum/Philadelphia: Fortress, 1984.

Kaiser, *Isaiah 1–12*
> Kaiser, O. *Isaiah 1–12.* OTL. Translated by R. A. Wilson. Philadelphia: Westminster, 1972.

Käsemann, "Beginnings"
> Käsemann, E. "The Beginnings of Christian Theology." Pages 82–107. In *New Testament Questions of Today.* Philadelphia: Fortress, 1969. Originally published in *ZThK* 57 (1960) in German.

Kealy, *Apocalypse*
> Kealy, S. P. *The Apocalypse of John.* MBC 15. Wilmington: Glazier, 1987.

Kee, "Testaments"
>   Kee, H. C. "Testaments of the Twelve Patriarchs." *OTP*. 1.775–828.
Keil, *Minor Prophets*
>   Keil, C. F. *Minor Prophets*. Translated by J. Martin. In *Commentary on the Old Testament* by C. F. Keil and F. Delitzsch. 10 vols. Grand Rapids: Eerdmans, repr. 1984.
Kelber, *Kingdom*
>   Kelber, W. H. *The Kingdom in Mark: A New Place and a New Time*. Philadelphia: Fortress, 1974.
Kilpatrick, "Gentile Mission"
>   Kilpatrick, G. D. "The Gentile Mission in Mark and Mk 13:9–11." Pages 145–48. In *Studies in the Gospels: Essays in Memory of R. H. Lightfoot*. Edited by D. E. Nineham. Oxford: Blackwell, 1955.
Klijn, *Lateinische Text*
>   Klijn, A. F. *Der lateinische Text der Apokalypse des Esra*. TUGAL 131. Berlin: Akademie, 1983.
Klijn, "Recent Developments"
>   Klijn, A. F. J. "Recent Developments in the Study of the Syriac Apocalypse of Baruch." *JSP* 4 (1989) 3–17.
Klijn, "2 Baruch"
>   Klijn, A. F. J. "2 (Syriac Apocalypse of) Baruch." *OTP*. 1.615–52.
Knibb, "Exile"
>   Knibb, M. A. "The Exile in the Literature of the Intertestamental Period." *Heythrop Journal* 17 (1976) 253–72.
Knibb, "Date"
>   Knibb, M. A. "The Date of the Parables of Enoch: A Critical Review." *NTS* 25 (1978–79) 345–59.
Knibb, "Martyrdom"
>   Knibb, M. A. "Martyrdom and Ascension of Isaiah." *OTP*. 2.143–76.
Koch, *Prophets*
>   Koch, K. *The Prophets*. Translated by M. Kohl. 2 vols. Philadelphia: Fortress, 1984.
Koch, *Rediscovery*
>   Koch, K. *The Rediscovery of Apocalyptic*. Translated by M. Kohl. London: SCM, 1972.
Kolenkow, "Assumption"
>   Kolenkow, A. B. "The Assumption of Moses as a Testament." *STM*. 71–77.
Kraft, *Offenbarung*
>   Kraft, H. *Die Offenbarung des Johannes*. HNT. Tübingen: Mohr, 1974.
Krentz "Thessalonians"
>   Krentz, E. M. "Thessalonians, First and Second Epistles to the." *ABD*. 6.515–23.

Kuhn, *Enderwartung*

Kuhn, H-W. *Enderwartung und gegenwärtiges Heil: Untersuchungen zu den Gemeindeliedern von Qumran mit einem Anhang über Eschatologie und Gegenwart in der Verkündigung Jesu.* Studien zur Umwelt des Neuen Testaments. Göttingen: Vandenhoeck & Ruprecht, 1966.

Kümmel, *Introduction*

Kümmel, W. G. *Introduction to the New Testament.* Translated by H. C. Kee. Nashville: Abingdon, rev. 1975.

Kümmel, *Promise*

Kümmel, W. G. *Promise and Fulfillment: The Eschatological Message of Jesus.* Translated by D. M. Barton. London: SCM, 1961.

Kutsch, *Verheissung*

Kutsch, E. *Verheissung und Gesetz: Untersuchungen zum sogenannten Bund im Alten Testament.* ZAW. New York: De Gruyter, 1973.

Ladd, *Presence*

Ladd, G. E. *The Presence of the Future: The Eschatology of Biblical Realism.* Grand Rapids: Eerdmans, 1974.

Ladd, *Revelation*

Ladd, G. E. *A Commentary on the Revelation of John.* Grand Rapids: Eerdmans, 1972.

Lambert, "Destiny"

Lambert, W. G. "Destiny and Divine Intervention in Babylon and Israel." *OTS* 17 (1972) 65–72.

Lambrecht, "Discourse"

Lambrecht, J. "The Parousia Discourse: Composition and Content in Mt. 24–25." Pages 309–42. In *L'Evangile selon Matthieu: Redaction et Theologie.* Edited by M. Didier. Gembloux: Duculot, 1972.

Lambrecht, *Redaktion*

Lambrecht, J. *Die Redaktion der Markus-Apokalypse: Literarische Analyse und Strukturuntersuchung.* Rome: Pontificio Instituto Biblico, 1967.

Laperrousaz, *Testament*

Laperrousaz, E.-M. *Le Testament de Moïse (généralement appelé Assomption de Moïse): Traduction avec introduction et notes.* Semitica 19. Paris: Adrien-Maisonneuve, 1970.

LaSor, *OT Survey*

LaSor, W. S. , D. A. Hubbard, and F. W. Bush. *Old Testament Survey: The Message, Form, and Background of the Old Testament.* Grand Rapids: Eerdmans, 1982.

LaSor, *Scrolls*

LaSor, W. S. *The Dead Sea Scrolls and the New Testament.* Grand Rapids: Eerdmans, 1972.

Lebram, "Perspektiven"

Lebram, J. "Perspektiven der genenwärtigen Danielforschung." *JSJ* 5 (1974) 1–33.

Lebram, "Piety"
   Lebram, J. C. H. "The Piety of the Jewish Apocalyptists." *AMWNE.*
   171–210.
Levenson, "Davidic Covenant"
   Levenson, J. D. "The Davidic Covenant and its Modern
   Interpreters." *CBQ* 41 (1979) 205–19.
Lewis and Reinhold, *Roman Civilization*
   Lewis, N., and M. Reinhold. *Roman Civilization: Selected Readings
   Edited with Introduction and Notes.* 2 vols. New York: Columbia
   University, 1955.
Licht, "Taxo"
   Licht, J. "Taxo, or the Apocalyptic Doctrine of Vengeance." *JJS* 12
   (1961) 95–103.
Liddell and Scott, *Lexicon*
   Liddell, H. G., R. Scott, and H. S. Jones. *A Greek-English Lexicon.*
   New (9th) ed. with a supplement. Oxford: Clarendon Press, 1968.
LJSTT
   Literature of the Jewish People in the Period of the Second Temple
   and the Talmud.
Lohmeyer, *Offenbarung*
   Lohmeyer, E. *Die Offenbarung des Johannes.* 3d ed. Tübingen: Mohr,
   1970.
Lohse, *Die Texte aus Qumran*
   Lohse, E. *Die Texte aus Qumran: Hebräisch und Deutsch.* Munich:
   Kösel, 1971.
Maier, *Temple Scroll*
   Maier, J. *The Temple Scroll: An Introduction, Translation & Commentary.*
   JSOT Suppl 34. Translated by R. T. White. Sheffield: JSOT, 1985.
Marshall, *Luke*
   Marshall, I. H. *Commentary on Luke: A Commentary on the Greek Text.*
   NIGTC. Grand Rapids: Eerdmans, 1978.
Marshall, *Luke: Historian*
   Marshall, I. H. *Luke: Historian and Theologian.* Grand Rapids:
   Zondervan, 1971.
Martin, *Mark*
   Martin, R. *Mark: Evangelist and Theologian.* Grand Rapids:
   Zondervan, 1972.
Marxsen, *Mark*
   Marxsen, W. *Mark the Evangelist: Studies on the Redaction History of the
   Gospel.* Translated by J. Boyce et al. Nashville: Abingdon, 1969.
Maurer, "Apocalypse of Peter"
   Maurer, C. "Apocalypse of Peter." Hennecke-Schneemelcher, *NT
   Apocrypha.* 2.663–83.
Mays, *Amos*
   Mays, J. L. *Amos.* OTL. London: SCM, 1969.

Mays, *Hosea*
  Mays, J. L. *Hosea*. OTL. Philadelphia: Westminster, 1969.
Mays, *Micah*
  Mays, J. L. *Micah*. OTL. Philadelphia: Westminster, 1976.
MBS
  Message of Biblical Spirituality
McCarthy, *OT Covenant*
  McCarthy, D.J. *Old Testament Covenant: A Survey of Current Opinions.*
  Richmond, Va.: John Knox, 1972.
McCarthy, *Treaty*
  McCarthy, D. J. *Treaty and Covenant*. AnBib 21. 2d ed. Rome:
  Biblical Institute, 1981.
McCullough, "Israel's Eschatology"
  McCullough, W. S. "Israel's Eschatology from Amos to Daniel." In
  Studies on the Ancient Palestinian World. Edited by J. W. Wevers and
  D. B. Redford. University of Toronto Press (1972).
Meeks, "Social Functions"
  Meeks, W. "Social Functions of Apocalyptic Language." *AMWNE,*
  687–705.
Meier, *Marginal Jew*
  Meier, J. P. *A Marginal Jew: Rethinking the Historical Jesus.* ABRL.
  New York: Doubleday, 1991.
Mendenhall, *Law and Covenant*
  Mendenhall, G. E. *Law and Covenant in Israel and the Ancient Near
  East.* The Bible Colloquium, Pittsburgh (1955), repr. *Biblical
  Archeologist* 17/2,3 (1954) 26–46, 49–76.
Metzger, "Fourth Book of Ezra"
  Metzger, B. M. "The Fourth Book of Ezra." *OTP.* 1.517–59.
Milik, *Enoch*
  Milik, J. T. *The Books of Enoch: Aramaic Fragments of Qumran Cave 4.*
  Oxford: Clarendon, 1976.
Moltmann, *Crucified God*
  Moltmann, J. *The Crucified God: The Cross of Christ as the Foundation
  and Criticism of Christian Theology.* Translated by R. A. Wilson and
  J. Bowden. London: SCM, 1974.
Moltmann, *Future*
  Moltmann, J. *The Future of Creation.* Translated by M. Kohl.
  Philadelphia: Fortress, 1979.
Moltmann, *Hope*
  Moltmann, J. *Theology of Hope: On the Ground and the Implications of a
  Christian Eschatology.* Translated by J. W. Leitch. New York: Harper,
  1967.
Moltmann, *Spirit*
  Moltmann, J. *The Spirit of Life: A Universal Affirmation.* Translated
  by M. Kohl. Minneapolis: Fortress, 1992.

Moule, *Birth*
  Moule, C. F. D. *The Birth of the New Testament.* Revised ed. San
  Francisco: Harper, 1982.
Moulton and Milligan, *Vocabulary*
  Moulton, J. H., and G. Milligan. *The Vocabulary of the Greek
  Testament: Illustrated from the Papyri and Other Non-Literary Sources.*
  London: Hodder and Stoughton, 1930.
Mounce, *Revelation*
  Mounce, R. H. *The Book of Revelation.* NICNT. Grand Rapids:
  Eerdmans, 1977.
Mowinckel, *He That Cometh*
  Mowinckel, S. *He That Cometh.* Translated by G. W. Anderson.
  New York: Oxford; Blackwell, 1956.
Munck, *Paul*
  Munck, J. *Paul and the Salvation of Mankind.* Translated by F. Clarke.
  London: SCM, 1959.
Murphy, *Structure and Meaning*
  Murphy, F. J. *The Structure and Meaning of Second Baruch.* SBLDS 78.
  Atlanta: Scholars, 1985.
NCB
  New Century Bible
Neusner, *Eliezer*
  Neusner, J. *Eliezer ben Hyrcanus: The Tradition and the Man.* 2 Parts.
  Leiden: Brill, 1973.
Nicholson, "Apocalyptic"
  Nicholson, E. W. "Apocalyptic." In G. W. Anderson, ed., *Tradition
  and Interpretation: Essays by Members of the Society for Old Testament
  Study.* Oxford: Clarendon, 1979.
Nicholson, *God and His People*
  Nicholson, E. W. *God and His People.* Oxford: Clarendon, 1986.
Nickelsburg, "Apocalyptic"
  Nickelsburg, G. W. E., Jr. "The Apocalyptic Message of I Enoch
  92–105." *CBQ* 39 (1977) 309–28.
Nickelsburg, *Resurrection*
  Nickelsburg, G. W. E., Jr. *Resurrection, Immortality, and Eternal Life in
  Intertestamental Judaism.* Cambridge, Mass.: Harvard University
  Press, 1972.
Nickelsburg, "Riches"
  Nickelsburg, G. W. E., Jr. "Riches, The Rich, and God's Judgment
  in I Enoch 92–105 and the Gospel according to Luke." *NTS* 25
  (1978–79) 324–44.
NICOT
  New International Commentary on the Old Testament
Nikiprowetzky, *Sibylle*
  Nikiprowetzky, V. *La Troisième Sibylle.* Paris: Mouton, 1970.

Nineham, *Mark*
> Nineham, D. E. *The Gospel of Mark*. Harmondsworth: Penguin, 1963.

Noth, *Numbers*
> Noth, M. *Numbers*. Translated by J. D. Martin. London: SCM, 1968.

Noth, *History*
> Noth, M. *The History of Israel*. 2d ed. Revised translation by P. R. Ackroyd. New York: Harper, 1960.

NTS
> *New Testament Studies*

Osborne, *Spiral*
> Osborne, G. R. *The Hermeneutical Spiral: A Comprehensive Introduction to Biblical Interpretation*. Downers Grove: InterVarsity, 1991.

OTL
> Old Testament Library

OTP
> *The Old Testament Pseudepigrapha*. Edited by J. H. Charlesworth. 2 vols. Garden City, N.Y.: Doubleday, 1983–85.

OTS
> *Oudtestamentische Studien*

Pannenberg, *Jesus*
> Pannenberg, W. *Jesus–God and Man*. Translated by L. L. Wilkins and D. A. Priebe. Philadelphia: Westminster, 1974.

Perrin, *Jesus*
> Perrin, N. *Jesus and the Language of the Kingdom: Symbol and Metaphor in New Testament Interpretation*. Philadelphia: Fortress, 1976.

Perlitt, *Bundestheologie*
> Perlitt, L. *Bundestheologie im Alten Testament*. WMANT 36. Neukirchen: Neukirchener, 1969.

Pesch, *Markusevangelium*
> Pesch, R. *Das Markusevangelium*. 2 vols. 2d ed. HTKNT. Freiburg: Herder, 1977.

Pesch, *Naherwartungen*
> Pesch, R. *Naherwartungen: Tradition und Redaktion in Mk. 13*. Düsseldorf: Patmos, 1968.

Plöger, *Theocracy*
> Plöger, O. *Theocracy and Eschatology*. Translated by S. Rudman. Oxford: Blackwell, 1968.

Porter, "OT Historiography"
> Porter, J. R. "Old Testament Historiography." Pages 125–62. In *Tradition and Interpretation*. Edited by G. W. Anderson. Oxford: Clarendon, 1979.

Prévost, *How to Read*
> Prévost, J.-P. *How to Read the Apocalypse*. Translated by J. Bowden and M. Lydamore. New York: Crossroad, 1993.

Priest, "Testament"
> Priest, J. "Testament of Moses." *OTP*. 1.919–34.

PTMS
> Pittsburgh Theological Monograph Series

von Rad, *Deuteronomy*
> von Rad, G. *Deuteronomy*. Translated by D. Barton. OTL. London: SCM, 1966.

von Rad, *Genesis*
> von Rad, G. *Genesis: A Commentary*. Translated by J. H. Marks. OTL. 3d rev. London: SCM, 1972.

von Rad, *Theology*
> von Rad, G. *Theology of the Old Testament*. Vol. 2 of *The Theology of Israel's Prophetic Traditions*. Translated by D. M. G. Stalker. Edinburgh: Oliver and Boyd, 1965.

von Rad, *Wisdom*
> von Rad, G. *Wisdom in Israel*. Translated by J. D. Martin. London: SCM, 1972.

Ramsay, *Letters*
> Ramsay, W. M. *The Letters to the Seven Churches of Asia and Their Place in the Plan of the Apocalypse*. London: Hodder and Stoughton, 1904.

Reid, "Ten Week Apocalypse"
> Reid, S. B. "The Structure of the Ten Week Apocalypse and the Book of Dreams." *JSJ* 16 (1985) 189–201.

RevQ
> *Revue de Qumran*

RGG
> *Die Religion in Geschichte und Gegenwart*. 7 vols. 3d ed. Tübingen: Mohr, 1957–65.

Rigaux, *Thessaloniciens*
> Rigaux, B. *Saint Paul: Les Epîtres aux Thessaloniciens*. Paris: Gabalda, 1956.

Ringgren, "Apokalyptik"
> Ringgren, H. "Apokalyptik," Part 2. *RGG*. 1.464–66.

Ringgren, *Qumran*
> Ringgren, H. *The Faith of Qumran: Theology of the Dead Sea Scrolls*. Translated by E. T. Sander. Philadelphia: Fortress, 1963.

Ritt, *Offenbarung*
> Ritt, H. *Offenbarung des Johannes*. DNEB. Würzburg: Echter, 1986.

Robinson, *Redating*
> Robinson, J. A. T. *Redating the New Testament*. Philadelphia: Westminster, 1976.

Rohde, *Rediscovering*
> Rohde, J. *Rediscovering the Teaching of the Evangelists*. Translated by D. M. Barton. Philadelphia: Westminster, 1968.

Roloff, *Revelation*
    Roloff, J. *The Revelation of John: A Continental Commentary*.
    Translated by J. E. Alsup. Minneapolis: Fortress, 1993.
Roth, "Era"
    Roth, C. "The Era of the Habakkuk Commentary." *VT* 11 (1961)
    451–55.
Rowley, *Jewish Apocalyptic*
    Rowley, H. H. *Jewish Apocalyptic and the Dead Sea Scrolls*. London:
    University of London, 1957.
Rowley, *Relevance*
    Rowley, H. H. *The Relevance of Apocalyptic: A Study of Jewish and
    Christian Apocalypses from Daniel to the Revelation*. London:
    Lutterworth, 1947.
Rubinkiewicz, "Apocalypse of Abraham"
    Rubinkiewicz, R. "Apocalypse of Abraham." *OTP*. 1.681–705.
Russell, *Disclosure*
    Russell, D. S. *Divine Disclosure: An Introduction to Jewish Apocalyptic*.
    Minneapolis: Fortress, 1992.
Russell, *Jews*
    Russell, D. S. *The Jews from Alexander to Herod*. Oxford: University
    Press, 1967.
Russell, *Method*
    Russell, D. S. *The Method and Message of Jewish Apocalyptic: 200
    B.C.–A.D. 100*. Philadelphia: Westminster, 1964.
Ryle and James, *Psalms of the Pharisees*
    Ryle, H. E., and M. R. James (eds.). *PSALMOI SOLOMONTOS:
    Psalms of the Pharisees, Commonly Called the Psalms of Solomon*.
    Cambridge: University Press, 1891.
Saggs, *Encounter*
    Saggs, H. W. F. *The Encounter with the Divine in Mesopotamia and
    Israel*. JLCRS 12. London: Athlone, 1978.
Sanders, *Jesus and Judaism*
    Sanders, E. P. *Jesus and Judaism*. Philadelphia: Fortress, 1985.
Sanders, *Paul*
    Sanders, E. P. *Paul and Palestinian Judaism: A Comparison of Patterns of
    Religion*. London: SCM, 1977.
SBLMS
    Society of Biblical Literature Monograph Series
SBLDS
    Society of Biblical Literature Dissertation Series
SBT
    Studies in Biblical Theology
Schiffman, *Eschatological Community*
    Schiffman, L. H. *The Eschatological Community of the Dead Sea Scrolls:
    A Study of the Rule of the Congregation*. SBLMS 38. Atlanta: Scholars,
    1989.

Schillebeeckx, *Jesus*
> Schillebeeckx, E. *Jesus: An Experiment in Christology*. Translated by
> H. Hoskins. New York: Crossroad, 1981.

Schmidt, *Apokalyptik*
> Schmidt, J. M. *Die jüdische Apokalyptic: Die Geschichte ihrer
> Erforschung von den Anfange bis zu den Textfunden von Qumran*.
> Neukirchen-Vluyn: Neukirchen, 1969.

Schüpphaus, *Psalmen*
> Schüpphaus, J. *Die Psalmen Salomos: Ein Zeugnis Jerusalemer Theologie
> und Frömmigkeit in der Mitte des vorchristlichen Jahrhunderts*. Leiden:
> Brill, 1977.

Schüssler Fiorenza, *Revelation*
> Schüssler Fiorenza, E. *The Book of Revelation: Justice and Judgment*.
> Philadelphia, Fortress, 1985.

Schüssler Fiorenza, "Revelation"
> Schüssler Fiorenza, E. "Apocalyptic and Gnosis in the Book of
> Revelation." *JBL* 92 (1973) 565–81.

Sherwin-White, "Early Persecutions"
> Sherwin-White, A. N. "Early Persecutions and Roman Law Again."
> *JTS*, n.s., 3 (1952) 199–213.

SJT
> *Scottish Journal of Theology*

Skinner, *Prophecy*
> Skinner, J. *Prophecy and Religion*. Cambridge: University Press, 1930.

Smith, *Micah*
> Smith, R. L. *Micah–Malachi*. WBC 32. Waco, Tex.: Word, 1984.

SNTS
> Society for New Testament Studies

Sparks, *AOT*
> Sparks, H. F. D. *The Apocryphal Old Testament*. Oxford: Clarendon,
> 1984.

Speiser, *Genesis*
> Speiser, E. A. *Genesis*. AB 1. Garden City, N.Y.: Doubleday, 1964.

Steudel, "4Q177"
> Steudel, A. "Eschatological Interpretation of Scripture in 4Q177
> (4Q Catena^a)." *RevQ* 14 (1990) 473–81.

STM
> *Studies on the Testament of Moses: Seminar Papers*. Edited by G. W. E.
> Nickelsburg. Septuagint and Cognate Studies 4. Cambridge, Mass:
> SBL, 1973.

Stone, "Apocalyptic Literature"
> Stone, M. E. "Apocalyptic Literature." *JWSTP*, 383.

Stone, " 'The End' in 4 Ezra"
> Stone, M. E. "Coherence and Inconsistency in the Apocalypses:
> The Case of 'The End' in 4 Ezra." *JBL* 102 (1983) 229–43.

Stone, *Fourth Ezra*
  Stone, M. E. *Fourth Ezra: A Commentary on the Book of Fourth Ezra.*
  Hermeneia. Minneapolis: Augsburg Fortress, 1990.
Stone, *Scriptures*
  Stone, M. E. *Scriptures, Sects and Visions: A Profile of Judaism from Ezra
  to the Jewish Revolts.* Philadelphia: Fortress, 1980.
Strack and Billerbeck, *Kommentar*
  Strack, H. L., and P. Billerbeck. *Kommentar zum Neuen Testament aus
  Talmud und Midrasch.* 6 vols. Munich: C. H. Beck, 1922–28,
  1956–66.
Strecker, *Der Weg*
  Strecker, G. *Der Weg der Gerechtigkeit: Untersuchung zu Theologie des
  Matthäus.* Göttingen: Vandenhoeck & Ruprecht, 1966.
Strobel, *Kerygma*
  Strobel, A. *Kerygma und Apokalyptik: Ein religiongeschichtlicher und
  theologischer Beitrag zur Christusfrage.* Göttingen: Vandenhoeck &
  Ruprecht, 1967.
Strobel, *Untersuchungen*
  Strobel, A. *Untersuchungen zum eschatologischen Verzögerungsproblem:
  auf Grund der spätjudisch-urchristlichen Geschichte von Habakuk 2,2ff.*
  Leiden: Brill, 1961.
Stuart, *Hosea–Jonah*
  Stuart, D. *Hosea–Jonah.* WBC 31. Waco, Tex.: Word, 1987.
Sturdy, *Numbers*
  Sturdy, J. *Numbers.* CBC. Cambridge: University Press, 1976.
Sweet, "Assumption"
  Sweet, J. P. M. "The Assumption of Moses." *AOT.* 601–16.
Swete, *Apocalypse*
  Swete, H. B. *The Apocalypse of St. John.* 3d ed. 1908. Reprint. Grand
  Rapids: Kregel, 1979.
Talbert, "Quest"
  Talbert, C. H. "The Redactional Critical Quest for Luke the
  Theologian." Pages 171–222. In *Jesus and Man's Hope.* Vol. 1. Edited
  by D. G. Buttrick. Pittsburgh: Pittsburgh Theological Seminary,
  1970.
TB
  Tyndale Bulletin
TDNT
  Theological Dictionary of the New Testament. 10 vols. Edited by
  G. Kittel and G. Friedrich. Translated by G. W. Bromiley. Grand
  Rapids: Eerdmans, 1964–76.
Testuz, *Jubilés*
  Testuz, M. *Les Idées religieuses du Livre des Jubilés.* Geneva: Droz,
  1960.

Thompson, *Responsibility*
> Thompson, A. L. *Responsibility for Evil in the Theodicy of IV Ezra: A Study Illustrating the Significance of Form and Structure for the Meaning of the Book.* SBLDS 29. Missoula, Mont.: Scholars, 1977.

Thompson, *Jeremiah*
> Thompson, J. A. *The Book of Jeremiah.* NICOT. Grand Rapids: Eerdmans, 1980.

Thompson, *Revelation*
> Thompson, L. L. *The Book of Revelation: Apocalypse and Empire.* New York: Oxford University Press, 1990.

Tigghelaar, "Apocalyptic"
> Tigghelaar, E. J. C. "More on Apocalyptic and Apocalypses." *JSJ* 18 (1987) 137–44.

TNTC
> Tyndale New Testament Commentaries

TOTC
> Tyndale Old Testament Commentaries

Trafton, "Isaiah"
> Trafton, J. L. "Isaiah, Martyrdom and Ascension Of." *ABD.* 6.507–9.

Trilling, *Israel*
> Trilling, W. *Das wahre Israel: Studien zur Theologie des Matthäus-Evangeliums.* Munich: Kösel, 1964.

TUGAL
> Texte und Untersuchungen zur Geschichte der altchristlichen Literatur

Ulrich, "Daniel Manuscripts"
> Ulrich, E. "Daniel Manuscripts from Qumran. Part 1: A Preliminary Edition of 4QDan^a." *BASOR* 268 (1987) 17–37.

VanderKam, *Enoch*
> VanderKam, J. C. *Enoch and the Growth of an Apocalyptic Tradition.* CBQMS 16. Washington D.C., 1984.

VanderKam, *Jubilees*
> VanderKam, J. C. *Textual and Historical Studies in the Book of Jubilees.* Missoula: Scholars, 1977.

de Vaux, *Archaeology*
> de Vaux, R. *Archaeology and the Dead Sea Scrolls.* Translated by D. Bourke. Repr. London: British Academy by the Oxford University Press, 1973.

Vermes, *DSSE*
> Vermes, G. *The Dead Sea Scrolls in English.* 3d ed. Harmondsworth: Penguin, 1987.

Vermes, *Perspective*
> Vermes, G. *The Dead Sea Scrolls: Qumran in Perspective.* Philadelphia: Fortress, rev. 1977.

Vos, *Synoptic Traditions*
Vos, L. A. *The Synoptic Traditions in the Apocalypse.* Kampen: Kok, 1965.

Vielhauer, "Apocalyptic"
Vielhauer, P. "Apocalyptic in Early Christianity: 1, Introduction." In *New Testament Apocrypha.* 2 vols. Edited by E. Hennecke, W. Schneemelcher, and R. McL. Wilson. Philadelphia: Westminster, 1965.

Violet, *Apokalypsen*
Violet, B. *Die Apokalypsen des Esra und Baruch in deutscher Gestalt.* Leipzig: Hinrichs'sche, 1924.

Volz, *Eschatologie*
Volz, P. *Die Eschatologie der jüdischen Gemeinde im neutestamentlichen Zeitalter.* Tübingen: Mohr, 1934; repr. Hildesheim: G. Olms, 1966.

Vriezen, *Outline*
Vriezen, Th. C. *An Outline of Old Testament Theology.* 2d rev. ed. ET: Newton, Mass.: Charles T. Branford. 1970.

VT
Vetus Testamentum

VTSup
Vetus Testamentum, Supplements

Wanamaker, *Thessalonians*
Wanamaker, C. A. *The Epistles to the Thessalonians: A Commentary on the Greek Text.* Grand Rapids: Eerdmans, 1990.

Watts, *Isaiah*
Watts, J. D. W. *Isaiah 1–33.* WBC 24. Waco, Tex.: Word, 1985.

WBC
Word Biblical Commentary

Weeden, "Heresy"
Weeden, T. J. "The Heresy that Necessitated Mark's Gospel." *ZNW* 59 (1968) 145–58.

Wenham, "Paul"
Wenham, D. "Paul and the Synoptic Apocalypse." Pages 345–75. In *Gospel Perspectives: Studies of History and Tradition in the Four Gospels.* Vol. 2. Edited by R. T. France and D. Wenham. Sheffield: JSOT, 1981.

Wenham, *Rediscovery*
Wenham, D. *The Rediscovery of Jesus' Eschatological Discourse: Gospel Perspectives* 4. Sheffield: JSOT, 1984.

Werner, *Formation*
Werner, M. *The Formation of Christian Dogma: A Historical Study of its Problem.* New York: Harper, 1957.

Westermann, *Genesis*
Westermann, C. *Genesis 37–50.* Translated by J. J. Scullion. Minneapolis: Augsburg, 1986.

Widengren, "Iran"
> Widengren, G. "Iran and Israel in Parthian Times with Special
> Reference to the Ethiopic *Book of Enoch*." In *Religious Syncretism in
> Antiquity: Essays in Conversation with Geo. Widengren*. Edited by B. A.
> Pearson. Missoula, Mont.: Scholars Press (1975) 85–128.

Williams, *Renewal*
> Williams, J. R. *Renewal Theology*. 3 vols. Grand Rapids: Zondervan,
> 1992.

Willis, "Prophetic Hope Oracle"
> Willis, J. T. "A Reapplied Prophetic Hope Oracle." *Studies on
> Prophecy*. VTSup 26 (1974) 64–76.

Willis, *Kingdom of God*
> Willis, W., ed. *The Kingdom of God in 20th-Century Interpretation*.
> Peabody, Mass.: Hendrickson, 1987.

Wintermute, "Jubilees"
> Wintermute, O. S. "Jubilees." In *OTP*. 2.35–142.

Wise, "Eschatological Vision"
> Wise, M. O. "The Eschatological Vision of the Temple Scroll."
> *JNES* 49 (1990) 155–72.

WMANT
> Wissenschaftliche Monographien zum Alten und Neuen Testament

Wolff, *Hosea*
> Wolff, H. W. *Hosea*. Hermeneia. Translated by G. Stansell. Edited
> by P. D. Hanson. Philadelphia: Fortress, 1974.

Wolff, *Joel and Amos*
> Wolff, H. W. *Joel and Amos*. Hermeneia. Translated by W. Janzen,
> S. D. McBride, Jr., and C. A. Muenchow. Edited by S. D. McBride,
> Jr. Philadelphia: Fortress, 1977.

Wright, *Environment*
> Wright, G. E. *The Old Testament against its Environment*. SBT 2.
> London: SCM, 1950.

Wright, "Psalms of Solomon"
> Wright, R. B. "Psalms of Solomon." *OTP*. 2.639–70.

Yadin, *Temple Scroll*
> Yadin, Y. *The Temple Scroll: The Hidden Law of the Dead Sea Sect*.
> Edited by M. Pearlman. New York: Random, 1985.

Young, *Isaiah*
> Young, E. J. *The Book of Isaiah*. 3 vols. Grand Rapids: Eerdmans,
> 1965–72.

Youngblood, "Prophecy and Apocalyptic"
> Youngblood, R. "A Holistic Typology of Prophecy and Apocalyptic."
> Pages 213–21. In A. Gileadi, *Israel's Apostasy and Restoration: Essays in
> Honor of R. K. Harrison*. Grand Rapids: Baker, 1988.

Zaehner, *Dawn*
> Zaehner, R. C. *The Dawn and Twilight of Zoroastrianism*. London:
> Weidenfeld and Nicolson, 1961.

ZAW
> *Zeitschrift für die alttestamentliche Wissenschaft*

Zimmerli, *Ezekiel*
> Zimmerli, W. *Ezekiel 2.* Hermeneia. Translated by J. D. Martin. Edited by P. D. Hanson with L. J. Greenspoon. Philadelphia: Fortress, 1983.

Zimmerli, "History"
> Zimmerli, W. "The History of Israelite Religion." Pages 351–84. In *Tradition and Interpretation.* Edited by G. W. Anderson. Oxford: Clarendon, 1979.

ZNW
> *Zeitschrift für die neutestamentliche Wissenschaft und die Kunde der älteren Kirche*

INTRODUCTION

The NEW TESTAMENT IS ESCHATOLOGICAL. THE EARLY CHURCH which gave us our NT saw itself as an end-time phenomenon (cf. 1 Cor 10:11; Heb 9:16; 1 Pet 1:20; 1 John 2:18). In fact the NT breathes the air of fulfillment of the OT prophetic (eschatological) hope; and beyond that, anticipation of a yet greater fulfillment. Therefore, to understand the eschatological orientation of the NT is essentially to understand the NT. Conversely, not to understand the eschatological origin of the NT is really not to understand the NT.

At the center of NT eschatology is expectation—that is, anticipation of the final victory of God in the parousia (coming) of Jesus Christ.[1] In this monograph I focus primarily on understanding the eschatological expectation of the early (NT) church. In the process we shall examine attending motifs that were part of that hope.

In exploring this theme, I shall trace eschatological expectation in the way in which I understand the early church to have interpreted Jesus' message, particularly as found in the eschatological discourse of the Synoptic Gospels, in 2 Thessalonians 2, and in the Apocalypse.[2] But since the origins of NT expectation are firmly rooted in the OT and apparently to a significant extent in Jewish apocalypticism, I shall first give attention to both of these relevant

---

[1] Cf. Moltmann, *Hope,* 325: "The risen Christ calls, sends, justifies and sanctifies men and in so doing gathers, calls and sends them into his eschatological future for the world." Eschatology "announces the future" of a present reality, ibid., 17.

[2] The homogeneity of these three main examples of apocalyptic in the NT has been recognized by scholars, cf. Vielhauer, "Apocalyptic," 2.624f.; Moule, *Birth,* 151; Jeremias, *Theology,* 124; Dunn, *Unity,* 326–34; Ford, *Abomination,* 254.

literatures. We must reckon with the fact that while early Christian hope is rooted in the prophetic hope of the OT, the NT reflects a *transformed* hope. In part this may be explained in light of apocalyptic Judaism, which both preceded and accompanied the Christian era. We will also consider ways in which the NT hope sharply contrasts with Jewish apocalyptic thought, and then ponder the reasons why.

In Part One I look at the development of the origins of expectation as found in the OT and especially in the writings of the prophets. In order to appreciate the fundamental role of the OT in NT eschatology, we will need to identify certain NT themes that are an extension of OT thought.

New Testament fulfillment largely centers on the messianic hope (e.g., Acts 3:18–26; 1 Pet 1:10–12). Behind this lies the fulfillment of a covenant relationship which Yahweh established with Israel. The early church traced the roots of its faith back to three prominent OT figures: Abraham, David, and Moses. A covenant relationship that distinctly determined the future of Israel is associated with each of these men. Consequently, the fulfillment of the covenants relates to these three pillars of OT faith. This may be seen in various ways.

(1) It is clear that realization of Israel's eschatological (messianic) hope amounts to fulfillment of covenant promises made to Abraham and to David (cf. Luke 1:32–33, 54–55, 67–79; Acts 3:26; Rom 4:13–18; Gal 3:6–9, 14, 19). The NT abounds with references to these two OT heroes to whom promises for Israel's glorious future were made. The critical role of Abraham and David in the NT hope is underscored by the linking of these two in the NT. They appear together in Matt 1:1 as heading the genealogy of Jesus the Messiah. Eschatological fulfillment revolves around these two in Luke 1 (vv. 32–33 with vv. 68–73). In Rom 4 Paul uses both (and only these) as models of justification by faith. In Acts 2–3 Abraham and David, along with Moses, are the key OT figures around which fulfillment of the messianic salvific blessing is interpreted.

(2) Fulfillment is also seen against the backdrop of Yahweh's covenant with Israel through Moses. But here the Sinaitic legal code is more conspicuous than is the covenant promise. Consequently fulfillment is more markedly type to antitype, with contrast highlighted (e.g., the new covenant versus old in 2 Cor 3:7–18; Heb 8–10). Nevertheless the new covenant with life in the Spirit provides fulfillment of the moral and ethical dimensions of the Mosaic law (e.g., 2 Cor 3:3–6 with Rom 8:1–4 and Gal 5:13–18). Jesus' own prophetic ministry is in fact understood as modeled after that of Moses (Acts 3:22f.).

(3) It is the uniform testimony of the NT that the messianic mission which started in the appearance of Jesus of Nazareth preaching the gospel of the kingdom will only be consummated with the future coming of the Son of man (the parousia) in his glorious kingdom. This will usher in the ultimate fulfillment of the OT eschatological hope, howbeit, a more glorious and radically transformed hope.

In Part Two I deal with selected Jewish apocalyptic documents, both canonical (Daniel) and extra-canonical. These help further to explain the background of early church eschatological expectation. At times there appears in the literature an apocalyptic hope wherein the present earth gives way to a future world that is radically different in its suprahistorical and transcendental character. It is somewhat more prominent in the later Jewish works that are contemporaneous with those of the late first century Christian church. This section is first concerned with the earlier Jewish works, starting with Daniel, and then turns to three late first century (or early second century?) Jewish apocalypses. The greater attention I give to Jewish apocalyptic literature is hopefully justified in the interesting and somewhat controversial background it provides to early Christian eschatology, especially since this is often not sufficiently considered in background studies of the NT.

In Part Three I trace eschatological expectation through the key NT writings (see above) in the chronological order in which I perceive them to have been written. The accent is clearly on apocalyptic, as a significant part of that worldview becomes the locus of NT expectation. To speak of the expectation of Jesus and the early church immediately raises a number of critical questions for scholars. Especially in the fore is the question of the extent to which the early church and the Evangelists have reinterpreted the original Jesus message. In this study, my intent is not to explore fully this relevant subject, though there is a brief discussion in an excursus at the end of Part Three. Rather, I shall work with the NT documents as they stand, but nevertheless do so with sensitivity to identifying the tradition which apparently lies behind the documents. We shall look at the use the Evangelists have made of the gospel tradition which they received, which is commonly called "the Jesus tradition."

With Part Four I summarize and draw conclusions from this discussion of the progressive development of eschatological expectation in its varied historical settings. Here I include hermeneutical implications for understanding the relevance of biblical eschatology today, along with a final challenge.

As we track eschatological expectation through the OT prophetic literature, through Jewish apocalyptic documents, and then
through the indicated NT literature, it will become evident that a
near-expectation/delay tension is often present. I believe that the
historical and theological reasons for this are instructive for us, as
we seek to relate to biblical hope today.

Our investigation leads to several questions. Why is the NT hope
so different from that of ancient Israel? What are the pivotal points
which account for a transformed hope by the time of the Christian
era? How decisive was Jewish apocalypticism in shaping early
church expectation? What hermeneutical implications might there
be for the church today in reckoning with a biblical hope? These are
not new questions. However, consideration of tension between near
expectation and delay, which occurs throughout much of the pertinent literature, has seldom received the attention that it deserves. I
believe that this is important for understanding NT expectation and
how this NT hope might inform the contemporary church.

I am aware that the contemporary background against which
explorations such as this are undertaken is that of a revival of
interest in apocalypticism.

On the scholarly level, there is much ongoing research in the
ancient literature, with at times a delving into the relevance of such
studies for the contemporary world. For example an international
colloquium on apocalypticism convened in Uppsala, August 12–17,
1979 resulted in a work first published in 1983 and revised in 1989,
entitled *Apocalypticism in the Mediterranean World and the Near East*.[3]

On the popular level, we have witnessed great interest in "end
of the world" predictions, especially as we approach the end of the
century and another millennium. For example, in 1993 Russell
Chandler, formerly a religion writer for the Los Angeles Times,
published a book entitled, *The End of the World: A View Through
Time*.[4] This volume surveys end time predictions historically and
reflects current interest in the same. In an earlier work, the bulk of
which was submitted as a doctoral dissertation to the University of
Chicago in the '70s, Timothy P. Weber observes that "premillennialism suddenly became big news" after 175 public radio stations in

---

[3] Edited by D. Hellholm (Tübingen: J. C. B. Mohr [Paul Siebeck], 2d
ed., 1989).

[4] Ann Arbor, Mich.: Servant Publications, 1993. Cf. Cohn, *Pursuit*,
which surveys movements of eschatological anticipation in Europe in the
latter Middle Ages.

1984 aired a documentary on "Ronald Reagan and the Prophecy of Armageddon."[5] In *When Time Shall Be No More: Prophecy Belief in Modern American Culture,* Paul Boyer, history professor at the University of Wisconsin, asserts that "prophecy belief is far more central in American thought than intellectual and cultural historians have recognized."[6] He further states that since World War II popularizers of dispensational premillennialism have played a large role in shaping public opinion on a wide range of topics, such as the Soviet Union and the Common Market.[7]

For the following study the English biblical quotations are from the New Revised Standard Version of the Bible, unless otherwise indicated. Similarly, for the pseudepigraphical references I commonly use *The Old Testament Pseudepigrapha,* two volumes, edited by James H. Charlesworth (1983, 1985). The Dead Sea Scroll references are from Geza Vermes, *The Dead Sea Scrolls in English,* 1987 edition, unless otherwise indicated. When Hebrew is given for the Scrolls, I refer to Eduard Lohse, *Die Texte aus Qumran* (1971). For the ancient historians Josephus, Tacitus, Plutarch, Suetonius, Dio Cassius, and Eusebius, I have used the Loeb Classical Library series.

---

[5] *Living in the Shadow of the Second Coming: American Premillennialism, 1975–1982* (Chicago: University of Chicago Press, 1979, expanded edition 1983, 1987), viii.

[6] Cambridge, Mass.: Harvard University Press, 1992, ix.

[7] Ibid.

Part One: The Roots of New Testament
Eschatology: The Old Testament Hope

1

EMERGENCE OF EXPECTATION

AMONG ITS SEVERAL NEIGHBORING NATIONS IN THE ANCIENT world, pre-exilic Israel was evidently the only culture which had a growing national eschatology that was rooted in history.[1] Despite its disappointed hopes over the centuries, from the pre-exilic era on, Israel never lost hope of a revival of the Davidic-Solomonic kingdom in all its grandeur and dominance. Furthermore, a radical reinterpretation of this hope in early Christianity in relation to the kingdom of God eventuated in both a vivid awareness of fulfillment and also further expectation within NT Christianity. In fact, the faith of OT Israel has resulted in three great world religions: Judaism, Christianity, and Islam. Nothing of the sort can be said of the religions of the ancient Egyptians, Mesopotamians, Hittites, Canaanites, or any other culture of the ancient Near East. Why did Israel's monotheistic faith remain, and in particular why did its eschatological expectation continue to thrive, eventually giving birth to Christianity?

---

[1]Working from an OT perspective, our definition of "eschatology" includes the last days of history as well as a new world that is inaugurated by God through human mediation. At the same time our definition allows for an "apocalyptic" eschatology that is an outgrowth of Israel's earlier hope. Some scholars have defined "eschatology" solely in apocalyptic terms, with a "cosmic" and "catastrophic" end of the world and an entirely new order emerging independent of human activity, e.g., Mowinckel, *He That Cometh,* 125f. Such OT prophecies are regarded as post-exilic, ibid., 126–33. For our use of the term, see cf. e.g., von Rad, *OT Theology,* 2.113–19, esp. 118; cf. Bright, *Covenant,* 18f.; Clements, *Prophecy,* 113f.; Koch, *Prophets,* 2.117f. McCullough says the term is relative and conditioned by the age in which it appears, "Israel's Eschatology," 86.

Israel's Sense of Salvation History

Israel's awareness of history as the scene of God's mighty acts in its past was the backbone of faith for the future. The exodus deliverance was *the* act to which Israel looked back. The monumental importance of the exodus for Israel is underscored in the attention given it in the Pentateuch. The account covers Exodus 1–15, culminating in a hymn of praise to Yahweh in chapter 15. Except for the Joseph story in Genesis (which explains why Israel was in Egypt), no other single episode within the first six books of the OT receives the same amount of attention.[2] Memory of the exodus events was preserved in Israel's annual Passover observance (e.g., Exod 12; Deut 16:1–8; Josh 5:10), although for some centuries the Passover was apparently not observed (2 Kgs 23:21–23). The prophetic writings helped to preserve memory of the exodus (e.g., 1 Sam 2:27; 10:18; 12:6–8; 1 Kgs 8:9, 16; 2 Kgs 17:7; Hos 11:1; Isa 11:16; Jer 2:6; 11:7). Also the exodus was commemorated in Israel's hymnology (e.g., Pss 78:9–20, 42–53; 105:26–45; 106:6–33; 114:1).

The deliverance by Yahweh from Egyptian captivity was the foundation of Israel's national birth, which in turn formed the basis for covenant relation with its God (cf. 2 Sam 7:6, 23–24; 1 Kgs 8:53; Jer 7:25). Yahweh's prior saving act was followed by a covenant, often called the Mosaic or Sinaitic covenant, in which Israel pledged obedience to the God who had rescued them out of bondage (cf. Exod 19:4–6; 20:1ff.; 24:1–8). But deliverance was at the focal point of its faith.[3] Yahweh was the God who saves his people. Subsequent acts of Yahweh on behalf of his people would form a path of salvation history and thus stimulate hope for the future.[4] Eventually Israel's sense of destiny would clearly extend far beyond its ethnic boundaries and include other peoples.

Israel's Covenant Initiated

At the heart of ancient Israel's tradition and expectation is the idea of covenant. Covenant promises to the Patriarchs are rehearsed

---

[2]Dentan, *Knowledge of God,* 52.

[3]Hanson says that Israel's origin through the Egyptian deliverance is "the most ubiquitous theme of Hebrew scripture, permeating hymns, historical narrative, and legal documents from the earliest to the latest point of oral and then written transmission," *People Called,* 11. See also Noth, *History,* 111f.

[4]Cf. von Rad, *OT Theology,* 2.411.

again and again in Genesis. Then initial fulfillment of covenant promise is detailed, as Yahweh enters into covenant with the descendants of Abraham, Isaac, and Jacob (esp. Exod 19–24).

The Hebrew term for "covenant" (בְּרִית) is found frequently throughout much of the OT as descriptive of Israel's relation to Yahweh. Even where the term is absent the concept is often presupposed. There are of course several closely related themes that run throughout the OT such as election, promise—fulfillment, communion, and redemption. These themes speak of Israel's special relationship with Yahweh, which the OT specifies as a covenant relationship.[5] While recognizing that there are various themes which unify the OT (and in fact the Bible), we may not be too far from the mark in saying that more than any other single theme, the idea of covenant comes the closest to explaining the events and the significance of those events from the standpoint of the biblical authors.[6]

We have already seen how Israel's national identity as a covenant people was anchored in its memory of the exodus event. In order to explain why this covenant relationship between God and the ancient people of Israel was established in the first place, the Pentateuch introduces covenants made centuries earlier between God and the patriarchal ancestors of the Israelites.[7] Here the focus is not mainly

---

[5]Kutsch, *Verheissung*, contends in a widely recognized study that the biblical meaning of בְּרִית is "duty" or "obligation," note summary on 203, 205. This speaks of promise with reference to God and of law with reference to humankind. At this point Nicholson critiques Kutsch for holding that a bilateral significance of "covenant" between God and Israel is only a secondary or exceptional use of the term, *God and His People*, 89–109.

[6]Cf. Nicholson, *God and His People*, esp. vii–viii; Goldingay, *Theological Diversity*, 60; Eichrodt, *Theology*, 1.17f. Note Hubbard, "Hope," 47: "Scarcely anything more firmly underscores the historical nature of Israel's eschatology than [the] emphasis on covenants." The concept of "covenant" seems to have been a metaphor rather analogous to treaty in the ancient world. Mendenhall's seminal work, *Law and Covenant*, orig. published in the *Biblical Archaeologist*, 1954, argued that the concept was borrowed from the ancient world. Since, his theory has come under heavy fire, see survey in McCarthy, *OT Covenant;* however McCarthy himself argues for the "analogy" theory, *Treaty and Covenant*, esp. ch. 13; cf. Levenson, "Davidic Covenant," 205. In assuming as an underlying unity of the OT we are not discounting the diversity which has provided much grist for the mill for OT specialists.

[7]Some scholars have turned in part to the old Wellhausen hypothesis that a well-developed covenant theology in ancient Israel does not pre-date the eighth or seventh centuries, cf. Nicholson, *God and His People*. This is based on: (1) a particular source critical interpretation and late dating of relevant Genesis and Exodus texts, (2) observation that בְּרִית is scarce in the

upon the demand of obedience, but upon the promises of God for
Abraham, Isaac, Jacob, and their descendants. The promises pertain
largely to having: innumerable descendants (cf. Gen 12:2; 13:16;
15:5; 17:2, 4–6, 16; 18:18; 22:16–17; 26:3–4; 28:13–14; 35:11; 46:3);
a homeland (Gen 12:1, 7; 13:14–15; 15:7, 13, 16, 18–19; 17:8;
26:2–4; 28:13–15; 35:12; Exod 3:8, 17; 6:8; 23:23, 31; 34:24); to
being a source (or standard) of blessing to other peoples of the earth
(Gen 12:2–3; 18:18; 22:18; 26:4; 28:14);[8] to identifying a unique
relationship between God and his people. This last promise constitutes the very heart of covenant relationship, even if it identifies a
covenant relationship only in the broadest sense. It is found repeat-
edly throughout the OT in various phrases such as "your God," "the
God of Israel," "my people," etc. In the patriarchal covenant prom-

---

eighth-century prophets, and (3) the supposition that the Deuteronomist
literature (usually regarded as including Deuteronomy—2 Kings in the Hebrew Bible) dates from the seventh and sixth centuries. Cf. Nicholson;
Perlitt, *Bundestheologie*; Kutsch, *Verheissung*. However, Zimmerli, "History,"
378–80, understands the covenant concept to date from the Mosaic period,
but sees it receding and then reappearing in the Deuteronomic era.
McCarthy, *Treaty,* is convinced of the antiquity of the Sinai covenant which
has "very old origins and a long history of development," 277–79. Clements,
Abraham, stresses the influence of the Abrahamic covenant in Israelite tradition and its relation to the *later* Davidic covenant. In a review of Nicholson's
book, J. L. Mays in effect speaks to all theories which "post date" an Israelite
covenant tradition to the eighth or seventh century by stating, "the question
of emergence of Israel in history is left without a credible convincing
answer," *JBL* 107 (1988), 120. A careful investigation of covenant origins lies
beyond the scope of this study. It is important to note for our purposes
that the eschatological expectation which emerged from the times of the
pre-exilic prophets (to be discussed) was rooted in ideas that belonged to
Israel's awareness of a special relation to Yahweh. I take the position that this
in turn was determined by memory of its distinctive past.

[8]Albrektson indicates that it is debated whether these texts refer to
nations "being blessed" (cf. KJV, NASB, NIV, RSV for the Niphal verb, in a
note, NRSV) or in a proverbial way "blessing themselves" (RSV, NRSV for the
Hithpael verb, in a note) by Abraham and/or his descendants. The verb is in
the Niphal form in 12:3; 18:18; 28:14, and in the Hithpael form in 22:18 and
26:4. See his discussion in *History,* 78–81. The LXX however uniformly
renders the verb in these texts as passive, as does the NT when quoting (Acts
3:25; Gal 3:8). Favoring rather the reflexive sense, Albrektson contends that
no "divine plan" is suggested, as would otherwise be the case. We may say
that either way Abraham and his descendants (from the Genesis texts alone)
are seen as in some manner positively affecting the peoples of the earth,
either as the source or the standard of blessing. As time passed the idea at
least included Abraham's descendants being the *source* of blessing to the world
(cf. Isa 19:24 and the LXX of the Genesis texts), cf. von Rad, *Genesis,* 160.

ises the idea is introduced in Gen 17:7f. ("to be God to you [Abram] and to your descendants after you. . . . I will be their God."). It recurs in the patriarchal narratives in phrases such as "the God of Abraham"; "the God of your father"; "the LORD your God" (e.g., Gen 27:20; 28:13; 31:29; 49:25). In 22:17b Yahweh also promises that Abraham's descendants will possess the gate of their enemies. This particular promise will later be recognized as noteworthy when we track the eschatological hope of ancient Israel.[9]

From the above we can see how the covenant promises explain to Israel the mighty acts of Yahweh on its behalf. This is plainly stated in the Pentateuch itself (e.g., Exod 2:6–8, 16–18; 6:2–8; Num 14:22–25; Deut 6:20–23; 9:4–5). Probably more than anything else, this understanding of covenant relationship with Yahweh served to define Israel's national consciousness. Wedded as it was to the history of Yahweh's mighty acts on Israel's behalf, awareness of such covenant relationship made possible expectation of the future great event often referred to as the day of Yahweh. In fact this consciousness eventuated in an eschatological hope which was evidently unprecedented in the ancient Near Eastern world, however imperfectly it may have been popularly held in its earliest forms. Other peoples, particularly in Mesopotamia, may have had some awareness of an unfolding of their history under the hand of their pagan gods; but Israel's sense of destiny remained unparalleled in notable ways, as far as we know.[10]

---

[9]Clines has extensive listings of pentateuchal references to covenant promises, including a large number of "allusions," *Theme*, 32–43. Clines understands the theme of the Pentateuch to be fulfillment (or partial fulfillment) of the patriarchal promise; ibid., esp. 31, cf. 60, 89, 91.

[10]Cf. Hubbard, "Hope," 46f. It has been common to assert Israel's historical uniqueness and its unique sense of history, e.g., Noth, *History*, 2f.; Vriezen, *Outline*, 39; Wright, *Environment*, esp. 71f. Others have critiqued this approach for not sufficiently acknowledging an ancient sense of divine activity in history elsewhere and especially in Mesopotamia, e.g., Albrektson, *History*, much of the book, but note esp. 95–97. However Albrektson himself is inclined to conclude that historical events were perceived in Israel as divine manifestations in a way unparalleled among Israel's neighbors (115). He adds that "the deity's saving acts in history are nowhere afforded so central a position in the cult as in Israel," where they dominate in festal celebration (116). Saggs, *Encounter*, supports Albrektson's main critique, but also says that in Israel's prophetic movement the bounds of Near Eastern religions were burst (and also those of traditional Yahwism) in the universality of the messages, chs. 3, 5, and in particular pp. 151f. Somewhat less sympathetic responses to Albrektson may be found in Porter, "OT Historiography," and

Development of a "Golden Age" of Hope

Three Early Oracles

There are three poetical portions of the Pentateuch which
reflect confidence for a successful future, portions which are often
recognized as derived from ancient tradition prior to being re-
corded. These are the Blessing of Jacob (Gen 49); the oracles of
Balaam (in Num 23–24), and the Blessing of Moses (Deut 33).

The so-called Blessing of Jacob ("blessing" is not in the text
itself) is a mixed bag, but it emphasizes Judah's rulership (vv.
9–12) and Joseph's help and blessing from the Almighty (vv. 22–26). The
possibility or likelihood of a pre-monarchic life setting of the Gen
49 oracles is often acknowledged, based on internal evidence of the
sayings themselves.[11] Thus these oracles provide some reason to
trace a future hope to the earlier history of Israel.

In the Balaam oracles the prophet finds it impossible to pro-
nounce misfortune on Israel, for God is with them (23:7–10,
18–24); Balaam desires an "end" (אַחֲרִית) for himself like that destined for Israel, who are like the dust of the earth for number
(23:10; cf. the promise to Abram in 13:16 and repeated in 28:14);
Israel will destroy her enemies and those who bless her will be
blessed, even as those who curse her will be cursed (24:3–9, especially vv. 8f.; cf. Gen 12:3; see also Num 24:17–19 with the promise
to Abraham in Gen 22:17b). The canonical context is very appropriate, as Israel is about to enter the land of promise and experience
fulfillment of covenant blessings. The feeling of national confidence, success, prosperity, and contentment in the poems has been
considered a strong point in favor of their antiquity.[12]

Lambert, "Destiny." The latter concludes "it is a fact that many prophets
looked forward to something that had not occurred in human history prior
to their time. It is this idea which gave to the Hebrews a real concept of
history, which the ancient Mesopotamians lacked," 72.

[11] Cf. Bright, *Covenant,* 45; Speiser, *Genesis,* 371; Westermann, *Genesis
37–50,* 221. Aalders says: "It is generally accepted that we are dealing with some
of the oldest records that were incorporated into the 'J' source,"*Genesis,* 2.267.

[12] Gray, *Numbers,* 313f., who sees these poems closely connected with
the Blessing of Jacob, (Gen 49) and the Blessing of Moses (Deut 33).
Albright, "Oracles," has had some following in understanding these oracles
to predate the "J" and "E" documents, in which they are usually considered
to be found, cf. Budd, *Numbers,* 258f.; Bright, *Covenant,* 45; Noth, *Numbers,*
189 with 8, on the ch. 24 discourses. In fact Albright has said that the oracles
are most likely a reflection of Balaam's day ("Oracles"). Sturdy, *Numbers,* 158,
suggests the eleventh or tenth century and composed by "J" himself.

In the Blessing of Moses (Deut 33), both success against enemies and agrarian prosperity are reflected (vv. 7, 11–16, 24f.). Verses
26–29 emphasize these blessings for all Israel, with prime attention
given to its success over enemies. For a variety of historical and
linguistic reasons some scholars prefer a date around the tenth
century or earlier. The positive anticipation of the future well suits
the early history of the monarchy.[13]

A number of poems, including those presented above, have
been placed in "the earliest period of Israel's history" in light of
similarities with Canaanite literature from Ras Shamra (fourteenth
century).[14]

We thus see the makings of a golden age hope from possibly a
pre-monarchic period. This in turn is all the more understandable
if Israel was aware of being in covenant relation with Yahweh, as we
have discussed above. In any case the hope represented in the above
three pentateuchal poems became part of the written tradition of Israel.
This should help us to appreciate the strength of Israel's eschatological hope when it fully blossomed in the exilic and post-exilic times.

The Davidic Throne and Covenant

More than any other, the Davidic-Solomonic era proved to
establish a golden age hope in Israel. The territorial boundaries of
Israel were greatly enlarged. King David had subjugated vast territo-
ries in victory after victory (2 Sam 8). Twice in this chapter the
author of Samuel says that Yahweh gave victory to David "wherever
he went" (vv. 6, 14). Subsequently the nation flourished in many
ways in the reign of Solomon. This is graphically implied in the
concise statement of 1 Kings 4:20–22:

> Judah and Israel were as many as the sand by the sea; they ate and
> drank and were happy. Solomon ruled over all the kingdoms from the
> Euphrates to the land of the Philistines and to the border of Egypt;
> they brought tribute and served Solomon all the days of his life.

This era of political and economic greatness was undoubtedly
viewed in succeeding generations as a considerable fulfillment of

---

[13] E.g., Driver, *Deuteronomy,* 387f.; von Rad says the ninth or early eighth
century, *Deuteronomy,* 208. All do not agree on the linguistic evidence, see
Mayes, *Deuteronomy,* 397, who puts the collection as a whole in the eighth
century, but with the collection also in existence a considerable time prior
to its later incorporation.

[14] Bright, *History,* 143, with notes. Bright provides representative docu-
mentation from the secondary literature for the various poems.

covenant blessing, and in particular, fulfillment of the Abrahamic
covenant. In the text itself the narrator makes a "fulfilled covenant"
interpretation of the Solomonic era fairly apparent.[15] In chapter 4 a
detailing of Solomon's servants and of provisions for the royal house-
hold is twice interrupted with descriptions of Judah and Israel which
hark back to covenant promises (vv. 20f. and vv. 24f.).

First, the population count is compared with the innumerable
sand of the sea (v. 20 with Gen 22:17; 32:12 [MT 32:13]. Although
"sand by the sea" is used a few times elsewhere in the OT to indicate
population proliferation (or a large crowd) without covenant fulfillment being indicated or made clear (Jos 11:4; Jud 7:12; 1 Sam 13:5;
2 Sam 17:11; Hab 1:9), the phrase is also found in the eighth
century prophets and later, with covenant associations (Hos 1:10
[MT 2:1]; Jer 33:22; and possibly Isa 10:22; 48:19). In view of other
covenant comparisons in our 1 Kings 4 passage, the likelihood is
that "sand by sea" is to be interpreted similarly.

Second, the territorial boundaries now under Solomon's rule
compare with those mentioned in the Abrahamic covenant (cf. Gen
15:18; Josh 1:4). It is true that Israel itself does not occupy land
from the Euphrates to the border of Egypt. But does not reference
to these boundaries at least indicate movement toward covenant
fulfillment? This appears to be the point of the author in stating
these particular boundaries.[16] At this point we also note that partial
fulfillment could easily stimulate hope toward greater fulfillment in
the ensuing generations.

Third, Israel's hegemony over surrounding peoples and the
resultant security is emphasized in 1 Kings 4 (vv. 20b–21, 24f.) and
corresponds with Abraham's descendants possessing the gate of
their enemies (Gen 22:17).

This high point in Israel's history would serve as a kind of
model for centuries to come. David's throne would endure and

---

[15] From a source critical or at least a tradition historical viewpoint, this
of course presupposes the prior existence and awareness of the Abrahamic
covenant in some form, cf. Clements, *Abraham,* ch. 4. The alternative would
probably be to understand later authors composing the Abrahamic covenant
almost entirely in light of the glories of the Davidic-Solomonic era, and thus
reversing the canonical context. Cf. note 9 above.

[16] Cf. Bright, *Covenant,* 55, with n. 4. By the same token, scholars have
dated the "J" source of Genesis from the tenth century, partly because the
land-promises in Genesis are "fulfilled" in this period, e.g., Clements, *Abraham,*
ch. 2, and pp. 59f. Clements also believes an earlier form of the land promise
was limited to south Canaan, 21.

future kings would sit upon it (e.g., Isa 9:7 [MT 9:6]; 16:5; Jer 13:13; 22:2, 4; 33:15, 17). With the emergence of an eschatological hope, a new "David" would sit on the throne (Jer 30:9; Ezek 34:24; 37:24; Hos 3:5). The hope became messianic at this point and of course reaches into the New Testament, where Christ is the "son of David" (e.g., Matt 1:1; 9:27 = Mark 10:48 = Luke 18:38, 39; Matt 12:23; 21:9, 15; cf. Rom 1:3; Rev 5:5; 22:16).

The enduring character of the Davidic dynasty is traced by biblical authors to a covenant which Yahweh made with David, a covenant apparently found first in 2 Sam 7:1–17 (though not termed a covenant there), and then in Pss 89; 132:10–12; Jer 33:19–21. These diverse references are further evidence that the Davidic covenant became quite well rooted in Israelite tradition.[17] The covenant has certain parallels with the Abrahamic covenant, as follows:

1. David's name is to be great, as was that of Abram (2 Sam 7:9; Gen 12:2);

2. Israel is to have its own dwelling place and is to be secure from/triumphant over its enemies (2 Sam 7:9–11; Ps 89:20–27 [MT 89:21–28]; Gen 12:3, 7; 13:14–15; 17:8; 22:17);

3. Perpetuity of the Davidic dynasty is underscored, as is perpetuity of the Abrahamic covenant (2 Sam 7:12–16; Ps 89:4, 20, 29, 36 [MT 89:5, 21, 30, 37]; Gen 17:7f., 19);

4. Intimacy of relationship with Yahweh is stated, although in 2 Sam this is *immediately* associated with chastisement when the relationship is violated (2 Sam 7:14; Ps 89:26; Gen 17:7f.).

It is evident that the Davidic covenant stresses what Yahweh will do, and thus it is a covenant of promise, as is the Abrahamic covenant. However, as with the Abrahamic covenant, the disobedient are punished (2 Sam 7:14; Ps 89:30–32 [MT 89:31–33]; cf. Gen 17:14). But neither covenant is ever to be finally abrogated (2 Sam 7:15f.; Ps 89:28–37 [MT 89:29–38]; Gen 17:7–9). In light of the foregoing similarities of the two covenants, it appears that the covenant with David afforded an *extension* of the Abrahamic covenant. It was for an age in which earlier promises of numerous descendants and acquisition of the land had been/were being realized, and in which a monarchy now existed.[18] The continuity between these two

---

[17] Cf. Hubbard's succinct detailed discussion in "Hope," 39–42. Clements refers to the 2 Sam 7 passage as "the seed-bed" of the messianic hope, "Messianic Hope," 12.

[18] Clements, *Abraham,* ch. 5, concludes that the form of the Davidic covenant was probably influenced by recollection in Jerusalem of the ancient

covenants highlights hope and thus helps to explain how the NT is able to understand both covenants together as pointing to the coming of Christ (e.g., Matt 1:1).

How does the Davidic covenant compare with the poems of Genesis 49, Numbers 23f., and Deuteronomy 33 (discussed above) in setting forth the hope of Israel? One theme is fairly pervasive: Israel's success over its enemies. With the success of the Davidic-Solomonic monarchy, coupled with the Davidic covenant which promised future success, hope for a golden age was set. In this age Israel would dominate over its enemies and enjoy prosperity.

Demise of the hegemony of Solomon's tenth century kingdom (cf. 1 Kgs 14:25–28), must have brought a longing for the "good old days." And the fact that the monarchy in the southern kingdom of Judah never departed from the Davidic line would seem to testify to the seriousness with which Judah took the covenant promise.[19] This promise, together with the frequent religious infidelity under succeeding kings in Judah, surely fueled, if not triggered, the eschatological and messianic hope of prophetic inspiration as generations passed (cf. Jer 23:5–6 = 33:14–16 with 23:1f.).

Israel's hope is also reflected in Psalm 72. The psalm (difficult to date) anticipates justice in the land, dominion over enemies, and agrarian prosperity. These themes became prominent in messianic expectation (cf. Isa 9:1–7 [MT 8:23–9:6]; 11:1–9; Jer 30:8–11, 18–22; 31:10–14; Ezek 34:24–28). Psalm 72 concludes with a prayer that through the rule of the king all nations will be blessed (v. 17). This corresponds with the Abrahamic covenant (Gen 12:3; 18:18; 22:18; 26:4) and helps to confirm that the Davidic covenant was regarded as an extension of the Abrahamic covenant.

---

covenant with Abraham. He speculates that the Abraham covenant tradition was located in Hebron (cf. Gen 13:18; 23:29; 35:27), where David had close ties at the start of his reign over Judah (cf. 2 Sam 2:1–4). I do not find Clements discussing how this might relate to the biblical explanation that the Davidic covenant came from the prophetic inspiration of Nathan (cf. 2 Sam 7:4ff.).

[19] Bright, *Covenant,* 57ff., regarding 2 Samuel 7:12–16. (This need not depreciate recognition of the divine hand in history sovereignly seeing through the promise made in 2 Sam 7:16.) Bright here reckons with the debate over the date of the passage, but observes that reference to the Davidic Covenant is found in 2 Samuel 23:5, "which is in all probability of tenth-century date," 57. Cf. Cross, *Canaanite Myth,* 234–37. Cross believes the oracle of 2 Samuel 7 "in poetic form . . . goes back to Davidic times," ibid., 255; see 241–64.

We ought not to think that the messianic hope was limited to what was experienced in the Davidic-Solomonic reign. Psalm 72 itself would seem to go beyond this in its prayer for a universal kingdom and blessing for all nations (vv. 8, 11, 17).[20] But the conception of Yahweh's promise to bless His people had now entered a new dimension, and hope for the future became more concrete along the lines so gloriously displayed in Israel's first golden age.

Expectation in Pre-exilic (Eighth Century) Prophets

The earliest evidence of truly eschatological expectation in Israel and Judah is probably in the eighth century B.C. prophets. There we first witness the prophetic warning of a dissolution of the existing kingdom(s), but also the promise of a new start.[21] Beyond judgment the prophets, both pre- and post-exilic, foresaw a new age. The former times would terminate in a display of Yahweh's righteous anger, but he would yet fulfill his covenant promises in the new day.

Amos

We begin with what is often considered the initial reference to the day of Yahweh, Amos 5:18–20. It is impossible to know just when Israel began to think of a day of Yahweh in conjunction with its hope. But it is clear that Israel anticipates Yahweh's blessing in such a day. We have already surveyed the likely reasons for this hope. In 5:18–20 the eighth century B.C. prophet points his finger at Israel for violation of its covenant vows.

> Woe to you who desire the day of the LORD! Why would you have the day of the LORD? It is darkness, and not light [v. 18].

The concept of a day of Yahweh seems to have its origin in the idea of Yahweh "visiting" (פָּקַד) his people or the nations. This was

---

[20] Cf. Bright, *Covenant,* 66. Bright also points to an allusion of the river of paradise in Psalm 46:4 (cf. Gen 2:10–14; Ezek 47:1–12; Zech 14:8; Rev 22:1), ibid., 68.

[21] Cf. our defnition of eschatology on p. 1. Vriezen finds four OT views of the future: "pre-eschatological" (prior to the eighth century prophets); "proto-eschatological" (eighth-century prophets to Jeremiah); "eschatological with reference to the near future" (exilic, including Deutero-Isaiah); "transcendental-eschatological" (the apocalyptic period of "dualistic eschatology"), *Outline,* 456–58; cf. Ladd, *Presence,* 55f.; Frost, *OT Apocalyptic,* 46–50, 233–44.

often for purposes of blessing or deliverance (e.g., Gen 21:1; Exod 3:16; Ruth 1:6; Jer 27:22; Zeph 2:7); but frequently it was for punishment, especially seen in the prophets (e.g., Exod 32:34; Ps 89:32 [MT 89:33]; Isa 13:11; 23:17; Jer 6:15; 13:21; 44:13; Hos 1:4; Amos 3:14; Zech 10:3). Note in particular Amos 3:14 (*"on the day* I punish [פָּקַד] Israel"). The prophets warned of a day of judgment that was coming instead of the golden age that was yet hoped for by a backslidden Israel. This is clearly the dominant message of Amos. See especially 3:1–2 and the themes of reproof and warning throughout the book. In the conclusion of the book (9:11–15) there is a sudden turn of events with the triumphant restoration of Davidic rule (v. 11, particularly interesting in that Amos addressed the northern kingdom of Israel) and the promise of agrarian prosperity.[22]

We should observe that the prophetic correction of popular expectation amounts to a delay in fulfillment of the popular hope. Apparently the political/military success and prosperity of the eighth century B.C. had rekindled "golden age" hopes.[23] Thus we see a significant number in Israel "desiring" the day of Yahweh, even though their era was already a time of national material success (Amos 5:18)!

Hosea

The prophetic linking of Yahweh repudiating faithless Israel with Israel's restoration in covenant faithfulness is seen most vividly in Hosea. Note 1:9 ("Then the LORD said, 'Name him Lo-ammi, for you are not my people and I am not your God' ") with the following verse ("Yet the number of the people of Israel shall be like the sand of the sea . . . and in the place where it was said to them, 'You are not my people,' it shall be said to them, 'Children of the living God' "). Both Israel and Judah were to be restored (1:11 [MT 2:2]). The salvation message of Hosea continues in 2:14–23 [MT 2:16–25]. But chapter 11 is even more revealing of Yahweh's love and compassion. Observe the abrupt sequence of ideas (dare we say emotion?) in

---

[22] Many think these verses are a later addition, as they are without analogy earlier in Amos, e.g., Wolff, *Joel and Amos,* 351–53. If this is correct, then there is no clear note of restoration in Amos. Note discussion in Hubbard, *Joel and Amos,* 236–39, who observes thematic contrasts with the earlier portions of Amos and holds out for the reasonableness of vv. 9–15 being original with Amos. Cf. Stuart, who cites orthographic evidence, *Hosea–Jonah,* 397.

[23] For the return of "success" in the time of Israel's Jeroboam II, note 2 Kings 14:23–29; cf. Amos 3:15; 5:11; 6:1, 4–6; Hosea 1:8–12; 4:7; 10:1, 13f.; 13:15.

verses 1–9: "When Israel was a child I loved him" (v. 1); "yet it was I who taught Ephraim to walk" (v. 3); "they shall return to the land of Egypt, and Assyria shall be their king, because they have refused to return to me" (v. 5); "how can I give you up, O Ephraim! . . . My compassion grows warm and tender. I will not execute my fierce anger" (v. 8f.); "they shall go after the LORD . . . they shall come trembling like birds from Egypt . . . I will return them to their homes" (v. 10f.). Hosea's own personal life was a kind of parabolic enactment of this covenant love of Yahweh for his people, which found expression in promises of salvation after judgment:

> And the LORD said to me, "Go, love a woman who has a lover and is an adulteress; just as the LORD loves the people of Israel, though they turn to other gods and love cakes of raisins" (3:1).

Thus Hosea is characterized more with the message of hope beyond judgment than is Amos. The sequence of judgment and then blessing is in fact in all the eighth century B.C. prophetic books as they now stand. Many contemporary scholars, however, believe that such passages are later additions to the respective works, with the post-exilic age often said to be reflected. Thus even though we have so far only examined (quite briefly) two eighth-century B.C. prophets, it should be useful at this point to examine critically the possibility of restoration oracles appearing amidst those of judgment. In so doing we shall at the same time note further judgment/salvation texts, including those in Isaiah and Micah.

A Critical Evaluation

We may make the following observations:

(1) The burden of the pre-exilic prophets was a message of warning and woe to both Israel and Judah who had consistently violated their national vows of allegiance to Yahweh (e.g., Amos 3:1–2; 5:18–20; Hos 4:1–3; Isa 6; Mic 3:8–12).

(2) The oracles of restoration which extol future glories for Israel and Judah under a new David, with blessings extended to the nations of the earth, would have been especially appropriate in the exilic and post-exilic periods.

(3) However, it is unlikely that later redactors of the eighth century B.C. prophetic books would have inserted extensive predictions of future glory into writings which were intended to declare only warning and judgment. Instead it is likely that there was at least some glimmer of such hope already present within the prophetic tradition which they received.

(4) There are passages within the eighth-century prophetic books that speak of future hope, which also have the appearance of being original and are taken that way by at least some scholars. (a) Amos 5:4–6, after lamenting the decimation of Israel in judgment (vv. 1–3), holds out hope ("Seek me [Yahweh] and live"), although "Gilgal shall surely go into exile, and Bethel shall come to nothing." This hope (repeated in v. 14) is only a glimmer; but it marks a departure from the usual severe denunciatory tone of the oracles.[24] (b) We have identified Hosea passages above.[25]

(c) Isaiah is very important because of its extensive development of salvation after judgment and its prophecies of the messianic era. Here we note 1:24–26:

> Therefore says the Sovereign, the LORD of hosts, the Mighty One of Israel: "Ah, I will pour out my wrath on my enemies. . . . [v. 24] I will turn my hand against you. . . . [v. 25] And I will restore your judges as at the first, and your counselors as at the beginning. Afterward you shall be called the city of righteousness, the faithful city." [v. 26]

From the context we see that the "enemies" of Yahweh are his covenant people (1:1–3; 2:6); it is they who are to receive the wrath. But restoration is seen in verse 26, where the ungodly rulers of verse 23 are replaced and Jerusalem becomes a city of righteousness.[26] It may be that Isaiah's call in chapter 6 anticipates the gathering of all nations to learn the torah, as seen in 2:1–4:

> And one [seraph] called to another and said: Holy, holy, holy is the LORD of hosts; the whole earth [אֶרֶץ] is full of the his glory" (v. 3).

Various scholars consider an eighth-century date possible or very likely for 9:2–7(MT 8:23–9:6) and 11:1–9.[27] Here themes of national deliverance from enemies (esp. 9:2–7) and messianic reign in righteousness on David's throne stand out. Not to be overlooked is the remnant idea in Isaiah 10–11. After punishment has been

---

[24] Cf. Mays, *Amos*, 87–90, 99–102; Stuart, *Hosea*, 346f., 349; Wolff, *Joel and Amos*, 237–39. On Amos 9:11–15, see note 14 above.

[25] For eighth-century authorship, though not necessarily Hosea himself, cf. Mays, *Hosea*, 31, 46f.; Wolff, *Hosea*, 12, 24–26.

[26] Cf. Bright, *Covenant*, 177; Clements, *Isaiah 1–39*, 35f.; Kaiser, *Isaiah 1–12*, 19.

[27] On 9:2–7, Bright, *Covenant*, 107, Clements, *Isaiah 1–39*, 104; von Rad, *Theology*, 2:171; Young, *Isaiah*, 1.324–46; on 11:1–9, Bright, *Covenant*, 108; Kaiser, *Isaiah 1–12*, 155; Young, *Isaiah*, 1.378–94; Clements, *Isaiah*, says "a large number of modern critical commentators" have regarded this "as authentic to Isaiah," though he himself demurs, 121.

accomplished against Assyria (the cruel eighth century B.C. nemesis of Israel and Judah), spiritual restoration with messianic blessing is destined for Israel and Judah (10:20–11:10).[28] The eighth-century life situation is prominent in that Assyria is the prominent heathen nation with whom Yahweh reckons (cf. 10:24; 11:16).

(d) Mic 5:5–6 [MT 5:4–5] is an oracle that promises deliverance from Assyrian invasion. This message of hope follows the burden of the prophet in 3:8–12, wherein the destruction of Jerusalem is envisioned. The important fact for our study is that the prophet proclaims deliverance for a people under the verdict of judgment, with eighth century Assyria and not sixth-century Babylon the aggressor (contrast 4:10).[29] Similarly, at least much of Mic 7:7–20 appears to be pre-exilic. The references to Assyria and Egypt in verse 10 fit that period (cf. Amos 4:9; Hos 11:5; Isa 7:18f.; 10:5–19), as do geographical references to northern Israel.[30] Themes of triumph over enemies and God's forgiveness are prominent. National physical and spiritual restoration occur together, with the latter seemingly explaining the former (note Mic 7:18–20).

Another solution to the problem of "hope" prophecies being juxtaposed with the calls to repentance and warnings of judgment is that the latter were given in public, while promises of restoration and salvation were privately given and incorporated into the original documents at the time of their composition.[31] But however we explain the matter, we may find enough evidence in the eighth-century prophets to consider them messengers of hope in the face of Israel's and Judah's national failure and prophesied collapse. Thus we may find true eschatological expectation in these prophets.

The themes that constitute Israel's eschatological hope are broadly: national physical restoration, with triumph over enemies and prosperity in the land; spiritual restoration, including renewal of covenant fellowship with Yahweh; and, if we allow Isa 2:1–4

---

[28] Vv. 20–23 speak of Northern Israel, if we follow Watts, *Isaiah,* 152f.

[29] The reference to Assyria points more to the era of Micah than much later, cf. Hillers, *Micah,* 69; *contra* Mays, *Micah,* 118f.

[30] Willis provides striking evidence (with abundant secondary references) for an original provenance in eighth-century northern Israel, but with a reuse of the essential pericope in Judah, perhaps by Micah himself, "Prophetic Hope Oracle"; cf. Hillers, *Micah,* 89; Mays, *Micah,* 152–56.

[31] Cf. von Rad, *Theology,* 2.171; Carroll, *Prophecy,* 19. Carroll argues for a dialectical tension of judgment and salvation in eighth-century prophecy, ibid., 16–21. However, I do not disallow the possibility of later editorial activity at points within the prophetic tradition.

(= Mic 4:1–5), the Torah ministry to the nations of the world out of Jerusalem.[32]

The *hope* expressed in these pre-exilic prophets is not particularly imminent. If in any sense it was so viewed, it would have been only by implication in light of the fact that judgment seemed fairly near at hand, the warning oracles being addressed to a people then deserving punishment. A common phrase in the hope oracles is "in that day"—not in itself very suggestive of imminence (e.g., Hos 2:16, 20 [MT 2:18, 22]; Amos 9:11; Mic 7:12; Isa 4:2; 11:10f). However the same phrase refers to the day of judgment in Isa 2:20 and 3:7, 18, where judgment does seem near at hand in the contexts of those passages. The "day" indicated is the day of Yahweh (cf. Isa 2:12 and our discussion under "Amos" above). In the case of Judah, delay could well have been apparent to later generations in that exile did not occur for over a hundred years after the eighth century. Thus an "imminent-delay" tension with respect to the day of Yahweh for judgment probably appears in Israel's experience at this point.

We should also keep in mind that the eschatological blessings of success against enemies and prosperity in the land are in continuity with ancient Israel's traditional golden-age hope (as discussed above), wherein a distinctive relationship with Yahweh may be presupposed. But with the pre-exilic prophets, such hope takes the form of restoration following judgment. Are not the prophets implicitly saying that Yahweh will be true to his covenant promises, even though Israel fails and comes under divine judgment (cf. 2 Kgs 13:22f.)?

Summary

We have considered the possibility that Israel's national hope for a bright and prosperous future is to be traced back to its pre-monarchical history. The subsequent golden-age hope was based upon the earlier splendors of the Davidic-Solomonic kingdom and anchored in the Davidic covenant. We clearly see eschatological expectation for the first time in the eighth century prophets. At this time the hope takes the shape of national physical restoration and spiritual renewal (with inclusion of the nations in Israel's blessings?). But the old order is first ended, as divine judgment falls upon Israel and Judah. Especially at this point we observe critical events in history as instrumental in the shaping of a developing eschatology.

---

[32] Cf. the careful but positive assessment by Hillers, *Micah,* 51–53.

2

EXPECTATION AND THE
CRISIS OF EXILE

THE NORTHERN TRIBES OF ISRAEL WERE EXILED IN 722/721 B.C.;
the southern Judean state collapsed in 587/586 B.C., though the exile
began earlier. In 598/597 B.C. some 10,000 persons were exiled by
Nebuchadnezzar according to 2 Kings 24:14 (Jer 52:28 has 3,023,
but this may be the count of males).[1]

Our concern at this point is the prophetic response to the crisis
of exile (seeing the crisis of Israel and Judah together) in relation to
the prophetic hope and the development of eschatological expectation in the covenant community. We shall examine Jeremiah,
Ezekiel, and Isaiah 40–55.

Prophecies of Exile and Return

Jeremiah

In Jeremiah prominence of the prophetic hope is clear from the
way that Jeremiah's call is described at the beginning of the book
(1:9–10). The prophet is not only to tear down and destroy in his
mission, but he is "to build and to plant." It is actually Yahweh who
will do this (24:4–7; cf. 31:27f.; 42:10).

The "building" and "planting" message is concentrated in chapters
30–33 (often called the Book of Consolation), where the restoration

---

[1]Bright, *Jeremiah,* 369.

of Israel and Judah in their land is vividly set forth in both poetry and prose.[2]

We make the following observations on the prophetic hope of Jeremiah 30–33:

(1) There is a repetition of themes from the pre-exilic prophets. (a) The restoration of both Israel and Judah (30:3f.; 31:1 with vv. 5f.; 33:14). (b) National physical restoration in the land (e.g., 30:3, 10, 18–22; 31:7–14, 16–22). In chapters 30–33 restoration includes security from enemies, the reconstruction of Jerusalem with rejoicing, reinstitution of the Davidic monarchy and Levitical priesthood, and agrarian prosperity. (c) Spiritual restoration (30:22; 31:6, 31–34; 32:38–40). This is essentially a new covenant relationship in which Yahweh forgives sins and provides a heart that fears him and does his will. (d) Covenant-relationship as the basis of restoration (31:2f.; 32:21–23; 33:19–26). (e) An interchange between announcements of judgment and future blessing in the text (e.g., 30:1–3 with vv. 4–7; vv. 8–11 with vv. 12–15). Both judgment and blessing are to occur "in that day" (30:7f., cf. the day of Yahweh in the earlier prophets).

(2) Amidst similarities with the pre-exilic prophets, one very significant difference is present. The day of judgment has in fact dawned in the Babylonian onslaught and "the end" for Jerusalem is at hand (30:4–7, 12–15; 31:15; 32:1–5, 24–35; 33:4f.). Against this background the new age of restoration and blessing is anticipated. The perpetuity of the new city and the new covenant is stated (31:40; 32:39–40, cf. 33:14–18). Thus with Jeremiah the realization of the prophetic hope becomes more imminent.[3]

(3) The dominance of this expectation in Jeremiah is to be observed, even though a human contingency which allows for non-fulfillment of what Yahweh initially announces is also found in 18:5–11. We should add that this contingency is in itself

---

[2] Editorial expansion in chs. 30–33 is possible, cf. Thompson, *Jeremiah,* 552f. Commentators appear more inclined to see the Jeremiah core in chs. 30–31, cf. Bright, *Jeremiah,* lix; Carroll, *Jeremiah,* 569 (though he himself is doubtful); Eissfeldt, *Introduction,* 361f. In any case the expectation during and after the exile of a restoration is reflected in the oracles of chs. 30–31, which introduce the prose portion of chs. 32–33, cf. Carroll, *Jeremiah,* 569.

[3] There is almost a similar imminence of judgment and restoration in at least the present form of (the late pre-exilic) Zephaniah, esp. 1:7, 14 with 3:8–20. On date and canonical shape cf. Childs, *Scripture,* 458–62.

significant, especially since the commission found in chapter 1 "to destroy and to overthrow" and "to build and to plant" is repeated here in chapter 18.

The prophetic hope of Jeremiah 30–33 is introduced by a curiously controlled imminent expectation in chapter 29. After refuting the false prophecy that Nebuchadnezzar's grip would be broken in two years (ch. 28; 29:1–9), Jeremiah prophesies that restoration is to occur "when Babylon's seventy years are completed" (29:10–14; cf. 25:11–14).[4] Whether this number of years was meant to be taken literally or symbolically, the fact remains that it became very important for expectation in Judaism in subsequent generations (cf. Zech 1:12; 7:5; 2 Chron 36:20–23; Ezra 1:1). We shall discuss the importance of this seventy-year prophecy in greater detail when we consider the apocalyptic movement within early Judaism. But here we observe that eschatological expectation took a giant step forward with the crisis of exile and then the prediction that after seventy years the hope of an idealized Davidic kingdom would become a reality. Thus we see a further development of eschatological hope in Israel in conformity with its profound conviction of being the covenant people of Yahweh.

Ezekiel

In Ezekiel the continuity of salvation themes with Jeremiah is remarkable, as Ezekiel likewise addresses the exiles.[5] We find Israel and Judah reunited (37:15–22; 48:30–34, cf. 36:10); national restoration to the land, with the Davidic monarchy reinstituted, cities reconstructed, security and agrarian prosperity provided (11:14–18; 34:11–16, 23–29; 36:10–12, 33–36); and spiritual restoration, including cleansing and a new heart of obedience through the impartation of God's Spirit (36:25–28; cf. 11:19f.; 39:29).

More distinctive to Ezekiel is Yahweh's "sanctuary" (מִקְדָּשׁ), which is to be in the midst of his people "for evermore" (לְעוֹלָם)

---

[4]The seventy-year prediction has been taken as a later addition to the text, Carroll, *Jeremiah*, 493f., 557f.; Skinner, *Prophecy*, 295f. However it was taken seriously in early post-exilic Judaism, as we discuss. Bright considers the prediction authentic, *Jeremiah*, 208f.

[5]Zimmerli sees Ezekiel frequently influenced by Jeremiah, *Ezekiel*, 2:214, 216. It is widely agreed that the book is a composite of prophecies which are at least based upon the oracles of Ezekiel himself, cf. Brownlee, *Ezekiel 1–19*, xxxv; Childs, *Scripture*, 366; Eissfeldt, *Introduction*, 372–74; Harrison, *Introduction*, 838–44; Zimmerli, *Ezekiel*, 1.62f., 67.

(37:26, 28, cf. 43:7, 9). This is apparently the eschatological "temple" or "sanctuary" in chapters 40–48 (note מִקְדָּשׁ in e.g., 43:21; 44:5, 8, 11; 48:8, 10, 21). The unending character of Yahweh's blessing is stressed in 37:25–28, with עוֹלָם (everlasting/forever) appearing five times. The extended visionary description with an apparent angelic guide approaches the character of apocalyptic literature (to be discussed in Part Two), 40:1–4 with 40:5–48:35.

Expectation of the prophetic hope being realized in the "near" future is indirectly present in that there is no hint of a distant fulfillment for the exiles who are addressed. Furthermore, expectation seems present with reference to the day of Yahweh being on the horizon. "The end has come," as climactic judgment is pronounced against Israel (Judah) in 7:6. This is graphically rendered in Hebrew: קֵץ בָּא בָּא הַקֵּץ ("An end has come, the end has come"). Thus, "the day is near [קָרוֹב]" (v. 7). The excitement comes through in verse 10: " 'See, the day! See, it comes!' " No doubt the abbreviated reference is to the day of Yahweh (cf. 30:2f.).[6]

The most explicit reference to the nearness of the time for the prophetic hope being realized is 36:8.

> But you, O mountains of Israel, shall shoot out your branches, and yield your fruit to my people Israel; *for they will soon come home* [קֵרְבוּ לָבוֹא].

Such an announcement would certainly have fueled anticipation for fulfillment of the prophetic hope on the part of those who would or who had already returned "home."[7]

In Ezekiel we find frequent mention of Yahweh's reputation among the nations. Yahweh's acts toward Israel are intended to preserve his honor before the nations (20:9, 14, 22; 36:20–23; 39:27;

---

[6]Zimmerli, *Ezekiel,* 1:207, who points out that the LXX translates the "day" in 7:10 as ἡμέρα κυρίου ("day of the Lord"). "The end" of 7:6 is apparently an imminent fulfillment of Amos 8:2, where "the end" is likewise foreseen (the same Hebrew term). Of course by the time the book of Ezekiel was compiled, this "day" had passed (33:21). But apparently the author wishes to preserve the heightened excitement of earlier times. Although Ezekiel does not explicitly identify the day of Yahweh with the promised hope of restoration, judgment and salvation were closely linked in the prophetic tradition, as we have seen. "The day" in Ezekiel may be a cipher to inspire expectation.

[7]We should keep in mind a distinction between the oral prophetic utterances and the later written oracles, which were eventually compiled in the book of Ezekiel. Certainly the returned exiles would have been influenced by the latter, if not the former.

cf. 20:41; 28:25). Yahweh's vindication before the nations is linked to the nations "knowing" that he is Yahweh (36:23). Six times from chapters 36 to 39 Yahweh's purpose that the nations know [יָדַע] that he is Yahweh is expressed (36:23, 36; 37:28; 38:23; 39:7, 23, cf. 38:16). This is the same desire that is expressed for Israel (e.g., 34:27; 36:11; 39:28)! Thus in the prophetic-hope chapters a knowledge of Yahweh by the Gentiles is included. This is developed further in Isaiah 40–55.

Before leaving Ezekiel we should note that the hope includes all exiles returning to the land of Israel (37:16–23; 39:28).

Isaiah 40–55

With the mid-sixth century orientation of Isaiah 40–55 (often designated "Second Isaiah"), near-expectation for fulfillment of the prophetic hope is further heightened.[8] It is not the day of judgment that has drawn nigh (as in Ezek 7:7, 10); the time for restoration is at hand. The prophet calls out: ". . . say to the cities of Judah, 'Here is your God!' " (40:9–11, cf. 44:26; 46:13). The Babylonian bars are about to be broken (43:14). Cyrus is Yahweh's "shepherd" to "carry out my [Yahweh's] purpose" (44:28). The time for the deliverance through Cyrus (the man from the east, 46:11) has drawn near:

> I bring near [קֵרַבְתִּי] my deliverance, it is not far off, and my salvation will not tarry; I will put salvation in Zion, for Israel my glory [46:13, cf. 51:5].

As with Jeremiah and Ezekiel, we find the prospect of national physical restoration. Much attention is given the theme of release

---

[8]The chronological and geographical setting is clearly that of the Babylonian exile, with an end to exilic chastisement on the horizon (cf. esp. 40:1f., 9–11; 43:14–21; 44:24–45:7, 13; 46:12f.; 48:20f.; 52:1–12). Largely for this reason a "Second Isaiah" has been posited as author of these chapters by most scholars. Conservative scholars have interpreted this portion of Isaiah as from the eighth-century prophet, writing toward the end of his life and anticipating this future judgment with restoration. Craigie holds that arguments for the minority view "are not without weight," *Old Testament*, 155. A mediating view holds that the book is a unity, with the eighth-century Isaiah reflected in the entire book, but with a school of Isaiah (cf. 8:16) preserving his oracles and later editing them, cf. LaSor, Hubbard, Bush, *OT Survey*, 371–78; cf. Craigie, *Old Testament*, 153–57. This latter standpoint recognizes arguments for the unity of Isaiah, while at the same time accepting the hermeneutical principle that "prophecy always arises from the historical situation and speaks to people of that situation," cf. ibid., 374.

from captivity (43:1–7, 14–21; 44:28–45:7, 13; 46:8–13; 48:20f.; 49:9–13, 22–26; 52:1f.). Yahweh is to act on behalf of the cities of Judah, and especially Jerusalem, as the land is repopulated (40:9–11; 44:3f., 26–28; 49:8, 19–29; 54:1–3). Israel's enemies are to be defeated by Yahweh (41:2–4, 11–13; 47:1–15; 48:14).

The prophetic hope includes a spiritual restoration of Israel, as in Jeremiah and Ezekiel. Israel's sin is pardoned (40:2; 43:25; 44:22, cf. 53:1ff.). Justice and salvation come not only to Israel but to the world, accomplished through the "Servant" of Yahweh (42:1–6; 49:5f.; cf. 45:8, 22; 51:4–6). Israel's deliverance is a witness to the nations and nations run to Israel (43:6–10; 55:5).

Physical and spiritual deliverance are so intertwined in Isaiah 40–55 that at times it seems inappropriate to distinguish them. Yahweh is "Redeemer" in 41:14; 44:6; 48:17; 49:7; 54:5, 8. Yahweh is Israel's redeemer and savior in every way. It is a time of exuberant rejoicing and everlasting salvation, as we have witnessed earlier in the prophetic hope (51:6, 8, 11; 54:8, 10; 55:3, 12f.). The "remnant" of Israel is the object of Yahweh's blessing (46:3 with 10:20–22; 11:11, 16; 37:30–32).

Does the prophet have in mind all the tribes of Israel, or only the southern kingdom of Judah? The focus is clearly on Judah (e.g., 40:2, 9; 48:1; 51:11). Apparently the only solid clue that Israel more generally is in view is the reference to the tribes (plural) of Israel being "raised up" (49:6). "Jacob" and/or "Israel" are always the objects of the redemptive blessings; but it seems that for Isaiah 40–55 Israel usually means Judah. Here is a difference from Jeremiah and Ezekiel, in emphasis if not in substance.

Post-exilic Expectation and Experience of Delay

Haggai and Zechariah 1–8

The origin of the books bearing the names Haggai and Zechariah is clearly identified with the remnant of Judah that has returned to the land of promise following exile (Hag 1:1f., 12; Zech 1:1, 12).

Within these prophecies is the expectation that Jerusalem and the temple will shortly be restored with the glory that had already been set forth in the prophetic hope. Particular attention is given to the eschatological temple, as in the Ezekiel prophecy. But now the returned exiles are chided and encouraged to get on with the job of temple reconstruction (Hag 1f.; Zech 4; 6:9–14)! Joyous national physical and spiritual restoration are again seen together, (Zech 2:3–5, 10–12; 3:9–10; 8:3–8). Restoration of covenant fellowship with Yahweh is envisioned for the returned exiles.

> I will save my people from the east country and from the west country; and I will bring them to live in Jerusalem. They shall be my people and I will be their God, in faithfulness and in righteousness [Zech 8:7f.].

Note that restoration is as yet outstanding for the returned exiles. The larger fulfillment of the prophetic hope is still anticipated (cf. the above promises of restoration with Isa 1:26 and 43:4–6). In Zechariah 1–6 the prophecies are through visions with the assistance of an angelic guide. The angelic inquiry "how long?" in 1:12 likely reflects the impatience of the returned exiles. On the other hand, full restoration seems quite imminent (Zech 2:6f. with vv. 8–12). The governor of the returned Jews, Zerubbabel, is the chosen of Yahweh and likened to a signet ring, while Yahweh will shake the heavens and earth and destroy the power of the nations (Hag 2:20–23). The passage apparently indicates that the day of Yahweh is near, with Zerubbabel referred to in messianic overtones.

Attention is given to the nations in these post-exilic prophecies. Not only is their power to be broken, as Yahweh delivers his people (also see Zech 1:21; 2:9), but their treasures will help to beautify the eschatological temple and they will worship Yahweh with his people (Hag 2:7–9; Zech 2:11; 8:22–23; cf. 6:15).

Judging from Zechariah 8:13, both the house of Judah and of Israel constitute the returned remnant.

Zechariah 9–14

Scholars generally consider the oracles in Zechariah 9–14 as originally separate from chapters 1–8.[9] In contrast to 1–8, these chapters contain no biographical or chronological references which anchor the oracles to specific historical contexts. Without developing the many hypotheses for dating, we shall conclude with the scholarly consensus that they are to be placed at some point (possibly at varying points) within the post-exilic era.[10] Certainly their

---

[9] Baldwin cites the "almost unanimous" opinion, *Haggai*, 62.

[10] In the first oracle (chs. 9–11) return from exile is yet outstanding (10:6–12), but the temple is erected (9:8 with 11:13f.); this suits a period well

place in the canon as part of Zechariah testifies that they were so regarded in ancient times.

Themes found in chapters 1–8 are again set forth in 9–14. Thus much attention is devoted to the nations in relation to Judah and Jerusalem. A future return from exile of those still in "far countries" is seen (10:6–12). Yahweh will subdue the nations, as Judah's king comes to her in triumph; he will bring peace to the nations (9:1–10). Interestingly, Judah and Israel are seen together in the messianic conquest (9:10, cf. v. 14 and 10:6).

In chapters 12–14 we find an attack on Jerusalem by the nations, engineered by Yahweh; but then Yahweh delivers his people (12:1–9 with 14:1–5). There is spiritual cleansing for Jerusalem (12:10–13:9). Yahweh becomes king over all the earth and Jerusalem is exalted, as the nations bring their wealth to Jerusalem and worship there (14:8–21). The broad themes of physical and spiritual restoration, in which the nations of the earth participate, is fundamentally a carrying forward of the prophetic hope which we have seen in earlier periods. Even the idea of a future attack on Jerusalem with Yawheh's intervention is in Ezekiel 38–39. What now seems to occupy a larger place in the prophetic outlook is the role of the nations in Israel's future hope.

Finally, we must emphasize that this repetition of the basic features of the prophetic hope comes after a remnant of Jews has returned from exile. Perhaps this is why the focus is on the nations of the world. Exile remains a critical factor in the post-exilic era.

Malachi

Post-exilic disappointments are even more pronounced in Malachi, which is often dated in the early fifth century B.C. prior to the reforms of Ezra and Nehemiah.[11] Israel doubts Yahweh's special love for her (1:2; 3:13–15). The prophetic word is given to reassure

---

after the return of 538 B.C. The second oracle (chs. 12–14) presupposes the (re)establishment of Jerusalem amidst eschatological events. According to Baldwin most present day scholars favor the Greek period, ibid., 65. In contrast Childs speaks of the inability of scholars to reach a consensus on the dating of Zechariah, *Scripture*, 476. Hanson sees an emerging apocalyptic eschatology to which various portions of chs. 9–14 relate from the sixth to early fifth centuries, *Dawn of Apocalyptic*, 280–401.

[11] Childs, *Scripture*, 489; cf. Baldwin, *Haggai*, 213; Smith, *Micah*, 298.

Israel (1:3–5). But then Israel's backslidden state is exposed in the balance of the book (1:6–4:6 [MT 1:6–3:24]).

The prophet announces the intervention of Yahweh, who will "suddenly come to his temple" (3:1). He is here described as "the Lord whom you seek." Ezekiel (43:2–5) and Haggai (1:8) had promised this day, which was still outstanding for the returned exiles.[12] The "messenger" who is to "prepare the way" before Yahweh (Mal 3:1) is apparently the "voice" who cries "prepare the way" in Isaiah 40:3, prior to the glory of Yahweh being revealed (Isa 40:5).[13] But the prophet now emphasizes that Yahweh will draw near to purify his people (3:2–5). This is the "great and terrible day" of Yahweh, wherein he destroys the wicked after the coming of Elijah (4:1–5 [MT 3:19–22]). Elijah is evidently the "messenger" of 3:1.[14]

In Malachi Yahweh's name is great among the nations (1:11, 14b). This may be a prediction of what is imminent with the coming of Yahweh (cf. 3:12).[15]

The post-exilic situation in Malachi reveals discouragement within the covenant community, while the prophecy itself sounds a note of imminent expectation, with a stress upon a purifying judgment.

For our purposes two significant prophetic works remain, both of which are difficult to locate chronologically: Isaiah 56–66 and Joel.

Isaiah 56–66

Isaiah 56–66, frequently designated "Third Isaiah" by scholars, has earmarks of pre-exilic Judah, especially in its exposure of moral failure and idolatry (56:9–57:13; 58:1–9; 64:1–65:16). And then there are passages which could be an exilic anticipation of restoration, often against the background of Judah's disgrace but also her repentance (56:1–8; 57:14–21; 58:9–63:9; 65:17–66:24). However other indicators point more to a post-exilic setting. Along with the

---

[12] Cf. Baldwin, *Haggai,* 242; Smith, *Micah,* 328.

[13] Cf. ibid.

[14] Of course the NT identifies the "messenger" as John the Baptist, who came prior to Jesus, and who is called "Elijah" in the Synoptic Gospels (Mk 1:1–8 = Matt 3:1–12 = Luke 3:1–20; Mark 9:11–13 = Matt 17:10–13; Matt 11:13–14; cf. John 1:19–23).

[15] So Baldwin, *Haggai,* 230; C. F. Keil, *Minor Prophets,* 437f.; apparently Smith, *Micah,* 313–16.

call to repentance in pre-exilic fashion (see texts above), there is an
apparent reckoning with *delay* in the coming of salvation in 56:1
and especially in 60:22b (cf. 59:1ff.). We do not find such a "delay-
imminence" motif, which seems to explain these texts, in the life-
situation of the eighth century B.C. Isaiah (cf. 6:9–13; 8:16f.). Rather,
given the return under Zerubbabel in 538 B.C. (though not specified
here), we see these texts making the most sense for a people already
"home," but nevertheless still waiting for (and wondering about?)
the promised redemption. Both reconstruction generally in Judah
and the rebuilding of the temple are necessary (58:12; 63:18 and
64:11–12 with 56:3–8). The need for moral rectitude and expectation of a glorious temple (cf. 60:7, 13) remind us of the life-situation
we found in Malachi, except for the references to idolatry in "Third
Isaiah." (However regarding idolatry, cf. Zech 13:2.) It is quite
possible that texts which originally came from an earlier setting have
been reapplied, since the fullness of redemption in the new age
was still outstanding.[16] Without specific individuals or surrounding
nations being identified, the chronological question is complicated.

In addition to the above themes in Isaiah 56–66, we should
mention others which reflect eschatological hope. Much attention
is given the role of the nations in serving and honoring Zion in the
day of salvation (60:1–16; 61:5–62:9; 66:12, 18–21). Instead of a
threatening relationship with surrounding peoples, Israel enjoys
peace; but she is clearly in the ascendancy. Also, even as the Spirit of
Yahweh was operative in earlier times, so he would be instrumental
in effecting this redemption (61:1–3; cf. 63:10–11, 14). Both of
these themes are found earlier in the Isaiah corpus, but are developed further here.

What is particularly significant for eschatological expectation is
the assurance that the eschaton will arrive in its time. This note,
perhaps implied earlier in Isaiah (e.g., 46:13), becomes more distinct, particularly in 60:22b. The question is, what led to this
prophetic word? Could it be an awareness of delay in eschatological
fulfillment on the part of the post-exilic community?

Joel

The book of Joel has no heading to suggest a date. Four periods
have appeared suitable to various scholars: early pre-exilic, late

---

[16] Cf. Childs, *Scripture,* 323, 337f.

pre-exilic, the last decade of the sixth century, and after 400 B.C.[17] However it is clear that Joel addresses Judah and Jerusalem (2:1, 15, 23, 32 [MT 3:5]; 3:1, 6, 17, 20 [MT 4:1, 6, 17, 20]).

For our purposes the following themes are important:

(1) An unprecedented invasion of locusts in the land signals the nearness of the day of Yahweh for judgment (1:2–2:17, esp. 1:15f. and 2:1f.).

(2) Judgment has been averted, evidently through repentance (2:12–17), and now agrarian prosperity is promised (2:18–27). The pivot is in verse 18, wherein Yahweh becomes "jealous for his land" and has "pity on his people."[18]

(3) Following the material blessing, a deluge of the Spirit "on all flesh" is foreseen, answering to the downpour in verse 23 which replenished the earth and brought prosperity (vv. 28f., [MT 3:1f.]). This apparently introduces the truly eschatological era in which the day of Yahweh finally is to arrive. The fortunes of Judah are to be restored, the nations of earth judged, with Yahweh dwelling in Zion (2:28–3:21 [MT 3:1–4:21]).[19]

Significant for our subject of expectation is the fact that at first the day of Yahweh is "near," with signs in the cosmos (2:1–2, 10–11, cf. Isa 13:9–11). Then, after Judah's repentance, the day is seen both as no longer at hand (though anticipated), 2:26–32 [MT 2:26–3:5]; 3:1, 18 [MT 4:1, 18], but also as "near," 3:14 [MT 4:14]. There seems to be an ambivalence in imminent expectation after the great day is postponed following Judah's repentance. Otherwise the hope remains the same as in other prophetic writings, though with the distinctive profusion of the Spirit on "all flesh," seen initially fulfilled in Acts on the day of Pentecost (2:17–21).

Summary

In the exilic and post-exilic oracles fulfillment of the hope at times is more or less imminent, with both Israel and Judah being recipients. There is also greater specificity in themes of national

---

[17] Allen, *Joel*, 22.

[18] Allen, *Joel*, 86f.; cf. Wolff, *Joel and Amos*, 57, 61; C. F. Keil comments that the imperfect verbs with the *vav* connective in vv. 18 and 19a should be taken "as statements of what actually occurred," *Minor Prophets*, 200. So, KJV, RSV, and NRSV; *contra* NASB, NIV.

[19] So Allen, *Joel*, 97ff.; cf. Wolff, *Joel and Amos*, 65.

reconstruction than in the pre-exilic era; Jerusalem is more sharply in focus. Spiritual renewal is emphasized and there is increasing elaboration on nations of the world participating in the blessing of the restored Davidic kingdom.

It is noteworthy that throughout the centuries in which Israel's hope finds expression, particular attention is given to Israel's success over its enemies.

Delay in fulfillment of the prophetic hope seems to be an issue, at least in the post-exilic period (also cf. Hab 2:1–3). Certainly non-fulfillment of the hope is fundamental in explaining its recurrence and further development in later times. This will be most important when we consider the more thoroughgoing apocalyptic reinterpretation of Israel's hope and then the expression of hope in early Christianity. Especially in the later prophets, we already find significant elements of the apocalyptic genre. Notable are visions and angelic guides of Ezek 40–48 and Zech 1–6.

Finally, the strength of Israel's awareness of a covenant relationship with Yahweh is underscored in the survival of its hope beyond exile and the updating of it as the centuries passed. The prophets of Yahweh continued to affirm that the mouth of Yahweh had spoken.

Part Two: Expectation and Delay
in Jewish Apocalypticism

3

PRELIMINARY CONSIDERATIONS

W̲E HAVE THUS FAR SURVEYED THE DEVELOPMENT OF THE
OT prophetic hope, with special attention given to expectation of its
fulfillment. It is in the so-called Jewish apocalyptic literature and
ideology that the continuing development of this hope is most
readily and vividly found. It will be important for us to see in what
way(s) apocalyptic Judaism may have been the mother of Christian
expectation, and in what way(s) Christian expectation differs from
Jewish apocalypticism.[1]

What Is Apocalyptic?

It is widely agreed that definition is a problem. At the center of
the problem is the fact that "apocalyptic" may be used to refer both
to a genre of literature (although opinion of the limits of that
literature varies) and to certain beliefs and ideas in the literature.
The issue is further complicated because such beliefs and ideas are
also found in works not strictly part of the apocalyptic genre, but
such beliefs and ideas are nevertheless considered "apocalyptic."[2]
Thus at the start a working definition is important.

---

[1] Many will recognize a play on the famous statement of E. Käsemann:
"Apocalyptic was the mother of all Christian theology," though here he
excepts the preaching of Jesus. The quote may be found in Käsemann,
"Beginnings," 102.

[2] Barr, "Apocalyptic," 18; Ringgren, "Apokalyptik," col. 464. Koch, *Rediscovery*, 28–33, emphasizes "apocalypticism" as a religious movement to which
the adjective "apocalyptic" refers, cf. Hanson, "Apocalypticism," 30f.; Collins,
Apocalyptic, 9–11. Hartman, "Survey," 329–41, discusses the issue in terms of

Since our purpose is to understand better the ideological milieu of NT expectation, the beliefs and ideas found in religious movements and expressed in varying types of literature are especially significant. Of fundamental importance is the suprahistorical transcendental perspective that is found in apocalyptic eschatology.[3] Although this is found most graphically in the apocalypses with their visionary distinctives, whether Jewish or Christian, this outlook exceeds the boundaries of the apocalypse genre strictly speaking. This is particularly true of our NT texts yet to be examined (Matt 24 = Mark 13 = Luke 21; 2 Thess 2).

The growing point of apocalyptic eschatology seems to be more than anything else the concept of two ages which are basically different. There is the present age entailing earthly life as we now know it with its weakness, sin, and death. But then, the age to come, consisting of a suprahistorical order of existence which at the appropriate time will break in from beyond and replace life of the present age.[4] The terminology of "this age/the coming age" surfaces in a more radical context in later works which are usually dated around the end of the first century A.D. (such as 4 Ezra 6:7–28 and 2 Bar. 44:8–15), but the basic idea of a new age in which sin and death are absent exists in earlier works (cf. Dan 12:2f.; 1 Enoch 91:15–17; T. Mos. 10:1). This same perspective is of course found in the NT, for example Mark 10:30 (= Luke 18:30); Luke 20:34–36; Rom 8:19–23; Rev 21f.

Certain supporting motifs appear: woes from abnormalities in nature and in society (especially warfare and extreme wickedness); an anti-god figure with far-ranging influence; apostasy; and extreme

---

defining genre. Charlesworth observes that some scholars deny that "apocalyptic" is a "specific genre," OTP, 3.

[3] Not all apocalypses have eschatology as a main theme. But frequently eschatology is a dominant concern and makes it viable for us to speak of "apocalyptic eschatology," cf. Collins, Apocalyptic, 8f. Other common literary features of many apocalypses include pseudonymous authorship, history in the guise of prophecy, dream-visions and angels as the media of revelation, much use of animal imagery and numerical symbolism. The following, for example, may be consulted for summary descriptions of apocalyptic literature: Russell, Disclosure, esp. 60–115; Osborne, Spiral, 221–30; Dunn, Unity, esp. 309–16.

[4] Cf. Russell, Method, 264–71; Mowinckel, He That Cometh, 266; Hanson, "Apocalypticism," 30; Vielhauer in Hennecke-Schneemelcher, NT Apocrypha 2.588; Dunn, Unity, 312. Collins, "Transcendence," 30ff. esp., pinpoints "transcendence of death" as the distinctive feature. Stone posits expectation of an imminent end independent of human action, "Apocalyptic Literature," 383.

persecution of the righteous. Such end time woes are found in much of the literature, including Dan 7:19–27; 12:1, 10–13; Jub 23:12–14; *1 Enoch* 91:6f.; 99:4f.; *Sib. Or.* 3:562–572; 601–604; *T. Mos.* 8; 4 Ezra 11:40–46; *2 Bar.* 25:1–27:6. New Testament references include Mark 13:7–23 and parallels; 2 Thess 2; Rev 6ff. It is the collage of such motifs along with the introduction of a heavenly new age (often preceded by a judgment-scene), which produce "apocalyptic eschatology" or the ambiguous shorthand term "apocalyptic." These various related motifs are seldom all present in a single work. It is likely that the canonical Daniel was the inspiration behind many apocalyptic themes in the available literature, as we shall explore later.

From Whence Apocalyptic?

The origin of Jewish apocalyptic themes has been greatly debated. Some have placed much stock in Persian or Zoroastrian thought.[5] In favor of possible Persian influence is the presence of diaspora Jews in the East for generations following exile in the sixth century B.C. However while observing parallels with Iranian mythology, several scholars understand apocalyptic as an interpretation of *essentially* Hebrew ideas. Even after granting interesting similarities with Iranian thought, one authority on Zoroastrianism says that in many instances we cannot be certain whether Jews borrowed from the Zoroastrians, the Zoroastrians from the Jews, or whether either in fact borrowed from the other.[6]

Another explanation for Jewish apocalyptic is that it was birthed by the Hebrew wisdom movement. Elements of the "wisdom" phenomenon have been observed in apocalyptic.[7]

---

[5] E.g., Bousset, *Apokalyptik*, 36–51; cf. Widengren, "Iran." Regrettably, Norman Cohn's *Cosmos, Chaos and the World to Come: The Ancient Roots of Apocalyptic Faith* came to my attention too late to include in my discussion.

[6] Zaehner, *Dawn*, 57f.; cf. Hengel, *Judaism*, 1.193f, who mentions the chronological difficulties of the Iranian apocalypses, which are relatively late.

[7] Notably, G. von Rad. He grants the apocalyptists' use of prophetic tradition, but believes the apocalyptic viewpoint is too far removed from the prophetic tradition to derive from it. In particular he cannot reconcile the prophetic view of Israel experiencing "saving history" as God's elect with the apocalyptic perspective of history being already determined from the distant past, *Theology*, 2.301–15, esp. 303, 313f.; cf. von Rad's *Wisdom*, 263–83.

However a majority of scholars seem agreed that the most viable explanation for the birth of apocalyptic is the influence of the prophetic tradition. Eschatology is prominent in both.[8] It is best to see the prophetic tradition taking a radical turn in the direction of a transcendental worldview, and being joined to other distinctives in apocalyptic literature such as visions, mythological imagery, determinism, and usually use of pseudonymity.

A strong argument for this explanation of apocalyptic is found in the overlap of prophetic with apocalyptic motifs, which becomes evident in a careful reading of both literatures.

The following themes common in apocalyptic can be traced to the OT prophets, at least in germinal form:[9]

1. Radical destruction of the present earth and/or sinful humankind:

Apocalyptic
> 1 *Enoch* 1:7; 45:4–6; 69:27f.; 91:14; 100:4f.
> *Sib. Or.* 3:77–92; 4:71–78
> 4 Ezra 6:20–29; 7:28–30
> 2 *Bar.* 70
> 1QH 3:29–36

Prophetic
> Isa 13:9–13; 24:1, 3, 18–23
> Jer 4:23–28; cf. Isa 66:16

2. Physical resurrection of human beings:

Apocalyptic
> Dan 12:2f.
> 1 *Enoch* 20:8; 51:1; 61:5
> *Sib. Or.* 4:181–83
> *Apoc. Mos.* 10:2; 28:4

---

[8]Cf. Nicholson, "Apocalyptic," 207–11; Koch, *Rediscovery,* 45f.; Hengel, *Judaism,* 1.209; Barr, "Apocalyptic," 24f.

[9]Hubbard, "Hope," 47, in fact observes a convergence of prophetic themes that draw from the Exodus, Moses, David, and Zion, especially from the time of the later prophetic tradition on into apocalyptic. Collins, *Apocalyptic,* 20, speaks of post-exilic prophecy sharing significant features of apocalypses, but lacking in the generic framework of apocalyptic thought. From our following data it is possible to observe similar themes germinating even earlier in the prophetic tradition.

4 Ezra 7:32, 35 (cf. 7:112–14)
2 *Bar.* 30:2; 42:8; 50:2–51:6

Prophetic
>   Isa 25:8(?); 26:19, cf. v. 14
>   Hos 6:1–2(?)
>   Ezek 37:1–14

3. Heavenly new age/world

Apocalyptic
>   1 *Enoch* 91:16f.
>   4 Ezra 7:31, 50, 112–14; 8:52–54
>   2 *Bar.* 39f.; 44:12–15; 48–50
>   *Apoc. Ab.* 31

Prophetic
>   Isa 25:6–8; 65:17ff.; cf. Zech 14:6–9

4. Determinism and expectation of an imminent end[10]

Apocalyptic
>   Dan 7–12 (esp. 9:24, 27; 11:36)
>   1 *Enoch* 85–90 (esp. 89:68–90:5)
>   4 Ezra 4:26, 48–50; 5:55
>   2 *Bar.* 27:1–28:2; 53–74 (esp. 54:1, 17; 70–74); 85:9–15

Prophetic
>   Isa 13:6; 40ff.; 55:10–13
>   Jer 25:8–14 with 29:10–14
>   Zeph 1:14–18
>   Hag 2:20–23

On the other hand there are of course eschatological themes in the prophetic literature which are in accord with a more earth-centered hope; but these at times also surface with little change in apocalyptic literature.

1. Defeat or removal of ungodly earthly kingdoms

Prophetic
>   Isa 13:23
>   Jer 46–51

---

[10] On the relationship of these two ideas see Vielhauer in Hennecke-Schneemelcher, *NT Apocrypha,* 2.590–93.

Ezek 38f.
Amos 1f.
Obad 15f.
Zech 9

Apocalyptic
   Dan 7–8
   1 Enoch 91:14
   4 Ezra 13:1–38
   2 Bar. 39:7–40:4; 72
   1QM 1:5–7; 15:1–2

2. Earthly blessings for the godly, sometimes depicting Messiah
   reigning

Prophetic
   Isa 2:2–4; 9:1–7; 32:15–20; 35
   Amos 9:11–15
   Mic 4:14–5:3
   Jer 30:18–31:40
   Ezek 36
   Zech 14:9–21

Apocalyptic
   1 Enoch 5:6–9; 48:2–5; 51:4f.; 90:20–42
   4 Ezra 7:26–30
   2 Bar. 73
   1QM 1:8f.
   Sib. Or. 3:616–23, 702–19

3. Repentance/exaltation of Israel

Prophetic
   Isa 4:2–6; 40: 44:21–45:13; 59:20–60:22; 61:5–7
   Jer 31:31–34
   Ezek 36:24–38
   Zech 13

Apocalyptic
   Dan 7:27(?); 9:1–27
   As. Mos. 1:18 with 10:9f.; cf. *T. Dan* 6:4
   T. Levi 16:1–5
   2 Bar. 78:6f.; 84:6–85:5

4. Conversion of Gentiles

Prophetic

 Isa 2:2–4 (= Mic 4:1–4); 11:9f.; 42:1–4; 49:6f.(cf. 60:3)
 Mic 7:16

Apocalyptic

 1 Enoch 48:2, 4; 90:30, 33, 35; 91:14d.

This interchange of eschatological motifs in prophetic and apocalyptic literatures points to a relationship between the two. And in apocalyptic literature at times "the earthly and the heavenly are strangely combined in one," as in *1 Enoch* 37–71.[11] For the earthly prophetic and the transcendental apocalyptic views presented side by side, one may observe *2 Bar.* 29–30.

Various scholars have recognized a significant trend toward apocalyptic thought in the prophets from the exilic period.[12] However others who likewise appreciate the growth of apocalyptic in the prophets would give greater place to Daniel or part(s) of *1 Enoch* as the first bona fide apocalyptic literature.[13]

It is noteworthy that the promise of Israel's subjugation of its enemies and exaltation in the world under the blessing of Yahweh continues in apocalyptic from the future hope of earlier centuries, which hope we surveyed in Part One. However, it is now the godly within Israel who are promised such blessings, with the ungodly (whether Gentile or Jew) suffering judgment. This accords with the idea of the righteous remnant motif in the prophetic tradition. In apocalyptic these judgment and salvation themes often appear in drastic otherworldly proportions.

---

[11] Russell, *Method*, 270.

[12] E.g., Frost, *Apocalyptic*, 236–38; Bloch, *Apocalyptic*, Plöger, *Theocracy*, 27, 47–50; Hengel, *Judaism*, 1.194–96. Cf. the list in Schmidt, *Apokalyptik*, 166–70, 265–77. Youngblood, "Prophecy and Apocalyptic," 216–18, relates themes in Isaiah 24–27 (often considered apocalyptic) to non-apocalyptic parts of Isaiah and other prophetic books. P. D. Hanson, *Dawn*, 27f. traces apocalyptic from the sixth and fifth centuries with a "proto-apocalyptic" in "Second Isaiah's" incorporation of myth into eschatology, which added a cosmic dimension. Then he sees an "early apocalyptic" in "Third Isaiah," Zechariah 9f., and Isaiah 24–27. From there he finds a "transition to full-blown apocalyptic eschatology" in Zechariah 11–14, cf. Hanson's "Apocalyptic Re-examined," 473. Barr, "Apocalyptic," 19, stresses Ezekiel as "the fountain from which the apocalyptic river flowed."

[13] E.g., Rowley, *Relevance*, 41; Frost, *Apocalyptic*, 235; Russell, *Method*, 88–91; Hengel, *Judaism*, 1.180. There has been a growing tendency to date parts of *1 Enoch* in the third century B.C., e.g., Stone, *Scriptures*, 38, 41f.

A widely accepted explanation for the emergence of apocalyptic eschatology, as seen at least from the time of return from exile, is accommodation in Israel of non-fulfillment of the prophetic hope.[14] It is true that at best the hope was only partially realized in the post exilic period, with a remnant returning to the land of promise and inaugurating worship of Yahweh in Jerusalem. In other words, delay of the new age may have been a very significant underlying factor that contributed to the apocalyptic worldview. A partial fulfillment of the prophetic promises probably strengthened hope at first, but then led eventually to reckoning with delay in fulfillment. Lack of fulfillment was evident in that the Davidic kingdom was not restored. Instead Persia continued to rule the land of the returned exiles and their descendants for two hundred years. The national material prosperity that was to characterize the new era was hardly evident (cf. Ezra 4; Neh 2; 4–6; Mal 3:9–12). The restored temple never did attain the expected glory (cf. Tob 14:4f.; *2 Bar.* 68 with Ezek 40–48; Hag 2:6–9). Though there were times of spiritual revitalization (e.g., Ezra 5:1f.; Neh 8), the enduring kind of "new covenant" renewal did not arrive (e.g., Tob 14:5–7; *T. Naph.* 4:3f.).

This interpretation of the rise of apocalyptic perspective need not be seen as opposed to divine inspiration on the part of the canonical prophets. On the contrary, we can see an interplay between historical development and revelation as the matrix within which late Israel and early Judaism, or at least a part of Judaism, came to understand itself in the unfolding plan of God. It is remarkable that with centuries of non-fulfillment, earlier prophetic traditions were not abandoned, but rather reinterpreted for the needs of existing faith communities.

---

[14] Cf. e.g., Hanson, *People Called,* 269–77. Here Hanson denies Ezekiel 38–39 to Ezekiel. Though somewhat common, this seems unnecessary, cf. Zimmerli, *Ezekiel 2,* 302–4.

EARLY JEWISH APOCALYPSES

We NOW TURN TO TWO EARLY JEWISH DOCUMENTS WHICH are generally considered "apocalyptic" in terms of that literary genre. Our interest is in parts of these documents that especially address eschatological expectation.

We start with the canonical Daniel, an important source for NT apocalyptic, as well as for various extra-canonical apocalyptic writings. In addition to Daniel, parts of the non-canonical 1 (Ethiopic) Enoch that are surveyed in this section help us to reconstruct the ethos of expectation in early Judaism. It is this atmosphere, with attending apocalyptic ideas, that is important as background for understanding expectation in early Christianity.

Daniel 7–12

Daniel 7–12 (cf. ch. 2), had a notable influence on eschatological expectation from the second century B.C. on through the NT era.[1] This influence is most evident in the NT in three pieces of eschatological literature we are yet to examine: the synoptic apocalypse of Mark, Matthew, and Luke; 2 Thessalonians 2; and Revelation. The arrival of a spectacular anti-god figure and attending events are largely in the foreground in these eschatological units. Thus we will want to pay special attention to these related themes in the apocalyptic portions of Daniel.

Of pivotal importance is the angelic reinterpretation of Jeremiah's seventy-year prophecy into seventy heptads, or 490 years

---

[1] Esp. note Beale, *Use of Daniel*.

(9:23–27). A traditional interpretation from earlier post-exilic years was that the seventy years were to be an extended sabbath rest for the land. This seventy-year period (however symbolically it may have been originally intended) was to end at the time when Persian rule was established in the sixth century B.C. (2 Chron 36:21–23; Ezra 1:1; cf. Lev 26:34f). Impatience over delay is reflected in the sixth century in the angel's words of Zech 1:12 (cf. 7:5):

> O LORD of hosts, how long will you withhold mercy from Jerusalem and the cities of Judah, with which you have been angry these *seventy years*? [emphasis mine]

It appears that the issue of eschatological delay becomes acute in post-exilic Judaism as a result of Jeremiah's prophecy. Accordingly its prominence in Daniel is significant for us. This signals a concern to cope with what was perceived as eschatological delay. At the same time we may observe a sense of expectation for the fulfillment of the ancient prophetic hope. But before proceeding, we must seek to understand the life situation in the Daniel oracles themselves. This in turn raises the question of authorship and date.

The text of Daniel actually does not identify the author (or final author), although most of the last six chapters purport to give the words of the exiled Daniel of the sixth century B.C. Chapters 1–6 are mostly narrated in the third person. Such narration returns in 7:1 and 10:1.

It is well known that critical scholars usually date Daniel in its present form from the Maccabean crisis of about 167–164 B.C. The Maccabean setting seems fairly apparent, although there is reason to see the leading character as derived from historical tradition that lies behind the book as it now exists.[2] The distinctly apocalyptic section

---

[2] Particularly important in recognizing historical tradition behind our canonical Daniel is the prompt second century B.C. reception of the book, if we may judge from the Qumran literature, cf. Russell, *Jews*, 221; Bruce, "Daniel," 221–235; Childs, *Introd.*, 616–18. Hengel, *Judaism*, 1.176, speaks of a "whole series of Daniel fragments," which are "probably backed by a school." Lebram, "Perspektiven," 5, says that many authors suggest that the *Grundbestand* of the prophecies in Daniel stem from the historical prophet Daniel in exile. Ellis says that "to whatever degree the language of Daniel 7–12 reflects an origin in the second century B.C.E., it is best explained as a contemporization of an earlier prophecy," "OT Canon," 684. In an article that details various ancient interpretations of the date for "Messiah's" coming based on Daniel 9, R. T. Beckwith concludes that had the prophecy in fact been regarded as written after the event the chronological information would have been more precise, "Daniel 9," 541f.

(chs. 7–12) moves to a climax in chapters 11f. with an extensive portrayal of third and second century Hellenistic militarism in the Mediterranean. This issues in the Palestinian terrors of Antiochus Epiphanes (11:20–39; cf. 12:11f.) and "the time of the end" (11:40ff.). An unprecedented "time of trouble," resurrection and judgment occurs "at that time" (12:1–4). Thus the focus is upon what we often call the intertestamental centuries, with the climax largely entailing the Maccabean period.

Conservative scholars have generally assumed an authorship much earlier than the second century B.C. The author, usually taken to be Daniel of the sixth century B.C., looks ahead and projects the future down to the era of the Maccabean crisis and then beyond.

In any case, we gather from the data of the book itself, as well as from available evidence of ancient contemporary Jewish literature, that the actual importance of the book in the life of ancient Judaism dates from the second century B.C. This will be evident in our ensuing discussion.

At the end of chapter 7, with the vision of four kingdoms that culminate in one anti-god figure who persecutes the godly community, Daniel is in shock and keeps the vision to himself (v. 28). Two years later (8:1 with 7:1) Daniel has a vision of the temple being desecrated for a specified period of time by a powerful impious figure (8:1–14), but afterward restored by divine intervention (v. 25). Even after the vision is interpreted by the angel Gabriel, Daniel still does not understand the vision, since the revelation is for a later time. Daniel is overwhelmed (vv. 15–27). In chapter 9 Gabriel reappears to clarify the vision, and the revelation of the "seventy weeks" follows, with its reference to final redemption of Jerusalem after its destruction and temple desecration (vv. 20–27). In 10:1 Daniel finally understands "the vision." Verses 2–14 apparently explain how this understanding came about. Yet another vision is involved (v. 14), which seems to unfold in 11:1–12:3. Details of war between Persia and Greece are given, culminating (again) in the activities of the anti-god figure (and some apostasy), persecution of the faithful community, and temple desecration; but afterward, the deliverance and resurrection of God's people (esp. 11:29–12:3). After Daniel finally arrives at understanding of this "end time" (8:17; 11:40; 12:4, 13; cf. 8:26; 10:14), he is to seal up the words given him and they are to be kept secret until the time of the end (12:4, 9). This presumably would be after Daniel's death (12:13). Thus Daniel either does not understand the visions of the "end time," or he is to keep them secret for posterity.

The oracles of Daniel are called a "prophecy" only in 9:24, and there they concern not what he proclaims. Rather Jeremiah's prophecy is reinterpreted for him by the angel Gabriel. Nowhere in this book is Daniel himself called a "prophet," although Mark 13:14 (= Matt 24:15) so refers to him. The difference between Daniel and the canonical prophets is striking. Daniel does not address his own people, as a prophet customarily did. He interprets for heathen kings divine messages addressed to them. He keeps private the divine messages given him. They are for a later time. It should be no surprise that the Hebrew canon places Daniel among the Writings instead of with the Prophets.

With the "publication" of Daniel by the second century B.C., it is understandable that pious Jews of that time and afterward would perceive themselves to be living in the days foretold by Daniel. The events were unfolding before their eyes! Such interest in Daniel is evident from the Dead Sea Scrolls of Qumran, other Jewish literature, and of course the NT documents.[3] This substantially helps to set the stage for our recognizing eschatological expectation within Judaism in the centuries immediately preceding the Christian era and afterward. But it also prepares us to recognize a coping with delay as "the end" continued to remain outstanding. In a sense "the exile" was not yet really over. Thus we have a continuation of the expectation/delay tension found earlier in the canonical literature.

Awareness of eschatological delay must have been marked for the second century B.C. community in which Daniel was published. In the canonical context of Daniel there is a great tension between a sixth century B.C. expectation of final restoration and blessing, based on Jer 25:11–12 and 29:10–14, and the visions Daniel receives of great distress in "days yet to come" (10:14). In his intercessory prayer of confession in chapter 9, Daniel had prayed, "do not delay"

---

[3] Although Daniel is commonly viewed as pseudonymous and as history written in the guise of prophecy, the book was hardly taken that way in the second century B.C. and afterward by contemporaries of that time. See note 18 above. Also, Ulrich, "Daniel Manuscripts," 17ff.; Bruce, *Biblical Exegesis*, esp. ch. 6; Bruce, "Daniel," 221–35. In an "additional note" in the last essay, Bruce refers to the Qumran text 4QFlorilegium (he says fully published just after his article was written) which speaks of "the book of Daniel the prophet." He says that "this expression (cf. Matt 24:15) should put an end to doubts about the canonical status of Daniel in the Qumran community,"235. Cf. Ellis who cites this evidence and argues that Daniel was most likely considered among the Prophets at the time of the Qumran community, "OT Canon," 683f.

(v. 19)! Now in the time of Maccabean crisis every Jew who serves Daniel's God not only shares his hope but also his quandary. If Daniel was published during the crisis, the prayers of "how long" in the midst of the tribulation described in 8:13 and 12:6 must surely reflect the existential agony in the community of those who remain faithful at that time. Most scholars understand the faithful to be the Hasidim (forerunners of the Pharisees in the NT) as they painfully resisted capitulation to the worldly Hellenistic influence on the part of foreigners and even many Jews (cf. Dan 11:29–35).

But Daniel concludes on a note of hope for those who persevere (12:12–13). Certainty of the good outcome is implied in the stated (determined) waiting periods, whether taken symbolically or more literally: 8:14 (1150 days); 9:24 (seventy weeks); 7:25; 12:7 (a time, two times, and half a time); 12:11f. (1290, 1335 days). In the context of persecution and delay we find expectation of the promised good end, which is not too far off. The themes of persecution, apostasy, expectation/delay, and a divine determinism found in Daniel recur in Jewish apocalyptic. Such will be important to keep in mind as we move toward establishing the background of NT expectation. In Daniel we find the critical immediate situation triggering the assurance of imminent divine intervention. This was the revealed word to Daniel. We know historically that the Jewish community had good reason to believe that such intervention had come, as they threw off the heathen yoke and restored and rededicated the defiled sanctuary (1 Macc 1–4). But "the end" did not come. Thus the eschatological hope within the seventy-weeks prophecy became the expectation of future generations. It is noteworthy that the lack of names and other such specific details in the predictions themselves prepared the way for a reuse of the predictions in later times.

1 Enoch: Two Apocalypses

The composite work known as *"1 Enoch"* is generally considered to derive in its various parts from the third or second century B.C. to perhaps the first century A.D. Important motifs parallel those of NT eschatology, and there is evidence that the work was influential in early Christianity.[4] The full text is only extant in Ethiopic, with the most readily accessible and up-to-date translations

---

[4]Isaac, "1 Enoch," 8. Most explicitly, Jude 14 comes from *1 Enoch* 1:9.

in English those by E. Isaac in J. H. Charlesworth's *Old Testament Pseudepigrapha* and M. A. Knibb in H. F. D. Sparks' *The Apocryphal Old Testament*. Fragments exist in Aramaic and Greek; scholars believe the original language(s) was Aramaic and/or Hebrew.[5]

The apocalyptic tone of *1 Enoch* is set from the beginning. Enoch is described in chapters 1–5 as seeing a vision in which judgment falls upon the distant ungodly generation in the day of tribulation (distant from his assumed vantage point, but not from that of the actual author!). The righteous inherit the earth in gladness and peace. For our considerations the most important sections of the composite work are the animal apocalypse in chapters 85–90 and the apocalypse of weeks (chs. 91, 93) in light of the broader context (chs. 91–107). Both apocalypses are historical surveys which eventuate in the eschatological judgment and heavenly kingdom. In both there is a periodization of events from Israel's early times to the fulfillment of the prophetic hope, especially in the apocalypse of weeks.

The Animal Apocalypse

The animal apocalypse progresses from the earliest times to the exile, and then has seventy "shepherds" who are responsible for the "sheep" (Israel) until the last judgment (89:59–90:27). The seventy shepherds serve in successive periods of time, apparently between the exile and the Maccabean period,[6] after which they are thrown into the "fiery abyss" (90:27) because of their destructive ways against the sheep. Then follows a triumphant scene in which a throne is erected in the "pleasant land" (90:20) and the Lord of the sheep provides a "new house" (temple) into which all surviving sheep and all the "animals" and "birds" gather (90:27–36). (The earlier "house" had been destroyed, apparently the temple destruction of 587 B.C.; 89:67). The animals and birds become subservient to the sheep (90:30–31).

---

[5]Cf. Black, "Bibliography," 3–6. Black says the most comprehensive edition of Ethiopic Enoch in the eighties, taking account of various extant fragments, is a German translation by S. Uhlig. On original language cf. Isaac, "1 Enoch," 6.

[6]Concerning the Maccabean era, cf. for example Hengel, *Judaism,* 1.187f. The seventy are usually taken to be angels who are responsible for controlling Israel's circumstances during this time, cf. Hengel, *Judaism,* 1.187f.; Charles, *Enoch,* 242f.; Knibb, "Exile," 256. VanderKam, *Enoch,* 166f., sees the shepherds as angels who represent seventy Gentile nations who have dominion over Israel for seventy years.

The posture of OT eschatology is evident, as a new temple is constructed (e.g., Ezek 40–48; Hag 2:7–9) and the nations of the earth eventually serve both Israel and Israel's God (cf. for example Isa 2:1–4; 55:5; 61:5–7; Amos 9:12; Zech 2:11).

But by far the most interesting corresponding OT references are in Jer 25 and Dan 7–8, 11–12. The seemingly predetermined seventy years of Babylonian domination in Jer 25 may have been filtered through apocalyptic Daniel (or the tradition behind Daniel) before resurfacing in a highly interpretive or midrashic form in *1 Enoch* 89–90. We apparently have the same extension of an original "seventy years" that we find in Dan 9.

In both Jer 25 and *1 Enoch* 89–90 we have a combination of seventy years chastisement and the pastoral imagery of shepherd/sheep.[7] As in *1 Enoch* 89–90, in Jer 25 those who have domineered over Israel are called "shepherds" (vv. 34–36). In both the seventy years of distress for Israel are followed by judgment on the oppressors (Jer 25:16–17, 27–29, 31, 38; *1 Enoch* 90:18–19). In *1 Enoch* the shepherds exceed their charge in destroying the sheep (89:59–67) and seemingly are punished for that. In Jer 25 Babylon is punished for its evil deeds (though the deeds are not specified in this context), verses 12, 14. Furthermore, in both cases the seventy years are predetermined (Jer 25:11; *1 Enoch* 89:59–60 with 68). Thus Jer 25 likely underlies the animal apocalypse of *1 Enoch*.

The possibility of apocalyptic Daniel also explaining the animal apocalypse is perhaps most vividly evident when comparing the themes of *1 Enoch* 90:20–27 with Dan 7:9–12; 8:9; 11:16, 41; 12:4, 9: judgment throne(s) set; venue as the "pleasant/beautiful land"; sealed books opened; the condemned thrown into the fire. More broadly the imagery and ideas of *1 Enoch* 90:9–27 may be compared with Dan 7–8, 11–12.[8]

A seemingly significant sub-theme is the fiery abyss for the "blinded sheep," who also are found guilty (90:26f.). Before the new temple is constructed, the blind sheep are judged (cf. 90:28f.). This apparently refers to apostates within Israel.[9] They hold forth just prior to the new age (cf. Dan 11:30b, 32 with 12:1–4).

---

[7]For calling my attention to the comparison of Jer 25 with *1 Enoch* 89–90 I am indebted to VanderKam, *Enoch,* 164–67. Reid, "Ten Week Apocalypse," 200, finds here a midrash on Ezek 34.

[8]Cf. Beale, *Use of Daniel,* 67–88.

[9]Cf. Sanders, *Paul,* 351.

A sense of delay triggered by the unfulfilled seventy-year prophecy of Jer 25 has evidently surfaced against a Maccabean backdrop, as it did in Daniel. And as in Daniel, eschatological fulfillment is seen as imminent. Judgment on Israel's enemies and Israel's exaltation are just around the corner. A common prophetic base for Daniel and *1 Enoch* 89–90 is probable.[10]

The Apocalypse of Weeks

The first seven weeks of "Enoch's" vision are in 93:1–10. The last three weeks constitute 91:12–17. There is little doubt that the contents of 93:1–10 originally preceded those of 91:12–17.[11] Furthermore, it has been widely held that this apocalypse was composed independently of the broader context of chs. 91–105.[12]

Our interest is mainly in the last three weeks. The periodization of events becomes progressively more "apocalyptic," though still rooted in the themes of the OT prophetic hope. We are evidently beyond the time of the (intertestamental) author. The motifs are as follows:

Eighth week, 91:12: Sinners punished by the righteous (cf. eschatological judgment on sinners, though not executed by the righteous, Jer 30:16; 51:36f.; Joel 3:1f.[MT 4:1f.]; Zech 12:1–4; 14:12–15). Then 91:13: Prosperity of the righteous (cf. Isa 58:8, 12; 60:21; 65:21f.; Jer 30:18) and a glorious "house" built for the "Great King" (cf. Ezek 40–48; Hag 2:1–9).

Ninth week, 91:14: The "whole earth" is purged of evil (cf. Isa 13:9–11; 24:1–3; Zeph 1:18) and all people follow righteousness (cf. Isa 2:2–4; 42:4; 49:6b).

---

[10] Without "proving" it, this agrees with our position that a Daniel tradition lies behind our canonical Daniel. Beale, *Use of Daniel,* argues for the animal apocalypse being dependent on Daniel, 88, n. 137.

[11] E.g., Charles, "Enoch," 264; Knibb, *Enoch,* 218. This order has been confirmed in the Aramaic of the Qumran scroll 4QEng, e.g., Milik, *Enoch,* 48; Dexinger, *Henochs,* 102–06.

[12] Cf. VanderKam, *Enoch,* 142f.; Nickelsburg, "Apocalyptic," 313, n. 15. Charles has suggested a pre-Maccabean date, as there is no reference to Maccabean persecution, with the remainder of chs. 91–104 in the early first century B.C., "Enoch," 171; cf. Eissfeldt, *Old Testament,* 619. Dexinger represents those who opt for a Maccabean crisis date, *Henochs,* 136–40, 187–89. The absence of warfare and temple desecration in this period of the apocalypse militates against this view.

Tenth week, 91:15–16: Eternal judgment conducted by angels and a new glorious heaven (powers shining "sevenfold") replaces the old heaven (cf. Isa 34:4; 65:17–19; 66:22). Eternity follows ("many weeks without number forever") in which is goodness and righteousness, with sin annihilated (91:17; cf. 32:16–18; Jer 31:31–34; Zech 13:1).

With the ninth-week purging of the entire world the eschatology becomes more "apocalyptic," though how this purging occurs is not given. Then with the brilliant new heaven in the tenth week, preceded with the eternal judgment by angels—not in the prophetic hope—we are apparently in the new age. This corresponds to the righteous shining like "the lights of heaven" (104:2; cf. 108:12–15; Dan 12:3).

The author seems to be speaking from the seventh week, during the time of apostasy (93:9), since the sixth week closes with the destruction of the temple and the dispersion (93:8). At the close of this week the righteous elect are illuminated with "sevenfold instruction" ("wisdom and knowledge," 4QEng).[13] We suspect that since the end-time is still outstanding by the seventh week, bestowal of fuller knowledge is appropriate. This reminds us of Daniel's need for further understanding to make sense of the prophetic hope being delayed (Dan 9:1f., 23–27). It is likely that the Enoch apocalyptist as well is keenly aware of eschatological delay and also finds the solution in divine instruction. The answer, then, comes with the sevenfold instruction just before the eighth week and the launching of the eschatological period with its prosperity and new temple. The "exile" has stretched down to the apocalyptist's own time, as in Dan 9, but it is soon to end.

Even though the eschaton is imminent, there is curiously still a delay within the imminent expectation! It is not until the tenth week that the new heaven arrives, and in fact it is the seventh part of the tenth week that is awaited (91:15).[14] We see the apocalyptist, and no doubt the godly community whom he addresses, struggling with delay in fulfillment of the prophetic hope. But hope is maintained despite delay. We also see the transposition of that hope into a definite apocalyptic register by this time.

---

[13] The Qumran reference is in a note on the verse by Isaac, *1 Enoch,* 74; cf. Milik, *Enoch,* 267.

[14] Reid, "Ten Week Apocalypse," speaks of a "three stage salvific eschatology" in the last three weeks, 195; cf. Hengel, *Judaism* 1.189.

What part of the intertestamental period are we witnessing?
This brings us back to the question of the relation of the apocalypse
of weeks to the broader context of chapters 91–107. (These chs. are
sometimes called the "epistle of Enoch" because the word "epistle"
occurs in 100:6 of a Greek text on this part of *1 Enoch*).[15]

There is considerable literary evidence that the last three
weeks (91:12–16) have been composed, possibly redacted, by the
author of the "epistle." Common key themes of retribution on
wrongdoers (cf. 94:6; 95:6f.; 97:8–10; 98:8; 99:12f., 15; 100:7),
worldwide judgment (cf. 99:4; 102:2f.), eternal judgment (104:5),
righteous shining like lights (104:2) may be more or less identified. Likewise there is some evidence of common themes in a
part of the epistle that precedes the apocalypse of weeks, but
which are not in the first seven weeks. Conversely, key themes
appear in the first seven weeks which do not appear in the ensuing
chapters. I believe that the author of the epistle betrays a very
special interest in the final three (eschaton) weeks, and may have
composed them himself.[16]

A composition date for the "epistle" (chs. 91–107) and with the
inclusion of the apocalypse of weeks in its final form is difficult to
determine. But there is reason to posit that the latter years of John
Hyrcanus toward the end of the second century B.C. or the earlier
years of Alexander Jannaeus (who ruled 103–76 B.C.) provided a
period likely to have produced the epistle. These were years when
the ruling classes in Judaism were considered to be wealthy and
oppressive. Social injustice was rank, with struggles belonging more
to an oppressed social group than to a sectarian or political conflict
(contrast the Maccabean years of 167–164).[17] The hellenizing faction in Palestinian Judaism was at odds with the more pious, poor,
and oppressed Jews, who probably at least included the Hasidim,
forerunners of the Pharisees.

In the Enoch "epistle" we find social injustice and persecution
of the righteous as causes for serious concern (95:5–7; 96:5, 7f.).
Murder is committed (99:15). Rulers are disinterested in the plight

---

[15] E.g., Knibb, *Enoch*, 8, who appeals to Qumran evidence for making
107 the last chapter.

[16] Detailed literary evidence for this conclusion is present in Holman,
"Eschatological Delay," 39–42.

[17] Cf. consensus at the Paris SNTS conference in Charlesworth, "Books
of Enoch," 322; Nickelsburg, "Riches," 326f. On the times more generally
cf. Russell, *Jews*, 66–73.

of the godly (103:14) and the wealthy are often the evil doers (94:7–11; 96:4–6; 97:8–10; 100:6; 103:5f.).

Another possibility is that the latter part of the third century B.C. or the pre-Maccabean second century is described. Scholars have contended that this period is to be preferred, with the same social-economic conditions prevailing in Palestinian Judaism.[18]

We may surmise that the prevalence of wickedness is vivid testimony that the apostate generation due to precede the eschaton is now alive (cf. Dan 9:27; 11:32, 34f.), even though still worse days of violence and bloodshed lie ahead (cf. "in those days" in 99:3–5; 100:1–4).[19] The apocalyptist exhorts his readers to "be hopeful" (96:1; 102:4; 104:2); "be confident" (97:1); "fear not" (102:4). Such entreaty probably reflects need for the community to become expectant (or to maintain expectation) for the eschaton, against a background of delay.

It would be helpful for us in tracking end-time expectation in early Judaism as a background to understanding New Testament eschatological expectation to have a more definite idea of the time period for the apocalypse of weeks. But we cannot go beyond the evidence available. At any rate we here note further evidence of the effects of a delayed fulfillment of the prophetic hope and a faith in a portion of Judaism (probably the Hasidim) in God's eschatological intervention in the not-too-distant future.

---

[18] VanderKam, *Enoch,* who cites a lack of "compelling evidence" for the later date, 143, 171; cf. Collins, *Apocalyptic Imagination,* 49–53; Hengel, *Judaism* 1.176, 188f. with 32–57.

[19] It may be argued that "in those days" is from the perspective of the antediluvian Enoch. However the hortatory and "woes" passages betray an immediacy that speaks of the actual author's times. Such passages may be contrasted with those pointing to the future. Note especially "in those days" in 102:1–3, where the cataclysmic worldwide judgment is portrayed. VanderKam helpfully suggests the apostates are the hellenizing party which existed at the beginning of Antiochus IV's reign, *Enoch,* 147, 149.

EXCURSUS: 1 ENOCH 37-71 (THE BOOK OF PARABLES)

Within this part of *1 ENOCH* are three "parables" (38–44; 45–57; 58–69). Eschatological expectation is implicit in that much attention is given themes which we can identify as "eschatological." Such themes include the extermination and judgment of sinners (e.g., 38:1; 47:2f.; 50:1, 4; 62:2f.). Often the judgment is against those who have oppressed the righteous (e.g., 47:1; 48:8; 62:11–13). The righteous have security and blessing forever (e.g., 39:7; 50:1; 51:2). These themes we have found earlier in apocalyptic writings; they show us the expectation of whatever godly community from which they derive.

The parables have received extensive study because of references to one denoted as "Son of Man," and who is apparently synonymous with the "Elect One" (cf. 48:2 with 48:6; 61:8 with 62:5). The descriptions are clearly messianic, including the eschatological role of judge (e.g., 49:3; 62:5–the "Son of Man" sitting on the throne of his glory, cf. Matt. 25:31). In 48:10 the ungodly are judged because "they have denied the Lord of the Spirits and his Messiah" (emphasis mine). In a fairly explicit reference to Dan 7, he is one "whose face was like that of a human being" and who was with "the One" who existed before time and whose "head was white like wool" (46:1 with v. 3; cf. Dan 7:9, 13).[1]

A major difficulty for NT backgrounds is the dating of the Parables. Options for dating usually run from the first century B.C.

---

[1] On the Parables of *1 Enoch* incorporating a midrash of Daniel, see Beale, *Use of Daniel,* 96–112.

to the first century A.D., with the possibility that they were composed beyond the first century A.D. by a Christian author(s).[2] There
is a good possibility that the reflected Danielic interpretation of one
who is like a "son of man" is pre-Christian. If so, this is significant
for eschatological orientation within Judaism in the time of Jesus.[3]

---

[2] E.g., Charlesworth, *Modern Research,* 98; Knibb, "Date," 358; Collins,
Apocalyptic, 143. The absence of the Parables from the extant Enoch Qumran
scrolls has contributed substantially to a date after the second century B.C.
This kind of evidence is not conclusive, however, cf. Black, "Bibliography,"
7. J. T. Milik represents a minority who date the Parables in the second or
third century A.D. and see it as Christian work, *Enoch,* 96; cf. comment by
Black, "Bibliography," 7.

[3] Cf. Hooker, *Son of Man,* 48. Dunn stresses the lack of evidence for a
Son of man concept in pre-Christian Judaism, *Christology,* 75–82; cf. Casey,
Son of Man, 112. Black points to the possibility of "fresh evidence" in recently
elucidated Qumran fragments (4Q Melchizedek), where there is a "remarkable parallel to the Danielic-Enoch-New Testament 'Son of Man' in Melchizedek who is identified with the Archangel Michael in a *judgmental and
redemptionist role*" (emphasis his), "Bibliography," 7–9.

5

APOCALYPTIC IDEAS IN OTHER EARLY WRITINGS

OUR LITERATURE IN THIS SECTION IS THAT WHICH IS MORE or less related to the apocalyptic genre and includes documents from the Qumran community. We shall continue to concentrate on themes most related to eschatological expectation.

Jubilees

This book, sometimes called "Little Genesis" or "Apocalypse of Moses," is largely a midrash on Genesis which sees history divided into "jubilee" periods (e.g., 1: 26, 29; 23:8f.; 50:4f. cf. Lev 25:10–15). *Jubilees* was most likely composed originally in Hebrew in the second century B.C., but the only extant complete version is in Ethiopic.[1] Several manuscripts have been found in Qumran caves and use of the same solar calendar has pointed to a possible Qumran origin, though a pre-Essene origin before the Qumran schism is also held.[2]

The kind of cosmic transcendental eschatology which we consider distinctly "apocalyptic" is lacking. But other motifs that are in apocalyptic thinking surface. These are in chapters 1 and 23. The prominence given these themes indicates eschatological expectation.

---

[1]Cf. Wintermute, "Jubilees," 41–44; Sparks, *Apocryphal,* 5–7; Collins, *Apocalyptic,* 67.

[2]For Qumran cf. M. Testuz, *Jubilés,* 33f., 179–95; Davenport, *Eschatology,* 16 (late second century redactor); Eissfeldt, *Old Testament,* 607f. For Essene or proto-Essene, VanderKam, *Jubilees,* 255–83; Wintermute, 46.

In addition we seem to find an explanation for eschatological delay. Thus this book becomes significant for us as possible background for understanding NT expectation.

The assumed life situation is Moses on Mt. Sinai, where he receives the law *and* the contents of *Jubilees,* with an accent on the future of Israel (e.g., 1:1–6). Forty-nine jubilees are specified from Adam to Moses and forty years are predicted before entering Canaan (50:4). Then an unspecified number of jubilees are anticipated before Israel is purged of all sin and the days of blessing arrive (cf. 50:5). The book closes on this note of eschatological expectation and an extensive midrash on sabbath keeping (50:5–13). Significant themes of expectation are featured as follows.

(1) A synopsis of Israel's reception of the law, failure to keep it and consequent captivity among the nations, and then return to God is climaxed with a "new creation." The latter includes the eternal temple and perennial days of healing, peace, and blessing on the earth (1:26–29 with 1:1–25; cf. Isa 65:17; Ezek 37:26, 28; 40–48; *1 Enoch* 89:28–36; 91:13).

(2) After arriving at chapter 23 the author interrupts his midrash on the Genesis history at the point of Abraham's death. The author looks ahead at future generations until "the great judgment" (v. 11). Evil in every way is predicted (e.g., shortened life span, sickness, famine, death, captivity, vv. 11–13), but the focus is on one generation—"the evil generation which sins in the land" (v. 14; cf. vv. 15, 16, 22). Then "in those days" when they begin to return to the law, longevity returns, Satan is removed, enemies are expelled, joy prevails (vv. 26–31). Following this excursus the narrative returns to Genesis where it left off. The author's interest in what lies ahead for his people is thus very evident.

(3) The portrayal of eschatological blessing that follows exile completely bypasses the new beginning in the sixth century B.C. when an incomplete new start was made. Israel goes into captivity; Israel returns to God; the new age arrives with the eternal sanctuary (1:13–18 with vv. 22ff.). It appears the author considers Israel to be still in exile and looking for the promised new day. The post-exilic return is treated as of no theological consequence. Thus eschatological delay must have been all the more acute.

Before we attempt to isolate a more exact life situation for *Jubilees,* the author's evident explanation for the delay merits our attention. We have observed that the cause of Israel's calamities is laid directly at the doorstep of its covenant infidelity. The author follows through by making repentance the route to fulfillment of the prophetic hope. The repentance must be thoroughgoing: "With all their heart and with all their soul and with all their might. . . . When they seek me with all their heart and with all their soul. . . ." (1:15, cf. vv. 20–25; Deut. 4:29). This is dramatically clear in chapter 23. The unanswered desperate cry of "that generation" of Israel is detailed in verses 22–25. Then we read: "In those days, children will begin to search the law, and to search the commandments and to return to the way of righteousness" (v. 26). It is after this statement that the days of blessings are vividly described (vv. 27–31). Since Israel is responsible for its continued "exile," the arrival of eschatological blessing is likewise its responsibility. This motif of repentance and then blessing is apparently firmly rooted in Jer 29:10–14. "Then when you call upon me . . . I will hear you. When you search for me, you will find me; if you seek me with all your heart . . . I will restore your fortunes and gather you from all the nations . . ." (vv. 12–14). It is fulfillment of the prophetic hope which *Jubilees* is anticipating. But the ball is in Israel's court!

What generation has given birth to such a document? Though a second century provenance is generally agreeable, a more exact origin is difficult to determine. We are on fairly safe ground to conclude that the author considers himself to be living in the evil generation which has captured his attention, or possibly that generation is just around the corner.

Although an editing of *Jubilees* perhaps occurred after the Maccabean era, a persuasive argument can be mounted for recognizing a Maccabean terminus a quo.[3] In the midrashic material the author's emphases are often evident at the point where he leaves the biblical narrative.[4] In particular the following motifs can be mentioned: Sabbath keeping (2:17–33; 23:21; 50; cf. 1 Macc 1:45; 2 Macc 6:6); circumcision (15:33f.; cf. 1 Macc 1:48, 60); commemoration of festivals (6:17–24; 16:20–27; cf. 34:18f.; 2 Macc 1:48, 60; warning against idolatry (20:7–9; 21:3f.; cf. 1 Macc 1:47); warning against nudity (3:31; cf. the Greek gymnasium in 1 Macc 1:14f.; 2 Macc 4:7–17).

---

[3] For a Maccabean dating, VanderKam, *Jubilees,* 207–85, esp. 283–85; Rowley, *Relevance,* 88–90; *Jewish Apocalyptic,* 10f.; Collins, *Apocalyptic,* 67. Testuz sees editing about 110 B.C. and a later redaction for 1:7–25, 28; 23:11–32; 24:28b–30 between approximately 65 and 38 B.C., *Jubilés,* 35, 39–42, 177, 197; Davenport holds to a late third or early second century date, with 1:4b–26; 23:14–20, 21–31; 50:5 redacted from the Maccabean wars, *Eschatology,* 2, 10–15, 74.

[4] VanderKam, *Jubilees,* 242.

References throughout to calendar changes may relate to the "little horn" of Daniel 7:25, who "shall attempt to change the sacred seasons and the law." Apostasy and conflict in 23:16f., 19f. correspond with the Maccabean scenario, including the "great wickedness in forsaking the covenant" and bloodshed in attempting to enforce return to the covenant way (cf. e.g., 1 Macc 1:42–53; 2:43–46; 3:4–6, 8).[5]

Two passages in chapter 23 point to a time after the Maccabean conflict. Verse 21 indicates that some who escape bloodshed (at the hands of covenant enforcers) will not forsake their evil ways but "will lift themselves up for deceit and wealth" and pollute the holy of holies with their corruption. This suggests the faction that compromised during the Maccabean resistance and later became powerful affluent Hasmonean priest-leaders (forerunners of the Sadducees in the NT).[6] And then verses 23f. speak of merciless slaughter by Gentiles, with "none" saved even though they cry out to the Lord. This cannot refer to the successful Maccabean resistance. It most likely is what the author envisions in the future, because of the continuing apostasy indicated in verse 21. (It hardly refers to the post-Maccabean era, when Israel was often successful against the Syrians.) In this case the Maccabean crisis prefigures events ahead, before the return to righteousness and God's blessing.

If the (final) author produced *Jubilees* in the latter part of the second century B.C. (or even somewhat later), his use of national repentance as an answer to eschatological delay is well explained against the background of an ongoing failure of the prophetic hope to be realized. He must have been part of the Hasidic or Essene community which sought to preserve the covenant traditions and hope of Israel.

Sibylline Oracles, Book 3

The genre known as sibylline oracles was indigenous in the Asiatic and Roman worlds of antiquity.[7] Those extant are formally

---

[5] Cf. Davenport, *Eschatology,* 41f.

[6] Cf. Davenport, *Eschatology,* 43f., who considers 23:21 probably an interpolation from Qumran. Charles dates *Jubilees* between 135 and 105 B.C., as authored by a Pharisee, "Jubilees," 1. Many hold to a date of around 100 B.C., cf. Sparks, *AOT,* 5. Qumran evidence makes it difficult to date *Jubilees* much earlier, cf. e.g., Wintermute, "Jubilees," 43f.

[7] Data on the sibyllines generally, and on which we are here dependent, may be found in Collins, "Sibylline Oracles," 317–24.

identified in fourteen "books." The Sibyl (of which there were several) was depicted as an old woman who was inspired to utter prophecies, frequently of gloom and doom that was to come on the world. Such prophecies were often taken seriously and served propagandist purposes.

What is now known as Book 3 is distinctly Jewish, along with Books 4 and 5. Most of Book 3 is generally dated around the middle of the second century B.C.[8] It is especially valuable for our purposes in that it reflects hellenistic Judaism of the diaspora (as do the other Jewish Sibyllina). The sibylline genre was employed by diaspora Jews to commend monotheism to a pagan world. These oracles were thus missionary writings. The Sibyl is identified at the end of Book 3 as the daughter-in-law of Noah (lines 823–27). Almost certainly the writing is from Egyptian Judaism.[9] Special attention is given Egypt, including references to the "seventh" king (cf. lns. 46, 159, 161, 193, 208, 314–18, 348, 608, 614).

The most pertinent passage for our consideration is lines 46–62. A longing for the day of judgment is expressed in a way that is somewhat reminiscent of Daniel's "how long?" statement (cf. Dan 8:13; 12:6). The particular lines are 55f.: "Alas, wretched one, when will that day come, and the judgment of the great king immortal God?" The signal for the anticipated judgment day to arrive, followed by God's kingdom on earth, is Rome's conquest of Egypt ("when Rome will also rule over Egypt," note lns. 46–50). As if to counter the disappointment of delay, we read in lines 57–59: "Yet for the present [ἄρτι δ᾽ ἔτι] be founded, cities . . . so that you may come to the bitter day."[10] Then the certainty of divine judgment is supported in line 60 ("For it will come" [ἥξει γάρ]), followed by the "Sibyl's" promise in lines 61f. to state the cities destined to suffer woe. Imminence seems suggested in line 50 ("as time presses on").

This passage (lns. 46–62) is usually dated in the first century B.C., in contrast to the balance of the book (most of lns. 97–829 and see above). Presumably Rome is at least on the move toward Egypt,

---

[8] Cf. Collins, "Sibylline Oracles," 354f.; Rowley, *Relevance*, 68; Russell, *Method*, 54f.; Volz, *Eschatologie*, 54; Eissfeldt, *Old Testament*, 616. Nikiprowetzky, *Sibylle*, ch. 7, argues for a first century date for the whole book.

[9] Cf. Collins, "Sibylline Oracles," 356; Denis, *Introduction*, 113; Charlesworth, *Modern Research*, 185 (probably Alexandria).

[10] Our Greek text for the third Sibylline book is that of Geffcken, *Oracula*.

which arouses expectation of the day of divine reckoning. This may be shortly after the second triumvirate ("Three will destroy Rome with piteous fate," ln. 52), that is, after 32 B.C., when Rome had already come to power in Egypt.[11] Even if the date should be placed somewhat earlier in the first century B.C., expectation would still be encouraged by all who took the Sibyl seriously and who could read the "signs of the times."[12]

But before we place too much stock in the above passage, we must allow for the possibility that the apparently impatient cry ("when will that day come . . . ?") and the dialectic between delay and imminent expectation is only a ploy in a missionary tract. Let us look more closely at the third Sibylline.

First, in the major portion of the book (clearly anchored in the second century B.C., as we have discussed), there is eschatological expectation within rather specific temporal boundaries. In three oracular addresses, after line 161, we find eschatological predictions (or predictions with eschatological overtones) in connection with, or immediately following, the reign of the seventh Ptolemy ("king"). Accordingly, in the first of these three oracles (cf. lns. 162–64), a renaissance of Israel as a power with (potential?) moral influence on all the world is effected (lns. 191–94; cf. Isa 2:1–4). In the next oracle (cf. lns. 295–99) slaughter and famine is predicted for Egypt in the "seventh generation of kings," but followed by "rest" (lns. 314–18).[13] These woes remind us of the woes preceding the end of the age in apocalyptic literature (cf. *2 Bar.* 25–27; *Apoc. Ab.* 30; Rev 6:3–8). In the third oracle (cf. lns. 489–91) there is a longer list of woes—retribution, famine, groans, war, pestilence, fearful calamities—imposed by God on "all mortals" at the time of the seventh Egyptian king (of Greek origin). Egypt falls and then humankind experiences great earthly blessings (lns. 601–23; cf. lns. 652–60; Mark 13:7f. = Matt 24:6–8 = Luke 21:10f.; Rev 6:1–8; Isa 65:17–23). Particularly in light of the first and third oracles, we are justified in

---

[11] Collins, *Oracles,* 64f., having done extensive work on the third Sibylline, claims to agree with most commentators at this point. According to Boak, *History,* the second triumvirate of Octavian, Anthony, and Lepidus was from 43 B.C. to 32 B.C., 188–94.

[12] Cf. Boak, *History,* 193–95 on events of that time.

[13] The verb (παύσῃ) in the middle or passive can mean "rest," Liddell and Scott, *Lexicon,* I, 1. This suits the context here and is so translated in our passage in the *OTP,* vol. 1.

understanding the eschaton to arrive by the seventh Ptolemy in the second century B.C.[14]

Secondly, the OT prophetic hope obviously lies behind the expressions of eschatological hope in Book 3. The Hebrew concept of history eventuating in both severe earthly judgment for the ungodly and great earthly blessing for the righteous punctuates the balance of the book (e.g., lns. 280–94, 545–85, 601–24, 767–95). Toward the end of the book the Sibyl predicts the end of war, but admonishes that "all must sacrifice to the great king," apparently to God who "will raise up a kingdom for all ages among men" (lns. 807f. with 767ff.). Supporting themes found in Book 3 and in the LXX include: the heavens rolled up as a scroll and the stars/firmament falling (lns. 81–83 with Isa 34:4; cf. Rev. 6:14); seventy years of exile followed by blessing (lns. 280–83 with Jer 36:10–12 [Hebrew text: 29:10–12]); men shall throw idols (χειροποίητος in Isa 2:18 and Book 3) into clefts of the rocks and hide them (lns. 605–7 with Isa 2:18f., cf. vv. 20f.; 31:7); attack on Israel after messianic age arrives, but divine intervention with rain, fire, and brimstone (lns. 657–97 with Ezek 38f. [with ch. 37]).

In view of the above data we conclude that at least a part of Hellenistic Judaism in the diaspora shared with at least a sector of Palestinian Judaism expectation of an eschaton in or near the second century B.C. This conclusion in turn leads us to believe that there existed a genuine imminence/delay tension in Judaism at large in the Hellenistic world. The cry "when will that day come" (ln. 55) was most likely important in the missionary purpose of the book, but there was more behind it than merely a propagandist tack. It reflects a heartfelt hope and ideological struggle in Hellenistic Judaism.

Carrying further our analysis of expectation in early Judaism, we are looking at hope deferred again. After centuries of waiting—up to the (mid?) second century—anticipation is re-expressed when Rome is about to conquer (or has conquered) Egypt a century

---

[14] Because of confusion in the listing of the Ptolemies it is difficult to be precise in dating. However Collins argues that the seventh Ptolemy cannot be later than 117 B.C., but with around the middle of this century being preferable, *Apocalyptic,* 95f. In harmony with his first-century dating, Nikiprowetzky opts for Cleopatra VII, the last queen of Egypt, in the guise of the second century Ptolemy Physcon, *Sibylle,* 215f. This view is unconvincing and not generally followed; cf. Collins, *Apocalyptic,* 95f., with n. 17; "Provenance," 3f., where Collins claims that seven was not part of Cleopatra's title in antiquity.

or so later (cf. above). The first-century passage in lines 46–62 thus likely has more *angst* behind it than would appear on the surface.[15] Our guess is that past delay has served to heighten present expectation.

Instead of deleting the expression of the second century hope from the later production of what we call *Sibylline Oracles*, Book 3, the redactor(s) has obviously reused the same texts (at least basically) and thus updated their central message with his contemporary message regarding Rome's designs on Egypt as a sign of the end times. We have seen the same hermeneutical method in the use of Daniel in *1 Enoch* and the use of Jeremiah in Daniel. What might be the implications of this for understanding the ongoing viability of the OT hope and particularly in relation to Christian hope?

Psalms of Solomon[16]

Fairly distinctive contributions to our interest in eschatolgical expectation are found in the themes of messianism, apostasy, and an anti-god antagonist in the *Psalms of Solomon*.

As we shall see, the final composition of this document is properly dated not long after Pompey's invasion of Jerusalem in 63 B.C. These psalms were evidently in Hebrew originally and later translated into Greek and Syriac, with the original work perhaps by various authors over a period of time. The authors (if we assume more than one) may be of Pharisaic or Essene background.[17]

---

[15] The importance of our assumption of a first-century dating for lns. 46–62 is now evident. In addition to the support we have already presented, there are other reasons for understanding lns. 46–62 to be originally separate from most of the book. First, Rome is not the object of the many warnings and woes found later in the book. Given Rome's prominence in world affairs in these early lines, oracles addressed to Rome would surely have surfaced again. Instead concern is with Greece (cf. lns. 537–72, 732–43, 809–13). Secondly, the list of Roman cities destined for judgment according to lns. 61f. is not forthcoming before this oracle concludes (cf. lns. 4–7 with 162–64).

[16] Wright, "Psalms of Solomon," 646, says these psalms "are a conscious imitation of the Davidic psalter." Nothing in the text itself indicates that the author(s) attributed these psalms to Solomon. This, then, is a later attribution.

[17] On language and authorship cf. Wright, "Psalms of Solomon," 640–42; Brock, "The Psalms of Solomon," 650–52; Eissfeldt, *Old Testament,* 611f.; Gray, "The Psalms of Solomon," 627f. Charlesworth denies "convincing evidence" that links these Psalms with a particular sectarian group, *Modern Research,* 195; cf. Sanders, *Paul,* 388.

End-time expectation is evident in chapters 17f. This is most clear in the lengthy confession of messianic hope in 17:26–46; 18:6–9. Illegitimate usurpers have set up the monarchy that belongs to David's descendants (17:4–7; cf. 1:1–8; 2:3–5; 8:1–13). The Hasmoneans are likely culprits. These arch rivals of the Hasidim/ Pharisees, and who have now taken over government and religion.[18] But these Jewish leaders were overthrown by the Romans when Pompey marched into Jerusalem in 63 B.C. at the invitation of those involved in an internecine struggle there (cf. 8:14–22).[19] Though regarded as divinely sent (17:7–10), the aliens are deplored, as they have massacred young and old, carried captives to the west (Rome?), introduced paganism in Jerusalem, and caused refugees to flee to the wilderness. The confession of hope is preceded by an earnest prayer for the Messiah: "See, Lord, and raise up for them their king, the son of David, to rule over your servant Israel in the time known to you, O God" (17:21). The Messiah will purge Jerusalem of all ungodly people and prepare the city for the arrival of those who are god-fearing from the nations to serve under him and see the glory of God. At the same time there will be tribal redistribution of the land to Israel. (See 17:26–31.) Eschatological anticipation is quite evident. Messiah is to rectify the present situation.

At the same time, imminent fulfillment is tempered with over-tones of a "delayed" intervention. The author proclaims, "Blessed are those born in *those* days" (17:44a, μακάριοι οἱ γενόμενοι ἐν ταῖς ἡμέραις ἐκείναις).[20] A prayer for hastening (ταχύναι) "those days" follows in verse 45. The question arises whether the present generation will witness the messianic deliverance. The beatitude of 17:44a is repeated in 18:6, but this time the verse goes on to specify "the coming generation" (ἁ ποιήσει γενεᾷ τῇ ἐρχομένῃ) as the recipient of the messianic blessing. Perhaps some of those alive in the present would see the messianic age in the next generation. Nevertheless expectation appears slackened. Hard lessons learned from the past, and most recently from the Maccabean era, would appear to have resulted in a cautious expectation, even though signs

---

[18] Wright, "Psalms of Solomon," 665.

[19] Josephus records that Pompey rewarded the high priest Hyrcanus for the latter's complicity with the Romans by restoring the high priesthood to him after the temple had been invaded by Pompey, *Ant.* 14.69–76; *J.W.* 1.52–54. We understand the internal struggle to be between two Hasmonean brothers, Aristobulus II and Hyrcanus II, cf. Russell, *Jews,* 76–81.

[20] Our Greek text is taken from A. Rahlfs' 6th edition of the LXX (1959).

pointed to the eschaton. We shall now consider such signs, namely apostasy and the anti-god antagonist.

First, the apostasy theme is prominent. In an eschatological context, apostasy itself assumes an eschatological character. We find the following development in the opening psalms (1f.) the middle (8f.), and the penultimate (17). The deeds of Israel as a nation or leaders within are described as lawless (ἀνομίαι/παρανομίαι are key terms), 2:3; 8:9f. (cf. 4:1, 12, 23). Such evil surpasses that of Gentiles (1:8; 8:13; cf. 17:15). When described as "lawless," Israel is identified with the pagan devastator (Pompey) who is "the lawless one" (17:11, ὁ ἄνομος).[21]

Secondly, The "lawless" antagonist referred to just above, "a man alien to our race" (17:7b), is portrayed as a powerful warrior who rivals God himself—an aggressive anti-god figure. As such he leads the Gentile forces, forces which must yield to the messianic rule. His significance in the eschatological picture is seen in the following ways.

(1) According to *Pss. Sol.* 2 this personage does not consider that he is only human (ἄνθρωπος) as he aspires to lordship over "land and sea," not recognizing that "it is God who is great" (vv. 28f.). Following sudden destruction, he is disgraced with lack of a proper burial, explained by God's rejection of him (vv. 26f.).[22] The anti-god exaltation and demise strikingly resemble that of the eschatological tyrants of Isa 14:3–20; Ezek 28:2–19, and Dan 11:36–45. In Isa 14:1–4 and Dan 11:45–12:34 (cf. 7:25–27) the covenant-people of God experience deliverance and the divine blessing (including restoration in the land in Isa 14) after judgment on the anti-god figure. The eschatological nature of the divine intervention is particularly evident in the Daniel passage.

(2) The rape of the temple by "Gentile foreigners," led by the anti-god figure, contributes to the eschatological scene (2:2; cf. 2:19; 17:22, 30). Especially with the "Let it be enough, Lord" (2:22) and "Do not delay, O God" (2:25, μὴ χρονίσῃς, ὁ θεός), evoked by the heathen rampage against Jerusalem (2:19–25), the emotion of the Daniel episode is replayed (cf. 8:13; 12:6; also, μὴ χρονίσῃς in Dan 9:19).

---

[21] Wright, "Psalms of Solomon," indicates that some MSS have "the storm" instead of "the lawless one," 666. Gray, "Psalms of Solomon," also prefers "the lawless one" in his translation, 648. So also Rahlfs' LXX.

[22] Plutarch describes the sudden death of Pompey on Egyptian shores and his subsequent disgrace before eventually having a proper burial, *Pompey*, 77–80.

(3) In *Pss. Sol.* 2:25 the antagonist is called "the dragon" (τοῦ δράκοντος). The dragon's arrogance (τὴν ὑπερηφανίαν) corresponds with the arrogance (ὑπερηφανίαν) of the antagonist (Pompey) in 17:13. The dragon imagery in the OT is found in passages with eschatological overtones (cf. Isa 27:1, "in that day"; Ezek 29:3, Pharaoh, with Ezek 29:12–30:4; Jer 51:34 [28:34 LXX], Nebuchadnezzar, with Jer 50 [27 LXX]:1–5, 17–20). The δράκων, found in each of the three texts (LXX), can apparently be identified with various individuals who epitomize opposition to God's people (cf. Rev 12:3–18 with 13:11). But it is a climactic opposition that is characteristic of the eschaton as variously described or alluded to in the above passages.

It is difficult to believe that the *Psalms of Solomon* are without a conscious Danielic scenario of persecution, apostasy, anti-god figure, "delay not" cry, and deliverance in mind, even though there is no explicit reference to Daniel. These same events are essentially repeated in garb of the first century B.C. and in what we take to be largely Hasmonean and Roman characters. However, there are explicit references to the OT hope, in which Daniel is also rooted (cf. Dan 9:1f.).

A prophetic base for the eschatological hope in the *Psalms of Solomon* is evident from *Pss. Sol.* 11. It can be demonstrated that language and ideas are drawn ultimately from the Prophets and especially from "Second Isaiah."[23] Key parallels are as follows. "Announce in Jerusalem the voice of one bringing good news" (v. 1b with Isa 40:9; 52:7); "Stand on a high place, Jerusalem, and look at your children, from the east and the west assembled together by the Lord. From the north they come in the joy of their God; from far distant islands God has assembled them" (vv. 2f. with Isa 43:5f.; 49:22; cf. Jer 31(38):8); "He flattened high mountains into level ground for them" (v. 4a with Isa 40:4; 45:2); "Jerusalem, put on (the) clothes of your glory, prepare the robe of your holiness" (v. 7 with Isa 52:1). The use of this part of Isaiah with its heightened

---

[23] Ryle and James, *Psalms of the Pharisees,* lxxiiif.; cf. Gray, "Psalms of Solomon," 643; Schüpphaus, *Psalmen,* 55f. *Pss. Sol.* 11 may be dependent largely on *1 Bar.* 4:36–5:9, cf. Eissfeldt, *Old Testament,* 593; or, vice versa, cf. Wright, who also observes connections with the Qumran literature, "Psalms of Solomon," 647f. They possibly share a common derivation, in light of differences. If the author of *Pss. Sol.* 11 was aware of the OT hope in Isaiah, as we suspect he was, then the prophetic base of *Pss. Sol.* 11 is particularly significant.

expectation is a hint for us that the hope so picturesquely announced there might have appeared well overdue for fulfillment to the author of *Pss. Sol.* 11.

In addition to *Pss. Sol.* 11 above, this document shows a prophetic consciousness in other ways. Its hope for the restoration of dispersed Israel points to this fact (cf. 8:28; 17:31). Certainly hope in the Davidic Messiah is founded in the prophetic tradition (cf. 17:4, 21; cf. v. 6). His rule is described in prophetic terms. For example he destroys evil with the word of his mouth (17:24; cf. v. 35, with Isa 11:4) and judges nations with the wisdom of righteousness and compassion (17:29, 34b with Isa 42:1–4).

In view of the above evidence it is feasible that the author(s) of the *Psalms of Solomon* had awareness of a delayed eschaton, with that delay reaching back into the early post-exilic generations. The recent desecration and slaughter in Jerusalem by Pompey must have brought the questions of "how long" and "when" to a fever pitch. Here, then, is imminent expectation which has accommodated itself to "delay," however impatiently.

What determines when the messianic era will finally dawn? Thus far we have observed two ways in ancient Judaism explained the delay of the eschaton: (1) God has his own time table (esp. Daniel, *1 Enoch,* and *Sib. Or.* 3); (2) Israel's repentance is determinative (esp. *Jubilees*). In the *Psalms of Solomon* national repentance is suggested as decisive. We find this in the following sequence. In *Pss. Sol.* 9, after rehearsal of the present national catastrophe in *Pss. Sol.* 8, the author justifies God for Israel's earlier exile (vv. 1–3). In verses 6f. he explains that God cleanses those who repent. Verse 8 is a plea for divine mercy on Israel. At this point the psalm concludes with reference to Israel's covenant relationship with God and a confession of hope (vv. 9–10). This sequence of sin, confession, mercy is reinforced in the final psalm with a prayer that God will "cleanse Israel for the day of mercy in blessing" (18:5a). It is the day when Messiah will reign (18:5b; cf. 17:32). This appears to be a way of explaining the heretofore delay of messianic blessing, while holding to expectation.

Qumran Scrolls

The Dead Sea Scrolls are in a class by themselves in the current research of ancient Judaism and NT backgrounds. Since the first discoveries in 1947, enormous interest, countless number of hours in

research, and heightened controversy have ensued. It is widely agreed
that the Qumran community existed from the mid-second century B.C.
to A.D. 68, when Roman troops probably destroyed the community.
The literature is in three areas: copies of the Hebrew Bible
(except Esther); copies of what is called the Apocrypha and Pseudepigrapha; documents composed by the Qumran community and
which reflect their history and beliefs. It is the last area that mostly
concerns us.

From documents thus far found, deciphered, and published, it
is certain that Qumranians had an eschatological "worldview" and
saw themselves as linked to the end times. There is some difference
of opinion as to how pervasive this was in the two centuries of their
community's existence at Qumran.[24] Nevertheless, the discovered
documents and fragments point to a heightened anticipation of a
fairly imminent end and also an explicit reckoning with delay in
realization of the prophetic hope. Adding to our interest is the fact
that there are several points of contact with the NT within the
eschatological framework.

The Damascus Rule (CD, also called Damascus Document/
Covenant or Zadokite Document) is the most helpful in providing
both a broad outline (if somewhat vague) of the community's existence and a mirror of its eschatological orientation.

Historical knowledge is sketchy, which invites difference of
opinion at several points.[25] However we may ascertain the following
from this document:

Some 390 years after Nebuchadnezzar took Judah captive, and
"in the age of wrath," God "visited" Israel and established a "root,"
the community (1:5–8).[26] After the community was "groping" like

---

[24] Davies chides scholars for lack of a sufficiently critical study of the
documents, which (he believes) indicates diversity of belief, "Eschatology at
Qumran," 39–55; cf. Steudel, "4Q177," 480; Dupont-Sommer, *Essene Writings,* 318f. Dimant stresses a basic unity of thought over the one or two
generations she allows for composition (170 B.C. to 100 B.C.), "Qumran,"532.
Note Collins' helpful discussion, *Apocalyptic,* 138–40.

[25] Davies maintains the document is a redaction from a pre-Qumran
period, *Damascus Covenant.* He begins with a lengthy history of study of the
text, 1–47.

[26] Dimant says the biblical terms "visitation" and "root" are "overlaid
with eschatological significance," placing the entire event in eschatological
perspective, "Qumran," 491f. The 390 years may not be a correct figure, cf.
Vermes, *Perspective,* 147f.; Ringgren holds the expression is ambiguous in
Hebrew, *Qumran,* 36f.

"blind men" for twenty years, God sent the community a "Teacher of Righteousness" (1:9–11). Through this Teacher God revealed to the "latter [אַחֲרוֹנִים] generations" what he [eventually] did to the "latter [last, אַחֲרוֹן] generation," the "congregation of traitors" (1:11–12).[27] The Teacher called his community to a "Covenant" of keeping God's commandments (e.g., 3:1–19). The document reveals a period of time that Israel has within which to comply with the divine order ("until the age is completed, according to the number of those years," 4:8–9, 10–11). This seems to be the period described as "about forty years" and begins with the death ("the gathering in") of the Teacher, in light of 20:13–15.[28] A "New Covenant" has been instituted in Damascus until "the coming of the Messiah out of Aaron and Israel" (19:33–20:1 [8:31–MS B, II, 1]; cf. 13:20–21), which possibly refers to two Messiahs (cf. 1QS 9:11). [29] This messianic arrival will result in the final separation of those who followed the villain known as "the Liar" from those who chose to keep the covenant and who then will know salvation (20:14–34 [MS B, II, 14–34]; cf. 1QS 4:23–25). The chronology of events is difficult, but enough is clear to indicate the heightened expectation for the arrival of the Messiah(s). The writer is apparently living in the last generation of wickedness, since the Teacher has died and the community is to be waiting for the last days, when "he comes who shall teach righteousness" (6:10f.).[30] The detailed statutes in 9–16 of the Damascus Rule are revealing in how the righteous are to keep the Covenant and be prepared for the messianic age.

We shall now refer to a few other documents which highlight themes not discussed as yet. (1) "The Messianic Rule" (1QSa, variously designated "Community Rule," "Rule of the Congregation" or "Rule Annexe") includes rather detailed dining instructions for the time when the Messiah will eat with

---

[27] On the "last" generation here cf. Davies, *Damascus Covenant*, 235. LaSor, *Scrolls*, 93–94.

[28] Cf. Dupont-Sommer, *Essene Writings*, 127, n. 5.

[29] Cf. e.g., Collins, *Apocalyptic*, 122–25.

[30] Dupont-Sommer understands a resurrection of the Teacher, *Essene Writings*, 131, n. 6. Collins says "the future messiah will fill the same role in the community as the historical Teacher," *Apocalyptic*, 126. In 6:11 the Hebrew participle יוֹרֶה is used; in 1:11, the noun מוֹרֶה. The Teacher ("Interpreter of the Law") is spoken of in messianic terms in 7:18–20 (cf. 6:7–11). In 4QPatriarchal Blessings 3 we have "the Messiah of Righteousness." Collins says the "scrolls are concerned with functions and institutions rather than with personalities," *Apocalyptic*, 126.

Israel (2:17–22). Such instructions presuppose near expectation, especially since carefully ordered common meals were already common among the Essenes (cf. 1QS 6:2–5, 20–23; Luke 14:15; Rev. 19:7–9).[31]

(2) Preparation for the end time war dominates the "War Rule" (1QM, variously called "The Scroll of the War Rule," the "War Scroll"). The outcome will be "salvation for the people of God" and "everlasting destruction for all the company of Satan" (1:5). Thus this is a "holy war." The battle apparently involves cosmic forces. For example, "Thou wilt muster the [hosts of] Thine [el]ect . . . with Thy Holy Ones [and with all] Thine Angels, that they may be mighty in battle" (12:4f.; cf. 15:1–18:14). On the other hand the final battle is earthly. The war is to result in "terrible carnage" (1:9) and in [great] tribulation for God's people (1:11f.). Much attention is given to battle formation, with priests in leadership (2:1–9:17). The war is to last for over thirty-three years (2:6). The enemy is several nations, with "the Kittim," generally taken to be the ruling world power, most prominent (e.g., 1:1f., 4, 6, 9).[32] These heathen powers come to the aid of the apostates in Judaism ("the ungodly of the Covenant") and fight against the "sons of light" (1:1–2), no doubt the Qumran community.

This document is perhaps from the latter part of the first century B.C. or early first century A.D. (at least in its final form), which would make the battle a Roman conflict.[33] The great attention to preparation for such a conflict is evidence that the final battle is just around the corner (cf. the eschatological battles of Dan 11:40–12:3; Rev 16:13–16; 19:11–21).

More could be said regarding Qumran expectation, and the volume of secondary literature is great.[34] But perhaps enough has

---

[31] Cf. Cross, *Ancient Library*, 87–91; Schiffman, *Eschatological Community*, 35, 53–67.

[32] Collins, *Apocalyptic*, 128f.; Dupont-Sommer says the Romans are always meant in the Scrolls, *Essene Writings*, 350.

[33] Vermes, *DSSE*, 104, who says he agrees with "Y. Yadin and other archaeologists and historians" in understanding the weaponry and warfare tactics in the War Scroll to be Roman. Cf. Davies on the date ("final redaction"), but he discounts Yadin's evidence, *1QM*, 123; Dupont-Sommer, *Essene Writings*, 167. Dimant says the second half of the second century B.C., but thinking of the original work, "Qumran," 517.

[34] Other Qumran passages with eschatological themes include:
(1) 4QFlorilegium (4Q174, "A Midrash on the Last Days" in Vermes, *DSSE*) 1:1–6, which appears to speak of the eschatological temple. Dimant sees three temples, with the eschatological temple in 1:1–3, "Qumran," 519. Cf. the more recently published "Temple Scroll" (11QT) 29:8–10

been presented here to identify primary motifs that are related to expectation and which are significant for NT backgrounds. Most of the relevant Qumran data are fairly explicit in eschatological anticipation, with some evidence for the belief that the eschaton (last generation) had already dawned.[35]

However before leaving Qumran, we must examine evidence for coping with delay. There is one document which quite clearly shows struggle with the lack of fulfillment of the prophetic hope, while at the same time seeking to retain expectation. This is the *pesher* (commentary) on Habakkuk (1QpHab) 7.

The text of 7:1–2 comments on Hab 2:1–2 and reads: "And God told Habakkuk to write down that which would happen to the final generation, but He did not make known to him when time would come to an end." Then follows a statement that "he who reads," considered prophesied in the Habakkuk text, is the Teacher of Righteousness, "to whom God made known all the mysteries of the words of His servants the Prophets" (1QpHab 7:3–4).

The Qumran text unfolds as follows:

Habakkuk: "For there shall be yet another vision concerning the appointed time. It shall tell of the end and shall not lie (2:3a)" [1QpHab 7:5b–6].

(in Maier, *Temple Scroll,* 20–57); Yadin, *Temple Scroll,* 112–15; Wise, "Eschatological Vision," 155–72.

(2) 4QpPsalm37 2:7–8a (in Vermes, 4Q171; in Dupont-Sommer, Frag. 1, 1:6–8a), which has all the wicked exterminated from the earth "at the end of the forty years."

(3) 5Q15, which is taken to be a fragment of the eschatological new Jerusalem, with measurements, with streets paved with white stone, marble, and jasper, and with twelve entrances (cf. Ezek 40–48; Rev 21).

[35] Cf. Dupont-Sommer, *Essene Writings,* 255; Stone, *Scriptures,* 67: "Eschatological tension was so high" that the community felt it was bridging as it were "the gap between this age and the age to come." Language in the Thanksgiving Hymns (1QH, the *Hodayot*) has been taken as at times approaching a realized eschatology, cf. Kuhn, *Enderwartung;* Collins, *Apocalyptic,* 133f.; Holm-Nielsen, *Hodayot,* 68, n. 11. This is to be contrasted with Jewish apocalyptic generally, cf. Kuhn, *Enderwartung,* 136–39. Perhaps the most graphic instances are those in which the author (The Teacher of Righteousness?) speaks of himself receiving the Spirit (esp. 7:6; 13:19; 16:12; 17:26; cf. 9:32; 12:11; 17:17). The references have messianic overtones. No one else in the community is said to have received the Spirit in like manner, that I see, though in the future the Spirit is for the community generally in 1QS 4:21. We note that the Hymns also speak of future judgment and destruction of the world (4:26; 6:29–30; 7:12).

Pesher: "Interpreted this means that the final age shall be prolonged, and shall exceed all that the Prophets have said; for the mysteries of God are astounding" [7:7–8].

Habakkuk: "If it tarries, wait for it, for it shall surely come and shall not be late (2:3b)" [1QpHab 7:9–10a].

Pesher: "Interpreted, this concerns the men of truth who keep the Law, whose hands shall not slacken in the service of truth when the final age is prolonged. For all the ages of God reach their appointed end as He determines for them in the mysteries of His wisdom" [7:10b–14a].

Here the Qumran commentator "reads into" the Habakkuk text a sense of eschatological delay that must have had increasing influence with the circulation of his commentary. The "final age" (literally, the latter end, [הָאַחֲרוֹן הַקֵּץ] is to be prolonged (7:7f., 12).[36] The Habakkuk text itself hints at delay (2:3a as quoted in 1QpHab 7:5b–6 above). But the Qumran text surpasses this with the final age itself being extended. No doubt the author is thinking of his own time, especially given the eschatological expectancy we have seen otherwise at Qumran. It is the present end-time that is being prolonged, with the "last days" (cf. 9:6, וּלְאַחֲרִית) still future.[37] This compares with the tension in 2:1–5, where some have betrayed the new Qumran covenant, but others will betray "at the ends of days."

The base for the Qumran delay awareness, while stemming ultimately from the prophetic hope, seems to be more immediate. The community had been founded with the arrival of the Teacher of Righteousness (cf. CD 1:5–12). It is conceivable that the final age was believed to have begun with the persecution of the Teacher by the Wicked Priest (8:16; 9:9f.; 11:4–6; CD 20:1, 4; 4QpPS37 4:8 = 4Q171 4 in Vermes).[38] This would correspond to the apocalyptic themes of apostasy and persecution in Jewish apocalyptic, documents which we know existed at Qumran.[39] It seems likely that with the passage of time, the end salvation and retribution was continuing to delay in pious Qumran expectation.

---

[36] On 7:7 cf. Dupont-Sommer who has "will last long" for the verb יֶאֱרוֹךְ, *Essene Writings*, 262; Fitzmyer, *Essays*, 22. Brownlee prefers "postpone" here, *Habakkuk*, 114f. In either case there is "delay."

[37] So Ringgren, *Qumran*, 166; cf. Elliger, *Studien*, 278.

[38] Dupont-Sommer thinks the Teacher was executed, *Essene Writings*, 114, 110, 266 (n. 3); *contra* Bruce, *Bib. Exeg.*, 25.

[39] Cf. Rowley, *Jewish Apocalyptic*, 18; Ringgren, *Qumran*, 164.

The question arises as to the era of which we are speaking. Most scholars identify the Wicked Priest as Jonathan (160–143 B.C.) or Simon (142–134 B.C.) of the earlier Hasmonean years.[40] In this case we come to the latter part of the second century B.C., the earlier part of the first century B.C., or even later, when the community would look back and reflect on the final age (generation?) time being "prolonged." If the Kittim are the Romans (e.g., 1QpHab 3:10; 4:5; cf. above), the latter two options are preferable.

It is noteworthy that rather than national repentance, judgment on apostates is anticipated. The time is in the hands of a sovereign God, who holds the answer to such mysteries. Meanwhile the faithful will keep the Law (7:10–12).

Testament of Moses

The *Testament of Moses* (also called the *Assumption of Moses*) purports to give Moses' last words wherein he prophesies the future of Israel up to the last days. The contents are apparently based on Deuteronomy 30f. (cf. *T. Mos.* 1:5). Despite defects in the only extant (Latin) manuscript, which is held to derive originally from Hebrew or Aramaic (via Greek),[41] key eschatological motifs are evident. Scholars generally consider at least the present form of the *Testament* as from the early first century A.D. Particular guide points are an apparent allusion to Herod the Great, his sons, and conflict with the Roman officer Varus in 4 B.C. that included burning a part of the temple and crucifixion of Jews (6:2–7; cf. Josephus, *Ant.* 17.10).[42]

This is the first Jewish document we have examined which places us quite clearly in the generation of Jesus. Thus eschatological expectation and attendant themes are all the more interesting to us.

---

[40] Cf. Charlesworth, "Scrolls," 218–22; de Vaux, *Archaeology,* 115–17, on grounds of internal evidence sifted by archeological evidence. A minority view places the Wicked Priest in the generation of the Jewish War; e.g., Roth, "Era," 451–55. For critique, de Vaux, *Archaeology,* 117–26.

[41] Cf. Priest, "Testament," 919f; Sweet, "Assumption," 601, 604. Laperrousaz speaks of the Latin translation as generally reliable, *Testament,* 13f. Our Latin text in this study is from R. H. Charles' *Assumption.*

[42] E.g., Charles, "Assumption of Moses," 411, 419; Priest, "Testament"; Collins, "Date and Provenance," 17. Charles argues the book was written before 30 A.D. because the "prediction" that Herod's sons would rule for shorter periods than he would have been shown false afterward (except for the rule of Archelaus), "Assumption of Moses," 411.

Anticipation of "the end" is set forth as follows:

(1) Moses' opening words of admonition to his successor Joshua conclude with instructions to preserve a document, probably the prophecy of Deuteronomy (cf. Deut 31:24–27; *T. Mos.* 1:5) and other writings ("the books," other parts of the Torah?). But the author has an eye toward "the day of repentance [or recompense] in the visitation" which will occur "in the consummation of the end of the days" (*consummatione exitus dierum*), 1:16–18.[43]

(2) Following what looks like an account of Nebuchadnezzar's invasion in the sixth century B.C. down to the time of Herod the Great (3:1–6:9), we read "the times will quickly come to an end" (7:1). Evidently "the times have passed and the author is convinced that he is living in the last days."[44] The eschatological period may be indicated as of "four hours" duration (7:2, *horae IIII venient*), suggesting a comparatively brief time.[45]

(3) After further events of the end time (to be discussed), the kingdom arrives (ch. 10:1–10). It appears "throughout the whole creation," with the devil being terminated (v. 1). Vengeance is taken on the enemies of God's people (vv. 2f.); there are cosmic phenomena, such as the sun being darkened (vv. 4–6); Israel is happy, exalted, and rejoicing over its enemies (vv. 8–10). This is all accomplished by "God Most High" who "will surge forth . . . in full view" (v. 7). Thus the *Testament* proper concludes on the note of expectant triumph for Israel. (Chs. 11f. conclude the *Testament* by resuming the dialogue between Moses and Joshua.)

With this outline in mind, the mood of imminent expectation is clear. We now need to look more closely at attendant themes which provide background to NT expectation, namely, apostasy, unprecedented tribulation with godly perseverance, and delay of the end.

Apostasy is part of the eschaton in chapter 7. "Destructive and godless men" who parade as "righteous" hold sway (v. 1). They are gluttonous and oppress the poor (vv. 4–8). (I see this description as perhaps extending into the future from the author's standpoint [cf. discussion above on 6:2–7:1], but with a setting that agrees with

---

[43] Translation is from Charles, "Assumption of Moses," 415, as this is more literal than that in the *OTP* and thus more useful for our purposes; cf. Priest, "Testament," 927, with n. 1k, which indicates a preference for "recompense" instead of "repentance."

[44] Priest, "Testament," 930, n. 7a; cf. Charles, "Assumption of Moses," 419; Janssen, *Das Gottesvolk,* 102, 106.

[45] Priest is less sure of this text, which is mutilated, *Testament,* 930, n. 7a.

Hasmonean and/or Sadducean rule in the second and/or first centuries B.C., cf. above.)[46] Pollution of the temple by would be priests precedes in chapters 5–6. In 6:1 those called priests are "powerful kings." This sounds like the Hasmonean priest-kings.[47] The "wanton king," not of the priestly family (Herod?), then follows. The apostasy is already underway from the Hasmonean era. Parallels and contrasts with NT eschatological apostasy are interesting, which we shall later examine.

The time of apostasy is succeeded by an outburst of unprecedented "wrath" from a heathen superpower, one who crucifies "those who confess their circumcision" and persecutes those who deny (or conceal) it (8:1–2).[48] Other means of persecution and torture are identified as well (8:3–5). The language of this great tribulation ("such as has never happened to them from the creation till that time") resembles that of Dan 12:1 with Dan 8:24–26; 9:26f.; 11:29–45 (cf. Matt 24:21). The leader of the persecution is "king of the kings of the earth" who has "supreme authority" (8:1). Herod hardly fits the description. This appears to be a future event from the author's standpoint.

An instance of perseverance during the time of severe punishment is seen in Taxo and his seven sons, who are admonished by Taxo to die rather than to violate the divine commandments (9:1–7; cf. Rev 13:1–10). We cannot identify an historical character as "Taxo," but the pericope appears to be exemplary of faithful behavior in such a time.[49] It is possible that expectation of divine retribution on the persecutors in verse 7 ("our blood will be avenged") is what precipitates the arrival of the heavenly kingdom, which immediately follows (10:1ff.; cf. Rev 6:9f.)[50]

This sequence of apostasy, severe tribulation, perseverance, and kingdom arrival constitutes the eschaton for the *Testament of Moses.*

---

[46] Cf. Charles, "Assumption of Moses," 419, who speaks of Sadducees. Priest is not certain, but sees the leaders as wealthy and apparently connected with the Temple, "Testament," 930, n. 7e. Alexander Jannaeus in the early years of the first century B.C. evidently was known for his indulgent and carousing ways, Russell, *Jews,* 71f. (cf. *T. Mos.* 7:4, 8 with Josephus, *Ant.* 13.379–383; 13.398–404).

[47] Cf. Charles, "Assumption of Moses," 418.

[48] The verb has been emended to read "deny" (Priest, Sweet) or "conceal" (Charles).

[49] So Priest, "Testament," 922f.

[50] Licht takes this position, "Taxo," 95–103. Priest believes this goes beyond the textual evidence, "Testament," 923.

Perhaps the most interesting aspect of this eschatological schema is that it replicates that of Daniel. Furthermore, it looks like a redaction of an earlier presentation. If so, we find evidence that the author (or redactor) is reckoning with eschatological delay in his updating of eschatological distinctives. He then is responding to the agonizing question in the covenant community: When will the kingdom come?

First, the *Testament of Moses* has several earmarks that strongly suggest a Dan 9 prototype.[51] After reference to Israel's captivity in 3:14, there is a strong intercessory prayer followed by divine deliverance (4:1–5). The one kneeling in prayer in the *Testament* reminds God of his covenant and begs for compassion (cf. 4:1f., 4 with Dan 6:10f.; 9:4, 9). Return to the land is stated in the *Testament* after the prayer (4:5–8) and the same is implied in Dan 9:25. In both passages there are turbulent times which follow return, until God intervenes (*T. Mos.* 4:8–10:1 with Dan 9:25b–27, cf. 12:1–3). In the *Testament* there is reference to Moses' earlier warnings (3:11–13), which essentially parallels Dan 9:11–13.

In addition the sequence of the four acts of the end-time drama (cf. above; the "four hours" of 7:1?) reminds us of Daniel's description of the last times. In Daniel there is apostasy (cf. 11:30b, 32; 12:10) and great tribulation (cf. 12:1, 7). The presence of sword, flame, and captivity in tribulation in Dan 11:33 seems to correspond to fire, sword, and imprisonment in *T. Mos.* 8:2, 4. We have faithful perseverance in the tribulation (cf. Dan 11:32b, 33; 12:2a, 3, 10, 12) and the appearance of God's kingdom (cf. Dan 2:44; 7:14, 27; 12:2f.). The similarity of Israel's exaltation to the stars (*T. Mos.* 10:9) with Dan 12:3 also makes some relationship with Daniel in *T. Mos.* 10 likely. Given all the above similarities, we must conclude that either Daniel itself or a tradition common to the book of Daniel underlay the *Testament*. Given the popularity of Daniel in early Judaism, it seems best to see Daniel behind the *Testament of Moses*.

So much for the similarities between Daniel and the *Testament*. It is when we observe important differences in the two eschatological schemes that we find evidence of a later updating of the message of Daniel. In the *Testament* the apostates are more distinctly identified with the leadership (probably priestly) of Israel. Their apostate deeds are more fully detailed. The time of

---

[51] Cf. Charles, "Assumption of Moses," 417; Charlesworth, *Pseudepigrapha,* 164; Kolenkow, "Assumption," 74. Collins is unsure, "Date and Provenance," 27.

great tribulation in *T. Mos.* 8 is more clearly the consequence of God's judgment ("punishment and wrath," v. 1) than it is in Daniel, although Daniel speaks this way of the captivity in the sixth century B.C. (9:16). The vexing conditions which describe the "wrath" in the *Testament* are more specific than the comparatively unadorned statements of the "fearful destruction" and the seduction that causes some to "violate the covenant" in Dan 8:24; 11:32f. The crucifixion of "those who confess their circumcision" in 8:1 of the *Testament* especially stands out, even in comparison with 1 Macc 1:10–15, 29–50, 58–61.[52]

Thus we have a broad outline of eschatological circumstances that accord with Daniel, but which also differs significantly in its presentation. It is conceivable that the eschatologies of the *Testament of Moses* and of Daniel emerged independently of one another. If so, it was undoubtedly still the same religious tradition of the Hasidim that promoted both.[53] Given the similarities with Daniel and also the popularity of Daniel in ancient Judaism, it seems more likely that the author of the *Testament* was responding to the eschatology of Daniel. In any case there seems to be a later use of eschatological motifs that were believed to be pertinent and interrelated in Maccabean times, as the author *now* in the first century A.D. confronts the problem of a delayed prophetic hope.

---

[52] But cf. Josephus, *Ant.* 12.255–56 on Jews crucified by Antiochus Epiphanes. However the fact remains there is no evidence of such in the Daniel and Maccabean traditions. Collins, "Date and Provenance," 19, questions Josephus' historicity at this point, though still allowing for the possibility of crucifixion by Epiphanes.

[53] Nickelsburg, *Resurrection*, 44f. suggests a priestly Hasidim (= Essene) origin for the (later) publication of the book, after interpolation of ch. 6. Daniel is hardly dependent on the *Testament of Moses.* The brief scenarios of the latter are too specifically arranged in terms of motifs and with concrete details to have preceded Daniel. Charles believes that chs. 8f. originally followed ch. 5, since Antiochus E. should immediately precede the Maccabean kings and Herod, "Assumption of Moses," 420; cf. Russell, *Method,* 58f. Chs. 8–10, however, are a unity of end time events, cf. Licht, "Taxo," 95f., 101f. It is possible that redaction by the first century author has occurred to make up the eschatological tableau of coming events.

CONCLUDING THOUGHTS ON EARLY JEWISH APOCALYPTIC ESCHATOLOGY

APPROXIMATELY 175 YEARS SPAN AUTHORSHIP AND/OR PUBLI-cation of the literature that we have surveyed. So we ought to be impressed with the virile hope that persisted in Judaism, probably most often in the Hasidim. As we have seen, this was a continual renewing and adaptation of the prophetic hope. On one hand it testifies to the non-fulfillment of that hope; on the other hand, to a deep-seated belief that God would yet fulfill the apocalyptic promise to the covenant people. In view of such an ongoing religious view-point within Judaism, we can see that expectation of fulfillment and reckoning with delay of that fulfillment are two sides of a coin. It is not too much to say that expectation may have been a way of reckoning with the delay.

Daniel (or the tradition behind Daniel) seems to set the pace for much of the apocalyptic thinking in early Judaism. Of course many ideas in apocalyptic go beyond Daniel. But the essential reinterpretation of the prophetic hope in more pronounced apoca-lyptic terms within Daniel evidently influenced subsequent Jewish literature.[1] We find the following ideas of Daniel also in other Jewish apocalyptic: (1) a consummate divine intervention against

---

[1] Other instances than those already mentioned include possibly *Sib. Or.* 3.397 with Dan 7:7; *Sib. Or.* 5.222 with Dan 7:8; most likely *1 Enoch* 40:1 with Dan 7:10; *1 Enoch* 62:5 with Dan 7:14. Also, the War Rule (1QM) with Dan 11:29–45 provides background apparently for 1:1–14, cf. Bruce, *Biblical Exegesis,* 67–74 on Daniel in Qumran generally. Daniel's seventy weeks appear in the *T. Levi* 16:1; 17:1. Regarding Daniel in *Sib. Or.* 3 and *1 Enoch* 1–16; 21–36; 72–105, cf. A. Hilgenfeld as cited in Schmidt, *Apokalyptik,* 134–37.

the world power that oppresses God's people; (2) preliminary woes before the final destiny of the righteous and before judgment on the ungodly; (3) a super power anti-god personage who opposes God's people; (4) apostasy on the part of the covenant people; (5) a glorious destiny for the godly; (6) a more or less determined time for the divine intervention; (7) a longing for the adjudication of the godly.

Other apocalyptic themes not in Daniel include a triumphant Messiah (curiously absent from a number of apocalyptic contexts); an earthly fulfillment of the prophetic hope; an eschatological temple; triumph of Israel among the nations; conversion of Gentiles to Israel's God; removal of Satan; Israel's repentance as instrumental for bringing the kingdom of God.

All of the above themes represent aspects of updating the prophetic hope for new generations who still looked for and longed for the promised kingdom of God. However, a diversity of approaches in interpreting eschatological expectation possibly suggests varied schools of thought. The following perspectives may be noted:

First, those documents which reflect a sharper "apocalyptic perspective" (Dan 7–12; 1 Enoch 91–107; Testament of Moses) more or less exude a strong sense of expectation in the face of delay. Some kind of timetable is utilized to underscore the certainty of the anticipated end. All three documents allow for further delay, though most minimal in Daniel and most prominent in the Testament of Moses. It is important to note, however, that a "day and hour" determination is lacking, except possibly in Dan 8:14 and 12:11f., depending on whether the "days" there were intended to be taken literally. God's sovereign intervention in his own time stands out.

Second, two documents that we have surveyed are less "apocalyptic" and lack a timetable for fulfillment—Jubilees and the Psalms of Solomon. Especially in Jubilees the contingency factor of Israel's repentance is set forth. Here, then, determination of the end is apparently more Israel's responsibility (cf. Dan 9:4–19; Tob 13:5 with 14:4b–5; 1 Bar 2:29–35). This probably explains why eschatological fulfillment seems more distant in Jubilees and the Psalms of Solomon. God's blessing on Israel in its earthly homeland is featured.[2]

---

[2]Though we are not detailing the data in this study, there is evidence that in the Testaments of the Twelve Patriarchs Jewish author(s) explained eschatological delay by Israel's need to repent. Apart from the numerous Christian interpolations, the Testaments were probably composed in the second or first century B.C., cf. Charlesworth, Modern Research, 212f.; Knibb,

Third, in the animal apocalypse of *1 Enoch* (89–90), the *Sibylline Oracles* 3, and the Qumran writings we find an emphasis upon the determined time of the end, but the hope is more earth-centered. Fourth, in two of our documents there is a messianic personage (*Psalms of Solomon; Damascus Rule*, perhaps two messiahs).

From this evidence it is clear that within Judaism (perhaps even one movement of Judaism) there was a diversity of eschatological expectation. But both ideas of God's sovereign intervention and the necessity for a national repentance have roots deep in the OT. In the seventy-year eschatological timetable of Jer 25:12; 29:10–14 the divine initiative is clear ("I will fulfill to you my promise," 29:10). But it is fascinating that in the very same context (29:12f.) Israel's promised blessing is combined with the announcement that it will wholeheartedly seek Yahweh (cf. *T. Mos.* 1:18). What seems to amount to an indirect admonition (cf. Deut 4:27–31; Isa 55:6–11; 59) may explain why later Jewish authors chose to identify failure to fulfill this obligation as the explanation of eschatological delay. Moreover in Jer 18:7–10 is a statement that the divine plan is contingent upon human decision:

> At one moment I may declare concerning a nation or a kingdom, that I will pluck up and break down and destroy it, but if that nation . . . turns from its evil, I will change my mind about the disaster that I intended to bring on it. And at another moment I may declare concerning a nation or a kingdom that I will build and plant it, but if it does evil in my sight, not listening to my voice, then I will change my mind about the good that I had intended to do to it.

Such a statement amounts to an explanation of unfulfilled prophecy. This is comparable to the prediction of disaster within forty days by the prophet Jonah (Jonah 3:4) but judgment was averted (3:10). From a canonical standpoint it actually delayed until 612 B.C. (cf. Nahum).

This mix of eschatological explanation is to some extent analogous with what we find in the NT (e.g., Acts 3:19–21 with Mark 13:30). Will this Jewish background of the eschatological hope help us in our understanding of the NT hope? Will the role of repentance

---

"Exile," 266; Becker, *Untersuchungen,* 373–77, 403, 404–6; Kee, "Testaments," 777f. Particularly important are the sin-exile-return pericopes, with a repentance motif present between "exile" and "return" in five of twelve such pericopes (*T. Jud.* 23; *T. Iss.* 6; *T. Zeb.* 9:5–8; *T. Dan* 5:4–13; *T. Naph.* 4:1–3, 4f.). The evidence points to these pericopes being Jewish in origin, cf. Holman, "Eschatological Delay," 75–86.

in the Jewish hope help us to understand the NT exhortation to repent in connection with kingdom expectation (e.g., Mark 1:14–15 [with parallels]; Acts 3:19–21)? We will return to such matters.

But before we conclude this section, we ought to say a further word concerning the reinterpretation of the prophetic hope with the passing of generations. That hope remained outstanding, with the result that expectation was refueled for the covenant people in later times. We have observed this in what we perceive to have been the updating of eschatological motifs in subsequent Jewish literature.

This is most poignantly seen with Daniel. We observed the fresh interpretation of Jeremiah's seventy-year prophecy in Dan 9, so that hope hinged on seventy heptads, or 490 years. This period then extended down into the Maccabean era, as the latter chapters of Daniel detail. With the evident proliferation of the book of Daniel in Judaism, there was reason for renewed eschatological expectation. Depending on the dating of this early Jewish literature, we see a continual return to Daniel. This is perhaps most vividly seen in the use made of Daniel in the *Testament of Moses.* If we are correct in dating the Testament in the early first century A.D., as do most scholars, then Daniel remains prominent in Jewish expectation as the Christian era draws nigh. Will the use of Daniel in pre-Christian Judaism help us in any way to understand better its role in the formation of early Christian eschatology? What are possible implications in the use of Daniel for a present-day hope that is in continuity with the NT?

7

LATER JEWISH APOCALYPSES (AFTER A.D. 70)

ALTHOUGH THESE WRITINGS ARE USUALLY DATED AROUND A.D. 100 or early in the second century, they reflect hopes of eschatological expectation which existed earlier. Thus they are important for understanding the background within which early church expectation existed. We are particularly interested in imminent expectation and reckoning with delay, and as part of this, the messianic hope, and "messianic" woes that are to come on the earth. Can the message of Jesus and that of the early church be better understood against this background?

We shall look at the apocalypses of 4 Ezra (2 Esdras in the Apocrypha) and *2 Baruch,* and the Apocalypse of Abraham, where the existential issues of perplexity and eschatological hope in Judaism of this era are largely developed. (Other themes are developed in these apocalypses, but we focus on the eschatology prominent in this literature.) The immediate background is Jewish distress following the destruction of Jerusalem in A.D. 70, though the pseudepigraphic context is the 586 B.C. destruction.

4 Ezra

The apocalypse portion of 4 Ezra[1] is divided into seven sections or "visions" (chs. 3–14). The first three sections (3:1–9:25) are

---

[1] This document is preserved in Latin and a few other ancient versions, with the original composed in Hebrew or Aramaic somewhere around 100 A.D. E.g., cf. B. M. Metzger, "Fourth Book of Ezra," 518–20; Collins, *Apocalyptic,* 156; Charlesworth, *Modern Research,* 112. The three heads in the

dialog, as Ezra asks vexing questions of theodicy and receives angelic replies. The pathos of the questions is vividly seen in 5:34: "Every hour I suffer agonies of heart, while I strive to understand the way of the Most High and to search out part of his judgment." Sections four through six are more visionary. The angel leaves the scene and the Most High communicates directly with Ezra through "dream visions" (cf. 9:38 and esp. 10:58f.). Important eschatological motifs in the earlier sections are developed further in the latter visions.

Questions related to why sin prevails in the world and particularly in Israel, as well as why Israel is punished rather than "Babylon" (Rome), dominate the earlier portions of the apocalypse. But an attendant theme is "how long?" This is clearly an eschatological question in the context of 4 Ezra (4:33, 35; 6:59; cf. 5:50; 6:7; 8:63). The apocalyptist ("Ezra") looks for the age to come, when God will act (6:7; 7:113; 8:52). At times the age to come seems near ("the age is hastening swiftly to its end," 4:26; the creation "already is aging," 5:55; cf. 6:20; "my judgment is now drawing near," 8:62).

An intimate connection between the "why" and "how long" questions is noteworthy. In 4:33 the apocalyptist asks: "How long and when will these things be? Why are our years few and evil?" In 6:59 he asks: "If the world [saeculum] has indeed been created for us, why do we not possess our world as an inheritance [the Abrahamic covenant? cf. 7:11; Rom. 4:13]?[2] How long will this be so?" As in earlier apocalyptic works, we see a close connection between a troubled oppressed community and a longing for eschatological intervention. Eschatological impatience is very evident among the disenfranchised.

The heavenly answers that come from the apocalyptist's probing not only speak of imminent divine action in some sense, but they also betray an uncertainty of the time and a reckoning with delay. This flipside to expectation is seen especially in two ways in this apocalypse.

---

vision of chs. 11–12 are considered to be the Flavian emperors, Vespasian, Titus, and Domitian; e.g., Gunkel, *Esra,* 352; cf. Rowley; *Relevance,* 102; Eissfeldt, *Old Testament,* 626; Stone, *Fourth Ezra,* 10 (says composed in time of Domitian, 81– 96). The approximate date of 100 seems confirmed in 3:1 with reference to the "thirtieth year after the destruction of our city," even though the book purports to speak of the 586 B.C. destruction.

[2] The Latin, taken from Klijn, *Lateinische Text,* speaks of "generation" or "age." We may compare the frequent translation of *aion* in Romans 12:2 as "world," e.g., NRSV, NASB, NIV.

First, perplexity of delay over *when* divine intervention will come is met with assertion of divine sovereignty. There are four main passages:

(1) 4:33–43. In verse 26 Ezra is told of the swift movement toward the end. When he asks "how long," he is told in effect to be patient, for the time is set. God has "measured the times by measure . . . and he will not move or arouse them until that measure is fulfilled" (v. 37). An analogy is drawn with the period of gestation for a pregnant woman (vv. 40–43). But the "how long" question is not really answered. Thus the time of the end is uncertain for Ezra, though known to a sovereign God.

(2) 5:41–49. Here the point is reaffirmed. Ezra assumes the world will last another generation, as he again expresses his impatience (vv. 41–43). To affirm God's sovereignty over the world the angelic reply is that "creation cannot make more haste than the Creator" (v. 44). A mother's successive bearing of children is compared to God not creating all generations of humankind at once and thus shortening the period of waiting for the end. The orderliness of a God in charge of his world is set forth to counter Ezra's impatience (vv. 45–49).

(3) 5:56–6:6. Ezra asks through whom the Lord will visit his creation (5:56). This is an unusual question in 4 Ezra and could be Ezra's way of keeping the dialogue going after reaching an impasse in his "why" and "how long" questions. (However he returns to his "how long" concern in 6:7!) The reply is a detailed and emphatic statement of God's sovereignty over creation and affirms that the end will come through God himself and not another.

(4) 6:19–20a. Ezra's desire for knowledge of when the end of the age is to occur takes the form of a request for signs in 6:11ff. But before the signs are given Ezra (vv. 20ff.), "a voice" equates the arrival of the end time with the time when Zion's "humiliation" is complete (vv. 17–19). This not only suggests delay and divine sovereignty over the end, but it gets at the heart of the whole delay problem. For as we have indicated, the fundamental question Ezra is asking in these sections is why must Israel be humiliated at the hands of the heathen. With affirmation that "the age . . . is about to pass away" (*saeculum quod incipiet pertransire,* v. 20a) we have imminence. This goes beyond a simple divine determinism of when Zion's humiliation is complete. Here is tension between an imminent end and delay of that time, but both answering to the problem caused by delay.

Second, "signs" (often technically called "messianic woes") are utilized to discover when the end will come, in view of delay. The author's desire to introduce such signs comes to light when the angel declares his intention to reveal signs for which he says Ezra has inquired, even though Ezra did not ask specifically for signs (*signis*, 4:52 with preceding vv.). The signs clearly belong to the end time, for they are a response to Ezra's inquiry regarding when the present age will end (4:26–51).

The most significant observation we can otherwise make regarding the signs is that they are a mix of possible events in the world as the author knows it and of fantastic or mythical developments. More credible occurrences (*signis*) are listed first in 5:1–3: "Those who dwell on earth shall be seized with great terror, and the way of truth shall be hidden, and the land shall be barren of faith. And unrighteousness shall be increased. . . . And the land which you now see ruling [Rome] shall be waste and untrodden, and men shall see it desolate." But some time later ("after the third period," v. 4) we have such things as the sun and moon reversing their luminary roles, blood dripping from wood, stones speaking, stars falling, and "menstruous women [bringing] forth monsters" (vv. 4–8). In 6:21 similar signs are found: one year old babies speak and prematurely born infants of three or four months "live and dance." More credible signs follow in this passage, in particular war among friends and terrified humankind (v. 24).

Even with many of the "credible" events projected, there is a dissimilarity with the world of the author. Certainly Rome is by no stretch of the imagination a wasteland. Such woes remind us of apocalyptic woes in earlier Jewish literature (cf. *1 Enoch* 91:5–7; 93:9; 100:1f.; *Jub.* 23:13–25; *Sib. Or.* 3:601–3, 632–51; *T. Mos.* 7–9). This at most speaks of a qualified "imminence," depending on the extent the beginning of such signs could be witnessed in the author's time.

On the other hand there are credible signs whose fulfillment is more of a possibility in the author's day than even the "credible" signs above. These are given in answer to Ezra's request for knowledge of when the signs will occur (8:63). Here earthquakes, international intrigue, indecision and confusion of world leaders are put forth (9:1–4). But alas these only indicate when the Most High is about to visit the world (*in quo incipiet Altissimus visitare saeculum*, v. 2)! If we may momentarily jump ahead, very credible signs are linked with other signs mentioned earlier: "Those who dwell on the earth" (cf. 4:39; 5:1, 6; Rev. 3:10; 6:10; 8:13; 11:10; 13:8 et al.) "make war against one another; city against city, place against place, people against people, and kingdom against kingdom" (13:30–32). These are a prelude to God's Son (Messiah) appearing (v. 32).

What are we to make of this wide variance between credible contemporary signs and fantastic or mythical signs? We probably have here another manifestation of the tension between imminence and delay. The signs of 4 Ezra appear to speak of an end to be anticipated because of a sovereign God who controls history, but an end which is nevertheless somewhat distant and certainly unpredictable.

Finally, we shall examine the latter part of this apocalypse, in which Ezra speaks directly with the Most High. Here we have a more definite answer to what "imminence" means, but at the same time the answer becomes more complex, as the dialectic between nearness and delay is heightened. The eschatology is developed around the Messiah. We now turn to the dream visions of 9:26–14:48.

A vision revealing agonizing grief over Zion's humiliation (A.D. 70) culminates in vision of the eschatological Jerusalem with the angel's interpretive word (9:38–10:59). This sets the stage for a final airing of "imminence," but tempered further with delay. The unstated question is: When will this all finally come to pass?

In chapter 12 three very oppressive kings rule in the last days of the "fourth kingdom," clearly the Roman empire and a reinterpretation of Daniel 7 (4 Ezra 12:10–25 with Dan 7:19–25). The kingdom is the "eagle" in Ezra's vision of 11:1–12:30 (note 12:10f.). It is generally agreed that 4 Ezra was composed in this period, when only two "kings" yet remained for a "brief" rule before the end of the empire (vv. 19–21, cf. vv. 1–3).[3] This period seems consonant for the author with that preceding the credible "signs" of the end in 5:1, 3 (great world panic and desolation of Rome). Thus we may note that in 12:3 the earth is terrified at the destruction of the eagle.

In 14:18 (within the last section of 4 Ezra) the "eagle" is "already hastening to come." In the time of the actual author the end must have seemed all the more imminent in comparison with Ezra's day, since the "eagle" (Rome) had now come![4] It is significant that expectation here is not modified as it is in 4:26 compared with 4:33–43.

But with the reintroduction of Messiah in chapters 12 and 13 (cf. 7:28–29), the end time is very explicitly drawn out for at least four hundred years. Actually in chapter 12 there are two "ends." The Messiah comes at the "end of days" (*quem reservavit Altissimus in finem,* v. 32). He then delivers the godly remnant and brings joy to

---

[3] E.g., Harnisch, *Verhängnis,* 256; cf. above n. 92.
[4] Cf. Harnisch, *Verhängnis,* 277.

them "until the end comes, the day of judgment, of which I spoke to you at the beginning" (*quoadusque veniat finis,* v. 34; cf. 9:8; 13:48). In 7:28–29 we learn that the Messiah will appear and bring rejoicing for four hundred years, then die, after which comes the resurrection and judgment (cf. Rev 20). Thus the appearance of the Messiah and Israel's vindication is conceivably imminent, but the incorruptible new age is still delayed.[5] It is noteworthy that the era of Israel's bliss includes the presence of the ten tribes taken captive in the time of Hoshea (13:39– 47; cf. Jer 33:14; Ezek 37:15–23).

All told, we may conclude that the author of 4 Ezra seeks to help his community to come to terms with delay as an existing fact of life, but within the framework of eschatological hope. (Ch. 14 speaks of "Ezra's" writings for public use.) Hope is softened rather than surrendered.[6] Once the matter of impatience is dealt with in the first three sections, the author focuses on expectation in the last four sections.

It is difficult for us to grasp the sense of discouragement and doubt that existed in at least a portion of Judaism in the author's time. We can see that the prophetic hope as funneled through Daniel is the basis of expectation, but also the cause of bewilderment in the community. Thus we may conclude that the crucial expectation theme of 4 Ezra betrays a concern that has strong roots in the earlier generations of Judaism, with the destruction of Jerusalem clearly a turning point in reckoning with delay in fulfillment of the prophetic hope.

2 Baruch[7]

Like 4 Ezra, this Jewish apocalypse was composed in reaction to the A.D. 70 destruction of Jerusalem, with the alleged setting being

---

[5] Stone, " 'The End' in 4 Ezra," discusses varied meanings of "the end" in 4 Ezra and concludes that it means "primarily 'the decisive turning point of history,' " esp. 241. Nevertheless, the fact that the term is associated with an imminent end of the age and yet allows for a four-hundred-year interval demonstrates an imminence/delay tension in this apocalypse. Stone rejects a theory formerly more popular that redaction of diverse sources explain inconsistencies, cf. Charlesworth, *Modern Research,* 112; Thompson, *Responsibility,* 107f.

[6] So Harnisch, *Verhängnis,* 318–20; cf. Lebram, "Piety," 173f.

[7] The complete apocalypse is extant only in Syriac and a recently translated Arabic manuscript, which appears to be based on another Syriac text, but similar to the one we have, Klijn, "2 Baruch," 615; Klijn, "Recent Developments," 3f. The extant Syriac is a translation from Greek, which

the destruction in 587 B.C. Baruch, Jeremiah's scribe, is in the forefront. The document is almost unanimously held to have been composed somewhere between A.D. 70 and 130.[8] The apocalypse clearly projects a time of worldwide disaster after the rebuilding of the temple in the sixth century B.C., followed by the arrival of the Anointed One, worldwide judgment, and then eternal peace (68–73). The theme of the end times surfaces in various ways throughout (e.g., 6:5; 10:3; 13:3; 29:8; 76:5; 85:8). *Second Baruch* thus exploits themes typical of apocalyptic which came to pervade such literature centuries after the sixth century B.C.

Like 4 Ezra, *2 Baruch* is commonly divided into seven parts. These parts may be identified by observing four references to seven-day fasts and passages entailing three community addresses by Baruch (chs. 1–9; 10–12; 13–20; 21–34; 35–47; 48–77; 78–87).[9]

Lamentation over the divine judgment on Jerusalem is the backdrop to the theme of eschatological hope that pervades *2 Baruch*. Future blessing for Zion is clearly rooted in the prophetic hope of the OT (cf. 1:5; 68:1–8). Jerusalem will be restored forever (6:9). Imminent expectation is seen as "the times will hasten, more than the former," and "the course of times . . . will come and will not tarry" (20:1, 6; cf. 83:1). "Salvation . . . is not as far away as before" (23:7). *2 Baruch* concludes with a letter to the nine and a half (dispersed) tribes (78–87). Within this letter is perhaps the strongest statement of imminent expectation in the document: "For the youth of this world has passed away, and the power of creation is already exhausted, and the coming of the times is very near and has passed by" (85:10).

Given the pseudepigraphic character of *2 Baruch,* expectation which is portrayed as very much alive in the sixth century would

---

probably is from an original Hebrew text, cf. Klijn, "2 Baruch," 615; Russell, *Method,* 64; Denis, *Introduction,* 184. Sparks gives credence to P. Bogaert's position of a Greek original addressed to the Jewish Dispersion, *AOT,* 836. Klijn argues reasonably for a Palestinian provenance, "2 Baruch," 617.

[8]Klijn, "2 Baruch," 616f.; Charlesworth, *Pseudepigrapha,* 84; Violet, *Apokalypsen,* xcii; Russell, *Method,* 65.

[9]Cf. Collins, *Apocalyptic,* 170. The seven divisions have been delineated in varying ways, however, Murphy, *Structure and Meaning,* 11–29. Similarities with 4 Ezra have led some scholars to project literary links, with 4 Ezra often considered to be first; e.g., Violet, *Apokalypsen,* lxxvii, lxxx; Rowley, *Relevance,* 103f.; Eissfeldt, *Old Testament,* 629. Klijn opts for dependence on a common source, "2 Baruch," 617, and says consensus has not been reached, "Recent Developments," 8.

obviously be a much greater issue in the time of the actual author centuries later. It may also be assumed that such heightened expectation which attended the traumatic destruction of Jerusalem in A.D. 70 must have been preceded by expectation in the earlier decades. We have seen as much in the apocalyptic literature already examined. This was the ideological climate that at least to some extent prevailed in the time of Jesus and the early church.

But with the expectation was a reckoning with eschatological delay. In fact the very expression of expectation itself appears to be a way of coping with delay in fulfillment of the hope. In the fourth section of *2 Baruch* (21–34) we have a concentration of themes contributing to the delay motif.

First, this section is preceded with the divine promise that the times "will come and *will not tarry*" (20:6, emphasis mine). The almost certain implication of this expression of imminence is that the eschaton still has not arrived. (Cf. 48:39c, "For the Judge will come and will not hesitate.")[10] Why does the apocalyptist ("Baruch") need to deny delay at these points? Because delay was an issue.

Section four begins with Baruch fasting and offering a lengthy prayer. After confessing the sovereignty of God and requesting enlightenment on the inequities of life (21:4–18), Baruch queries "how long" and prays for God's glory to appear (21:19–23). He concludes with the desperate prayer: "And now, show your glory soon and do not postpone that which was promised by you" (21:25). The author dramatically expresses the agony of delay through Baruch's prayer. With the conclusion Baruch becomes "very weak" (21:26).

The author also handles delay with a "woes" motif (25:1–29:2). At "the end of days" the Most High is to bring the "sign" of great tribulation on the earth (25:1–4). With indication that the time of this tribulation is to be in twelve parts and extended over the whole earth (27:1–15; 29:1), any thought of an imminent fulfillment of hope is slackened. Woes within the succeeding twelve parts include slaughtering, death, the sword, famine, earthquakes, demons, rape, and violence.[11] Those living in "this land" (apparently Israel) will be

---

[10] Cf. Strobel, *Untersuchungen*, 34, on 48:39. He says that twenty to thirty years after the Jerusalem catastrophe the delay issue must still have been burning.

[11] The kind of worldwide destructive upheaval indicated here was hardly in vogue in the first two centuries A.D., when the Roman empire maintained

protected (29:2, cf. Rev. 7:1–8). It is only after all has been accomplished that "the Anointed One [the Messiah] will *begin* to be revealed" (29:3, emphasis mine).

From another angle delay is seen in the elongation of the eschaton in chapters 29–30. With the arrival of the Messiah the earth will "yield fruits ten thousandfold" and "they will eat [manna] . . . in those years" (cf. millennialism)—this is "the consummation of time" (29:5–8). After this the Messiah "returns [to heaven] with glory" and the resurrection of the godly and ungodly occurs (30:1–5). This is "the end of times" (30:3). (If the difference between "the consummation of time" [singular] in 29:8 and "the end times" [plural] in 30:3 matters, it may be *2 Baruch's* way of avoiding what seems confusing in 4 Ezra.)[12] There is thus a stretching out of the eschaton. This is significant because *2 Baruch's* resurrection and judgment are the objects of expectation (21:21–25; 23:5–24:2); 32:2–4 [the temple will be renewed "in glory . . . into eternity"]; cf. 44:9; 48:48–50; 49:1–51:16; 74:2f.). Although the messianic era reverses the disgrace of Zion, it also serves to come between the corruptible present time and the anticipated incorruptible glory of the new age. In other words, it serves to delay the end.

There is evidence of a concern with eschatological delay elsewhere in *2 Baruch.* Summarily we may say the following. A divine determinism of time is a way of preserving hope when the time for fulfillment has become a conundrum. Time is viewed as under God's control (1:4; 4:1; 5:1f.; 39:3–7; 42:6; 48:2 with v. 12; 54:1; cf. 81:4). There is also further prediction of woes of world-wide proportions (48:31–41; 70:1–71:1). The "end" is frequently before the reader, as we have noted. Given the context of *2 Baruch,* this is another way of declaring God's sovereignty over history which has perplexed the godly community (or communities) addressed by the apocalyptist.[13]

There is little reason for those addressed to think the catastrophic situation will be immediately altered. But the community

---

a "nonaggressive foreign policy," cf. Lewis and Reinhold, *Roman Civilization,* II, 112, who allow for two exceptions to international warfare. The exceptions may have contributed to a sense of imminence in late Jewish apocalyptic.

[12] See above, pp. 89f.

[13] It is difficult to be sure just who is addressed. Klijn speaks of a small group of Jews in Jerusalem and of exiles in Babylon who are in danger of being absorbed by the pagan world, "Recent Developments," 10.

must brace itself to face the future with hope. To a significant extent this seems to explain the dialectic of imminence and delay in the apocalypse.

With the exposure of Israel's moral failure and a hortatory thrust to keep the law (e.g., chs. 44; 77), we might expect *2 Baruch* to make Israel responsible for the arrival of promised blessings in the new age. There is a connection between Israel's repentance and the new day ahead (44:7f., 13f.; 77:6; 83:8; 85:4). But *2 Baruch's* emphasis is that God will sovereignly bring about the fulfillment in his time.[14]

The prophetic hope as seen particularly in Jeremiah and re-interpreted in Daniel palpably lies behind the eschatology of *2 Baruch*. Besides the obvious reference to Baruch in Jeremiah (for example, Jer 32:12f.; 36:4ff.), the time references discussed above seem illuminated all the more when read against the background of the seventy years of Jeremiah 29:10 and as reinterpreted in Daniel 9:24–27.[15] The "time of the end" in Daniel is also of special interest (Dan 8:17; 11:35, 40; 12:4; cf. 8:19; 9:26; 12:13). Other points of contact with Danielic ideas are: (1) a court scene with "books . . . opened" (24:1 with Dan 7:10c, cf. Dan 12:1f.); (2) a great tribulation followed by resurrection of the righteous and unrighteous (25:1–30:5); (3) a "how long" question in the context of the tribulation (26:1 with Dan 12:6, cf. 8:13); (4) the identification of wisdom with those who "understand" in the context of the tribulation (28:1f., cf. 27:15 with Dan 12:10 with vv. 1–9); (5) four kingdoms lead to the revelation of the Anointed One, with the fourth "harsher" than the other three (chs. 39f. with Dan 2 and 7);[16] (6) a prayer involving divine mercy and the granting of revelation in *2 Bar.* 81:1–4 may be a compressed version of Daniel 9.

Given the above data, we may conclude that *2 Baruch* is dependent on Daniel or at least the tradition that lies behind Daniel. Behind Daniel lies the prophetic hope.

---

[14] Ladd speaks of "ethical passivity" in *2 Baruch* (and 4 Ezra), *Presence,* 99. If this is overstated, Murphy's contention that the primary purpose of *2 Baruch* is exhortation to obey the law may be saying too much, cf. *Structure and Meaning,* 28, 124, 136.

[15] Further evidence of a Jeremiah background is in my "Eschatological Delay," 29–31.

[16] Cf. Charles, "II Baruch," 501; Casey, *Son of Man,* 129; Beale, *Use of Daniel,* 145.

Apocalypse of Abraham

The *Apocalypse of Abraham*[17] is in two major parts: 1) the legend
of Abraham's conversion from idolatry (chs. 1–8), and the apocalypse proper (chs. 9–32), which is a midrash of most of Genesis 15.
In the midrash Abraham is promised revelation of ages to come
(9:6, 9f.). The destiny of those having done good and evil occupies
much of the apocalypse proper (chs. 21–31). Chapters 10–20 are
preparatory. The overt eschatological concern of the apocalypse is
reversal of the Jerusalem tragedy and retribution upon the heathen
(Roman) oppressors (chs. 27–31). The essential question is "how
long" must Abraham's seed endure the humiliation. Thus we find
similarity with 4 Ezra and *2 Baruch*.

I understand the author to speak of the destruction of Jerusalem in the sixth century B.C. which is now used as a backdrop for
vexation over the recent crisis (A.D. 70). The sixth century B.C. is
alluded to in the following ways: (1) idolatry is a problem (25:1–6;
with e.g., Jer 10:1–18; Ezek 6:13; 20:7–49); not so in later Judaism;
(2) godly kings are predicted (27:10f.), these possibly being David,
Hezekiah, Josiah (cf. Sir 49:4), or godly rulers just after the exile
such as Zerubbabel and Joshua; (3) retribution is for "four ascents,"
(or "descents") with the fourth ascent entailing one hundred years
(28:3–5a).[18] Four generations could well mean four hundred years
(based on Gen 15:13) and broadly or symbolically refer to the four
oppressive empires, beginning with Babylon in the sixth century
and ending with Rome (cf. 4 Ezra 12:10–13; *2 Bar.* 39).[19]

The (last) one hundred years (also called "one hour of the
age," 28:5) is what mostly captures the author's interest and which
therefore is no doubt his own time. The "hour" is also the twelfth
out of twelve hours of "impiety" and leads to the end of time
(29:2, 9). This final hour (cf. 1 John 2:18) is one when a wicked

---

[17] The extant text is in Slavonic, represented by six fairly complete MSS;
the original language is considered to be Hebrew and the provenance,
Palestine at the end of the first century, R. Rubinkiewicz, "Apocalypse of
Abraham," 681–83; cf. Sparks, *AOT*, 364–66 (though unsure whether original was Greek or Hebrew); Collins, *Apocalyptic*, 180f.; Russell, *Method*, 60.

[18] For "ascents" some MSS read "descents," Rubinkiewicz, "Apocalypse of
Abraham," 703.

[19] On four generations equal four hundred years, see Box, *Apocalypse of
Abraham*, 76, n. 8. Box quotes the Palestinian Targum to Gen 15:13: "And
behold, Abraham saw four kingdoms which should arise to bring his sons
into subjection," 74f., n. 7.

person is both insulted and worshipped by the heathen, insulted by some of the righteous, yet worshipped by others of the righteous (29:4–13).[20] The description in chapter 29 looks very much like the anti-god figure we have met elsewhere in apocalyptic and I take him as such. This last hour includes ten plagues, but is followed by "the age of justice," the arrival of God's chosen one (messiah?) and judgment (29:14–31:8).

With the above eschatological indicators (the last hundred years/last hour), imminent expectation is surely conveyed. The woes (plagues) are the usual: sorrow, conflagrations, pestilence, famine, earthquakes, slaughter (30:2–8). With some of these on the horizon, expectation would be encouraged.[21]

On the other hand, there is some reason to see an accommodation to eschatological delay. The "how long" concern in 28:2 ("Will what I saw be their lot for long?") and 29:1 ("How long a time is an hour of the age?") seems to betray an impatience for hope to be realized. The ten plagues in chapter 30 appear to point more or less to widespread calamities: "conflagrations for the cities" (plural), verse 4; famine "of the world," verse 5; "destroying earthquakes" (plural), verse 8. With greater calamities than existed in the late first or early second centuries anticipated, a slackened imminence within the "twelfth hour" is probably suggested.

Summary

The dialectic of expectation of an imminent fulfillment of the Jewish hope and a sense of delay in fulfillment of that hope continue to characterize Jewish apocalyptic. The delay seems to be in respect both to the past and to the present situation. This is especially seen in 4 Ezra and *2 Baruch*. In fact in later Judaism the delay issue comes even more into focus than in earlier times with the "how long" question, although the delay matter is secondary to the "why" question caused by the crisis of a ravished Jerusalem. This new crisis in Judaism makes postponement of eschatological blessings all the more painful.

---

[20] The translator in Sparks, *AOT,* 389, seems to allow for the heathen to worship but not necessarily insult this person. The passage is often obscure due to lack of certainty of the original text, as Rubinkiewicz, "Apocalypse of Abraham," 703f., especially indicates.

[21] Cf. below, ch. 8, on synoptic apocalypse.

Appeal to divine sovereignty is more frequent and explicit in later Jewish apocalyptic, as a way of countering the delay problem. This is most often seen in a temporal determinism and periodization of events which guarantees a good end, while accommodating the delay. Included in this periodization is an elongation of the eschaton to include in succession: the arrival of Messiah, a time of righteousness on the earth, and then resurrection with eternal judgment. We see this clearly in 4 Ezra and *2 Baruch*.[22]

As in earlier Jewish literature, the messianic woes motif is prominent. We saw in 4 Ezra that this could contribute both to imminence and to delay, depending on the nature of woes set forth—whether credible or fantastic. In *2 Baruch* and perhaps the *Apocalypse of Abraham* we see them contributing even more to delay, in that the woes are more evidently worldwide. This is especially true of *2 Baruch*. But in both *2 Baruch* and the *Apocalypse of Abraham* the godly are protected during the woes on the earth.

In the three apocalypses the "how long" question is consistently answered in an evasive way. To say this is to identify an anomaly. It is precisely the problem of delay (especially evident in 4 Ezra and *2 Baruch*) that motivates the apocalyptist in much of what he says. Yet in his concern to show that there is no real problem, he wisely avoids supplying the kind of answer to "how long?" which every devout Jew wishes to hear! Instead he answers in ways that encourage expectation, while at the same time seeking to prepare his audience to be able to handle further delay. Thus I conclude that the theme of an imminent end is basically a way of coping with delay.

As with earlier Jewish apocalyptic literature (cf. ch. 2), the responsibility for bringing in the new age through repentance is hardly if at all placed on Jewish shoulders. (This is in contrast to other earlier Jewish documents that we surveyed, which are farther from the *genre* of apocalyptic but which nevertheless incorporate apocalyptic motifs.)

This lack is striking, since the reason for Jerusalem's downfall is Israel's moral failure. Conceivably it would be a short step to say that blessing will come when failure is reversed. Furthermore, there is reason to think that the rabbinic evidence for the necessity of repentance stems from the first century A.D. This is seen primarily

---

[22] Klijn curiously says that *2 Baruch* rejected the idea of a messianic kingdom on earth, "2 Baruch," 619. *Second Baruch* 29:1–31:1 (cf. ch. 73) appears to contradict this.

in the well-known debate attributed to Rabbi Eliezer and Rabbi Joshua, whether or not the debate actually occurred.[23] In the shortest version R. Eliezer says: "If Israel repents, they will be redeemed." R. Joshua replies: "Whether or not they repent, when the end comes, they will forthwith be redeemed. . . ."[24] What originated in pre-Christian Judaism continued to have expression in the Judaism of the late first century and afterward. That is, responsibility for the delay of the eschaton is to be laid at Israel's doorstep.

Overall, the need to explain eschatological delay is quite obvious. Whether through a theism that rests itself in the knowledge of a sovereign God who controls the affairs of history, or through the ethic of human responsibility, an explanation must be forthcoming.

Various eschatological themes of the foregoing apocalypses are consonant with apocalyptic Daniel. We have noted that 4 Ezra and *2 Baruch* are particularly dependent on Daniel and/or the Daniel tradition.[25] Behind this lies the hope tradition of the canonical prophets. It is noteworthy that at least *2 Baruch* includes all tribes of Israel in the future blessing (cf. 78:2–7). That an eschatological repentance motif is found in *2 Baruch*, though not exploited by the author, is probably due to the tradition of such a theme, as we found it in our discussion of earlier Jewish literature.[26]

From this survey we may conclude that a significant part of Judaism participated in an apocalyptic hope. It remains for us to seek to understand the relation of this apocalyptic to the formation of early Christian eschatological expectation.

---

[23] For the traditional date of about 90 A.D. see Strack and Billerbeck, *Kommentar,* vol. 4, pt. 2, 992; cf. Bauckham, "Delay," 10–12. According to Strack and Billerbeck, *Kommentar,* vol. 4, pt. 2, 992f., R. Eliezer adopted the "repentance" explanation when the Danielic seventy-week prophecy failed to be fulfilled on 9 Ab A.D. 68.

[24] Midrash Tanhuma Behuqotai 5, in Neusner, *Eliezer,* pt. 1, 479, cf. 477–79. The debate is expanded in b. *Sanh.* 97–98a and attributed to the later authority of the Tannaim.

[25] Tigghelaar, "Apocalyptic," 141f.: "Because of their biblical canonicity, books like Daniel and the Apocalypse of St. John are more likely to have influenced the development of the genre in later times than other apocalypses."

[26] Klijn attributes the importance of *2 Baruch* to the way the author deals with traditional material, "2 Baruch," 618.

Part Three: Expectation in New Testament
Apocalyptic Writings

2 THESSALONIANS 2
(THE "PAULINE APOCALYPSE")[1]

APPARENTLY WITHIN A MATTER OF WEEKS OR MONTHS AFTER
evangelizing in Thessalonica around A.D. 50, Paul wrote what we
call 1 Thessalonians. He devoted considerable attention to correct-
ing a misunderstood eschatology that was playing havoc with the
congregation (esp. 4:13–5:11). In anticipating the Parousia (return
of Christ, cf. 1:10; 4:15; 5:2), many came to believe that the departed would miss the glorious day of the Lord (4:13–18) which was
soon to occur. Besides dealing with this misconception, Paul also
exhorts watchfulness for that day, apparently because a number have
become discouraged and perhaps disillusioned over when the
Parousia would occur (5:1–11).

In writing 2 Thessalonians, probably a short time later, Paul
faces a different situation.[2] Belief in a more or less imminent
Parousia had moved to a belief that the day of the Lord had actually
arrived; the community was greatly shaken (2 Thess 2:1f.). Since
the apocalyptic coming, with its cosmic upheaval, had obviously not

---

[1]The expression "Pauline Apocalypse" is borrowed from Jeremias,
Theology, 1.124. I am assuming the authenticity of 2 Thessalonians, as do
many others, despite a recent trend toward seeing the letter as a forgery (cf.
3:17). To posit pseudonymity presents more problems than it answers, in
my opinion. Cf. Jewett's survey of the discussion, while himself holding
to probable authenticity, *Correspondence*, 3–18; cf. Meeks, "Social Functions," 689.

[2]Some have held that 2 Thessalonians was the first letter. A survey of
the arguments is in Best, *Thessalonians*, 42–45, who favors the traditional
position. To me that order makes the better sense, though the reversal would
not substantially affect our study.

occurred, this belief was probably one that assumed that the day of
the Lord was *so* near that one could say the time had actually arrived
(cf. the false prophecy in Luke 21:8: " 'the time is near!' ")[3]
The dominant note of 2 Thessalonians is expectation of the
Parousia, as in much of 1 Thessalonians (2 Thess 1:5–10; 2:7f.; cf.
1 Cor 16:22; Rom 13:11f.; 16:20; Phil 3:20; 4:5), despite the errone-
ous belief in the community. But a moderating motif is introduced
in chapter 2 to counter the misunderstanding that the day had
already arrived. This amounts to Paul teaching a delay of the Parousia
from the Thessalonian perspective. Since the delay is described in
apocalyptic terms, it is especially relevant for our investigation. Thus
here we have a dialectic involving both expectation and the necessity
of reckoning with delay, as in apocalyptic examined earlier.[4]

The Apostasy and Man of Lawlessness

To diffuse the eschatological excitement Paul identifies two
very closely related events that must occur first before the Parousia:
"the apostasy" (ἡ ἀποστασία) and the arrival of the man of lawlessness (2:2–4). He reminds the Thessalonians that he had taught this
when with them (v. 3).

In biblical usage ἀποστασία (or ἀπόστασις) usually connotes
religious rather than political rebellion.[5] The most striking corre-

---

[3] The key verb is ἐνέστηκεν (2:2); the perfect tense of this verb is usually
rendered with a present sense. Rigaux, *Thessaloniciens,* 653, helpfully understands the meaning here to be "imminence," not for lexical, but for socio-
psychological reasons. It is possible that severe persecution contributed to
this belief (cf. 1:3–12), in other words, the apocalyptic woes had come, cf.
Wanamaker, *Thessalonians,* 240; Dunn, *Unity,* 326. Jewett posits the absence
of apocalyptic logic in the community in their thinking that the Parousia
could be present already, *Correspondence,* 191f. A more detailed discussion of
the options is in Holman, "Eschatological Delay," 181–86.

[4] The distinctive apocalyptic eschatology in 2 Thessalonians has been
used to deny Pauline authorship; e.g., Krentz, "Thessalonians," 6.521. However the turn of events in 2 Thessalonians adequately explains Paul's particular use of apocalyptic motifs, cf. Jewett, *Correspondence,* 191; Kümmel, *Introd.,*
265f.

[5] In six of the eight times that ἀποστασία or ἀπόστασις is used in the
LXX it clearly refers to religious apostasy (Josh 22:22; 2 Chron 28:19; 29:19;
33:19; Jer 2:19; 1 Macc 2:15). The terms usually refer to political rebellion
in Hellenistic Greek as seen in the works of Josephus (e.g., *J.W.* 2.39, 347;
7.83, 164; *Ant.* 8.223; 14.320; *Life* 17; *Ag. Apion* 1.238). This makes the
religious biblical usage all the more significant when it occurs.

spondence of the apostasy with our passage is in 1 Maccabees, in the context of the blasphemous acts of Antiochus Epiphanes and the revolt of pious Jews. Compulsion to commit (the) apostasy (τὴν ἀποστασίαν) with pagan sacrifice is in 1 Macc 2:15. In this context we also find reference to the "lawless" Jews (ἄνδρας ἀνόμους) who are executed by the faithful in Israel (2:42–44). Similarly in 2 Thess 2:3 the terms "apostasy" and "lawlessness" are wedded.

The narrative of the Maccabean event is found in an apocalyptic mode in Dan 11. The onslaught of a powerful king (vv. 20ff.) who seduces Jews to violate the covenant (vv. 31f.) is described against the background of the end time (v. 35).

Appeal to Daniel is confirmed in the reading of 2 Thess 2:4. The anti-god figure exalts himself above anything that speaks of God or worship and sits down in the temple, showing himself to be God. This comes close to Dan 11:36, where the king "shall exalt himself and consider himself greater than any god, and shall speak horrendous things against the God of gods."

The activity of the anti-god personage, the "lawless one," (ὁ ἄνομος) in 2 Thess 2:8, occurs with the apostasy (v. 3).[6] Therefore we may conclude that it is this lawless one who promotes the apostasy. The apostasy thus has primarily the character of religious rather than political rebellion.[7]

Although the origin of the apostasy and anti-god figure in 2 Thess 2 is best traced to Daniel, these related aspects of the end time were well represented in Jewish tradition besides. Apart from the Jewish literature where the themes are treated separately, we find them combined in the *Pss. Sol.* 17:11–20 (the Roman general Pompey is most likely the ἄνομος figure here); *T. Mos.* 8:1–5; 4 Ezra 5:1–12; the *Sib. Or.* 3:63–70. We have already mentioned 1 Macc 2. It is noteworthy that these Danielic end-time themes are updated after the Maccabean era and reapplied to later generations in the above documents.[8] It has been debated whether Paul is thinking of apostasy in the church in 2 Thessalonians 2, but it

---

[6]In 2:3 ἡ ἀποστασία and the manifestation of ὁ ἄνθροπος τῆς ἀνομίας (the man of lawlessness) are linked by καὶ (and) and both are governed by the subordinate conjunction ἐὰν μὴ (unless). There is some support for the reading "man of sin" (ἁμαρτίας instead of ἀνομίας), but this figure is clearly ὁ ἄνομος in v. 8.

[7]Cf. Wanamaker, *Thessalonians,* 244; Best, *Thessalonians,* 281; *contra* Bruce, *Thessalonians,* 166f., who stresses a "general abandonment of the civil order," though allowing also for religious apostasy.

[8]On dating of the pseudepigraphical works, see chs. 5 and 6.

seems clear that is the case in Matthew 24:10–12 and with the incarnate Beliar who turns most Christians aside to himself in the apocryphal work *The Martyrdom of Isaiah* 4 (cf. 3:21–31).[9] Apostasy in the "last days" is also found in 2 Tim 3:1–9 and the *Didache* 16:3–5 (cf. 2 Pet 2 and Jude 4ff.).

Belief in end-time apostasy and an anti-god figure derive from traditional Judaism and become part of early Christian eschatological teaching (cf. the "antichrist" of 1 John 2:18 and the "beast" of Rev 12:18–13:10). It is the non-fulfillment of the prophetic hope which becomes the grounds for a further revelation in Dan 9. As the hope remains outstanding at the end of the first century B.C., the same eschatological motifs are reapplied in the NT. Thus these apocalyptic themes are deeply rooted in the Judaism that lies behind Christian tradition and are occasioned negatively by delay in fulfillment of the OT prophetic hope which lies behind Jewish apocalyptic.

The Restraint/Restrainer

The most difficult part of 2 Thess 2 concerns the meaning of a Greek term: τὸ κατέχον (neuter) and ὁ κατέχων (masculine) in verses 6f. In most if not all standard versions of the NT (at least in English) the term is rendered something like "that which restrains" (v. 6) and "the one who restrains" (v. 7). However, of the fifteen or sixteen times the verb κατέχω is used in the NT, only three times at most does it mean "restrain" outside of 2 Thess 2 (Luke 4:42; Rom 1:18; Phlm 13). The more common meaning has the sense of "hold fast" or "possess."[10] Accordingly, a few scholars have seen this force/person contributing to rather than restraining the anti-god figure and the lawlessness associated with him (cf. vv. 6f.).[11]

---

[9] Trafton, "Isaiah," 3.507, says most scholars place the "Martyrdom" in the first century, by a Palestinian Jew; cf. Knibb, "Martyrdom," 2.149f., who says, the end of the first century for 3:13–4:22, a Christian addition often called the Testament of Hezekiah, cf. 143.

[10] Of some fifty occurrences in the LXX, κατέχω has this sense at least twenty-two times. At least ten times the idea is restraint. The papyri likewise indicate both meanings, cf. Moulton and Milligan, *Vocabulary*, 336f.

[11] E.g., Best, *Thessalonians*, 301 (though cautiously); Giblin, *Threat*, 202, 180, 192–204, who tentatively concludes the background is a pseudo-charismatic takeover of the congregation.

On the other hand, a critical consideration that favors the "restraint" translation is the fact that the sense conveyed in the verbal forms is better taken as something/someone opposed to the apostasy and man of lawlessness, since the κατέχον/κατέχων are withdrawn when the man of lawlessness is manifested, allowing lawlessness to have full sway (vv. 7f.). An alternative interpretation of something/someone in compliance with the initial expression of lawlessness (cf. v. 7) makes unnecessary the withdrawal of the κατέχον/κατέχων, since it/he would then be participating in the lawlessness. The translation is difficult, but this seems to make the better sense, in line with the standard NT versions and apparently most commentators.

Granted the restraint/restrainer translation, what and who are signified? When we recall the nature of the apostasy and lawlessness, this would need to be something and someone who restrains moral and religious evil. This matter has been a *crux interpretum* and any answer is difficult. A common answer has been the restraint of the Roman empire and emperor against lawlessness. This is attractive in light of Rom 13:1–5 especially, but falters when we remember that the main problem is religious evil, including blasphemy. Did Rome hinder this? Hardly. Another interpretation has been the end-time missionary preaching of the gospel with Paul himself the restrainer (the κατέχων). In Christian apocalyptic, universal gospel preaching is a sign of the end time (e.g., Mark 13:10ff. = Matt 24:14ff.) and Paul did have a lofty Gentile mission (e.g., Rom 15:17ff.). Furthermore restraint against religious lawlessness fits better here than with the prior theory mentioned. But this view places too much weight on the mission of Paul. Paul's death is assumed to signal the onslaught of the anti-god forces (2 Thess 2:7b, the restrainer departs or is removed). However Paul seems to have at least considered the possibility of being alive at the Parousia at this early date (cf. 1 Thess 4:15–17 [though 5:10]; Rom 12:11f.). (The difficulty is greater if we assume a late date for 2 Thess.)[12]

---

[12] The political explanation of Roman order is held e.g., by Bruce, *Thessalonians,* 171f., 188; Wanamaker, *Thessalonians,* 256f.; Betz, "Der Katechon," 276–91. The "gospel" explanation is offered by Cullmann, *Christ,* 157–67, and Munck, *Paul,* 36–43. Among other solutions is the mythological binding of the anti-god personage to explain the restraint, e.g., Dibelius, *Thessalonicher,* 40–43; cf. Bousset, *Legend,* 143–45, 164. This explanation does not really identify the *katechon* and does not allow for the present activity of lawlessness in 2:7a.

Any interpretation is difficult, given the veiled references in 2 Thess 2, including the cryptic phrase in verse 7b: ἕως ἐκ μέσου γένηται (lit. "until [he] is out of the midst"). But a promising approach lies in the view that the restraint and restrainer correspond to the activity and intervention of God in the world. This could include God's activity through the church (as in the "gospel" view above), but not necessarily restricted to the church. I find the following three considerations supportive.

First, though the linguistic evidence for verse 7b is slender for any interpretation, it is amenable to our suggestion. The phrase ἐκ μέσου (lit: from the midst) can refer to a person being removed or withdrawing.[13]

Second, in the OT God is spoken of as withdrawing, with evil usually following (e.g., Deut 31:17; Judg 6:13; 1 Sam 16:14; Jer 7:29; Hos 9:12; cf. Rom 1:24, 26, 28). Likewise, in other Jewish literature: T. Jud. 23:5; 2 Bar. 25:4; Mart. Isa. 3:26. Thus we may see 2 Thess 2:7b expressing God's passive action in what his absence allows, with 2:10–12 setting forth his active punishment, wherein God sends a "powerful delusion" on those refusing the truth.

Third, in the context of the Thessalonian letters God's action in the world is closely linked with the apostolic message (cf. 1 Thess 1:4f.; 2 Thess 2:13). Conversely, the apostasy would be promoted by false prophets and teachers (cf. 2 Pet 2:1–3; 1 John 2:26).[14]

For our purposes, more important than precisely identifying the κατέχον/κατέχων is recognizing the sovereign hand of God in the timing of such end-time events. This accords with apocalyptic, as we have seen. We may conclude that Paul has utilized certain apocalyptic ideas, which also include end-time apostasy and a monstrous anti-god figure. Likewise, his teaching the Thessalonians of an imminent salvation/end accords with Jewish apocalyptic (cf. 1 Cor 7:29; 16:22; Rom 13:11f.; 16:20; Phil 3:20).

On the other hand, there are ideas in 2 Thess 2 that are not found in Jewish apocalyptic and which show themselves as distinctly Christian.[15]

---

[13] Cf. LXX Isa 57:2; Dan 3:88; and Matt 13:49; Acts 17:33; 23:10; 1 Cor 5:2; 2 Cor 6:17. The glory of the Lord departs in Ezek 11:23.

[14] The entire subject of the κατέχον/κατέχων is analyzed in much greater detail with varying options presented in my thesis, "Eschatological Delay," 203–28.

[15] We do not examine Pauline eschatology further in this study. But we should mention that scholars have correctly qualified Paul's dependence on

1. The most important and obvious difference is that in Christian eschatology the apocalyptic event centers in the Parousia of "our Lord Jesus Christ" (v. 1). In Jewish eschatology the culminating events frequently have no mention of a messianic figure. By contrast, the NT hardly mentions the end time without reference to Christ as central, as for example in 2 Thess 2.

2. The idea of a restrainer who is actively involved on the earthly scene goes beyond Jewish apocalyptic, which less directly indicates divine intervention before the end of history, despite its deterministic statements and periodization of world history. If our interpretation of 2 Thess 2:6f. is correct, this is the activity of God in the world, rather than a God who is practically absent from the scene until the end arrives.[16]

3. The purpose of a delay theme in 2 Thess 2 is not first of all to encourage expectation (as we concluded was the case in Jewish apocalyptic), but to discourage an overly zealous and misguided expectation. There is hardly evidence of this in Judaism of this same era. In turn, our attention is directed to the strength of eschatological expectation in early Christianity.

As we move on to the synoptic apocalypse, found in NT documents which we date after the Thessalonian correspondence, we will again have occasion to go back into early Christian apocalyptic tradition. This should cast additional light on the origin and expression of the early Christian hope.

Conclusion

In the first-century early church there was a reuse and Christological interpretation of traditional Jewish apocalyptic motifs. Although we have only the Thessalonian congregation in view, the teaching is clearly traditional and thus common in early

---

usual apocalyptic themes. For example lacking are the periodization of history, extensive development of end time woes, and a sense of frustration over eschatological delay, cf. Baumgarten, *Paulus,* 229. With a present experience of the eschaton through the Spirit (e.g., 2 Cor 5:5), Paul is not so concerned over the length of time before the Parousia, ibid., 204–26. Most important, for Paul Christ is the first fruits of the resurrection (1 Cor 15:23). Resurrection was a Jewish apocalyptic theme, as we have seen earlier, (e.g., Dan 12:2f.; 4 Ezra 7:32; *2 Bar.* 30:1f.). But Paul places it in a Christian christological context.

[16] Cf. Ladd, *Presence,* 93–98.

Christianity. Since an eschaton rooted in the prophetic hope remains outstanding, an updated interpretation of that hope in light
of current developments in the early church becomes necessary.
We continue to witness a tension between eschatological expectation and delay, although the particular community situation in the
Thessalonian letters affects how that tension is expressed.

THE SYNOPTIC APOCALYPSE

Mark 13

We begin our study of the synoptic eschatological discourse with Mark 13. Like most scholars, I hold the priority of Mark in the attempt to unravel the Synoptic problem.

The Discourse as an Exhortation

It is important to recognize at the outset that the discourse of Mark is essentially an exhortation, not merely a prediction of future events. It takes the form of a private address Jesus gave four of his disciples a few days before his crucifixion (cf. vv. 3f. with 14:1).

The hortatory character of the Markan version of the discourse is evident in what may be called the βλέπετε ("take heed") structure. This imperative punctuates the discourse four times (vv. 5, 9, 23, 33) and in this way is unique to Mark. It not only points out major divisions, but since the term is distinctly Markan in the Synoptics,[1]

---

[1]On marking out divisions, Pesch, *Naherwartungen*, 77. Of the fifteen times Mark uses βλέπω, seven instances yield "take heed" (4:24; 8:15; 12:38; 13:5, 9, 23, 33). This contrasts with Matthew who uses βλέπω eighteen times, but only twice as "take heed" and significantly (I think) both times paralleling Mark (Matt 22:16 = Mark 12:14; Matt 24:4 = Mark 13:5). Luke also uses the term only twice out of fourteen times and only when paralleling Mark (Luke 8:18 = Mark 4:24; Luke 21:8 = Mark 13:5). On βλέπετε, cf. Beasley-Murray, *Jesus and the Kingdom*, 389f. It highlights his interest in key themes pertaining to eschatological expectation. This is important because it serves both to signal Mark's eschatological message to the Christian church of his day and to provide a basis for identifying likely eschatological teaching

it highlights his interest in key themes pertaining to eschatological expectation. This is important because it serves both to signal Mark's eschatological message to the Christian church of his day and to provide a basis for identifying likely eschatological teaching that was part of the Jesus tradition, in a possible pre-Markan formulation of the apocalypse.[2]

The motifs highlighted in the above manner by Mark are: (1) warning against deception from false christs (v. 5f.); (2) warning of severe persecution of Christians (vv. 9–13); (3) another warning against false christs, warnings of false (Parousia) prophets, and perhaps the appearance of an anti-god figure with great tribulation (vv. 21–23, and possibly vv. 14–23); (4) warning to be alert for the unknown but apparently imminent day of salvation (vv. 33–36). The βλέπετε of the last three warnings is unique to Mark, though his fourth βλέπετε somewhat parallels Matthew's γρηγορεῖτε (25:13, "keep awake") and Luke's προσέχετε (21:34, "be on guard"). Later we will consider Mark's purpose in underscoring the eschatological themes of false prophecy, persecution and (perhaps) anti-god tribulation, and alertness for the end. At this time we will only observe that the above themes are related to, if not always identical with, apocalyptic motifs that we have singled out earlier.

The question of when end time events are to occur is closely bound up with the themes of expectation and delay in Mark's discourse. There is a ὅταν (when)—imperative structure in verses 4, 7, 11, 14, 28, and 29. Whenever a temporal indication is given, an exhortation or command follows. This is another way in which we see the hortatory nature of the discourse. The teaching is meant to affect the lives of those exposed to it!

The "when" theme prepares us to examine the ideas of eschatological expectation and of delay in the discourse. I think both are present, as in earlier Jewish apocalyptic from Daniel on.

---

that was part of the Jesus tradition, in a possible pre-Markan formulation of the apocalypse.

[2]Various scholars have projected differing versions of a pre-Markan apocalypse. Cf. Weeden, "Heresy," 150, who says exegetes have generally held to vv. 7f., 14–20, 24–27. Hartman, *Prophecy*, 207–11, grants that a Jewish apocalypse may have been christianized before A.D. 50, though he prefers to speak of a "midrashic" substratum based on Daniel and going back to Jesus. Others reject the "little apocalypse" theory, e.g., Lambrecht, *Redaktion*; Gaston, *No Stone*, 47–51.

Near-expectation of the end

In the following ways we see anticipation of the Parousia and end of the world clearly set forth.

(1) Prediction of the destruction of Jerusalem and the temple is firmly rooted in the Jesus tradition (Mark 13:2, 14–20 and parallels; Mark 15:29f. and parallels; Matt. 23:37 = Luke 13:34f.; Luke 19:41–44; cf. 13:1–5). Contexts of these passages indicate that the destruction was imminent in terms of a life time (on this point, also Matt 23:34–36 = Luke 11:49–51).

Upon Jesus predicting the destruction of the temple (v. 2) the four disciples ask: " '. . . when will this be, and what will be the sign that all these things are about to be accomplished?' " (v. 4). The literal rendering is: when will *these things* (ταῦτα) be and . . . all these things (ταῦτα) . . . be accomplished (συντελεῖσθαι)?[3]

Furthermore, given the context of first century Judaism, it is likely that the predicted temple destruction would have elicited thoughts of the end time, since in Jewish expectation temple destruction was to be followed by construction of a new temple in the messianic era (cf. Dan 8:9–14; 9:26 with OT and non-canonical passages which more or less confirm this expectation (e.g., Hag 2:6–9; Zech 4:1–10; *1 Enoch* 90:28–36; *Jub.* 1:17, 27f.; *Sib. Or.* 3:273–94 [cf. 663–731]; *2 Bar.* 4:1–7).[4]

In Mark's perspective the temple destruction is part of the end-time agenda. Even though explicit reference to the temple destruction does not occur again in Mark 13, it is apparently part of the "all these things"(ταῦτα πάντα) in verse 30, since verses 5–37

---

[3] In Daniel the verb is used three out of six times in definitely eschatological contexts; the noun (συντέλεια), sixteen out of twenty-two times in such contexts. The most notable Daniel references are perhaps 9:26, 27 (four times); 12:4, 6, 7 (twice), 13 (twice). The noun is used six times in the NT, all in eschatological contexts. See Delling, "τέλος," 8:62–66; Lambrecht, *Redaktion,* 87; Dunn, *Unity,* 329. Hartman sees a likely "conscious allusion to Daniel 12:7" in Mark 13:4, *Prophecy,* 145, cf. 220f.; cf. Beasley-Murray, *Last Days,* 387. In other words the prediction of temple destruction was to involve a complex of events. This compares with the complex of events associated with temple destruction in Daniel 9:26 and with the "time, two times, and half a time" before "all these things would be accomplished"(Dan 12:7). The disciples' quest for a "sign" in Mark 13:4 when all these events would be "accomplished" surely signals their perceived eschatological interpretation of such events.

[4] Cf. our chapter 2, n. 71 for Qumran references. Also, Bousset, *Religion,* 238f.; Kümmel, *Promise,* 101; Hartman, *Prophecy,* 222; Dunn, *Unity,* 324.

are Jesus' reply to the question in verse 4.[5] Reference to the
βδέλυγμα τῆς ἐρημώσεως in verse 14 presupposes the temple's
existence (cf. Dan 9:27; 11:31; 12:11; 1 Macc 1:54), and verses
15–20 speak of critical events that attend its demise before the
coming of the Son of man (cf. vv. 24ff.). Thus the temple question
becomes the springboard for pursuing end time events and the
Parousia, which is really Mark's concern.[6]

(2) Jesus' reply to the disciples' query of "when" includes a brief
series of apocalyptic woes (vv. 5–8): warfare, earthquakes, famine.
The birthpangs of a new age are suggested in the capping statement
of verse 8d ("the beginning of the birthpangs"). Here Mark again
points to the end time. Of the numerous end time woes found in
Jewish apocalyptic, only a very few are present in Mark 13. These
would have been recognizable as at least incipient in the 50s and 60s.
Civil war (besides the Jewish rebellion) became rampant after
Nero's death; tremors were taken as an omen in Claudius' time;
famine was a threat and in Claudius' time one was taken as a
supernatural warning.[7]

(3) The most pointed near-expectation reference is verse 30:
"Truly I tell you, this generation will not pass away until all these
things have taken place." Emphasis is added with the opening:
"Truly I tell you"(ἀμὴν λέγω ὑμῖν). The logion climaxes verses 28f.
(the fig tree parable), which designates previously mentioned events
as signs of the nearness of the Parousia. (Note "these things taking
place," ταῦτα, in v. 29, which probably alludes to vv. 14–23.) If "this
generation" is to witness these events, the announcement is certainly pertinent for Mark's audience![8]

---

[5] Cf. Beasley-Murray, *Last Days,* 356, 384f.; Grässer, *Problem,* 155; Dupont, "Discourse," 226–43, 269; Ford, *Abomination,* 62–74.
[6] Cf. Beasley-Murray, *Jesus and the Kingdom,* 324f.; Hartman, *Prophecy,*
325f.
[7] On civil war see Henderson, *Civil War;* on earthquakes, Tacitus, *Annals*
12.43, 58; 14.27; 15.22; on famine, Tacitus, *Annals* 12.43; cf. Suetonius, *The
Deified Claudius* 17–19; Dio Cassius, *Roman History* 60.11. Lewis and Reinhold, *Roman Civilization,* 2.138, speak of famine as "an ever-present threat in
antiquity," with bread riots common.
[8] As a concordance will confirm, "this generation" throughout the
Synoptics clearly refers to Jesus' contemporaries, cf. Büchsel, "γενεά," 1.663;
Kümmel, *Promise,* 59–61. Most often the term is temporal and refers to
unbelieving Jews, Holman, "Imminent Parousia," 24f. The term as used in
v. 30 is a fitting climax to Mark's theme of opposition from and judgment
upon contemporary Judaism (note 2:6–11, 15–17; 2:23–3:6; 3:22–30; 7:1–3;
8:11–13; 10:2–9; 11:27–12:40; 13:1f.). It is debatable whether "all these

Delay of the End

Mark 13:5–13 composes the first part of Jesus' reply to the disciples' temple question (v. 4). Here there are three statements which serve to weaken significantly imminent expectation.

(1) In verse 7 the disciples are cautioned against alarm from the necessity (δεῖ γενέσθαι) of wars and rumors of wars (usual apocalyptic "signs") because "the end is still to come" (ἀλλ᾿ οὔπω τὸ τέλος). Expectation of "wars" is expanded in verse 8 with the additional mention of earthquakes and famines. Altogether this would make succumbing to the messianic deception predicted in verses 5f. easier for those anticipating such eschatological woes; perhaps the whole of verses 5–8, then, is to be included in the caution that *the end is not yet.*

(2) The thought that the woes of verses 5–8 are only the *beginning* of more to come is emphasized with "beginning" (ἀρχή) placed prominently as the first word in the last clause of verse 8 (contrast the parallel in Matt 24:8; the clause is absent in Luke 21:10f.). The "beginning" of woes in verse 8d parallels "the end is still to come" in verse 7c. The vivid metaphor of "birthpangs" is used in verse 8d to indicate what will eventuate in "the end." But the identifiable woes (already present, cf. above), are only the start. In other words, expectation should be moderated. Mark wishes to communicate this to his community.

(3) In his persecution paragraph (vv. 9–13), Mark interrupts his presentation with the missionary *logion* in verse 10 that "first" (πρῶτον) the gospel must be proclaimed to all the nations (ἔθνη).[9] A careful reading of the passage makes plain that there is really

---

things" in v. 30 includes the Parousia of vv. 24–27, or whether it only refers to the sign(s) behind the "these things" of v. 29. But the "in those days" of v. 24 makes a decision here less consequential, as far as Mark discourse is concerned. The message is actually implicit from v. 13, where endurance "to the end" in the midst of tribulation is addressed to Jesus' disciples. Watchfulness is not only the message for the disciples addressed by Jesus, but it is the message of Mark to the church.

[9] Mark's tendency toward parenthetical remarks is well known (cf. 2:10, 15; 3:30; 7:3f., 19; 8:14; 13:14). Considering 13:10 an insertion are e.g., Nineham, *Mark,* 640; Kelber, *Kingdom,* 118; Martin, *Mark,* 222f.; Dunn, *Unity,* 74, 320. Agreeing but suggesting authenticity or at least the presence in Mark's source are e.g., Beasley-Murray, *Last Days,* 360, 402f.; Pesch, *Markusevangelium* II, 285; Cranfield, *Mark,* 399f.; Wenham, *Rediscovery,* 268–80, who has a helpful source-critical analysis. Against v. 10 as parenthetical is Kilpatrick, "Gentile Mission," 145–58.

nothing in verse 9 to which the "first" can refer. It must refer to "the end," which has been the subject of the discourse. The idea of an interval of undetermined length, which has been already introduced, is here also. The *logion* of verse 10 is parenthetical, but it relates Mark's train of thought to verse 9 and to verses 11–13, in that gospel preaching is the cause behind the persecution until the end comes. Thus the disciples must be prepared to endure "to the end" (v. 13b).

From the foregoing analysis of verses 5–13, it becomes evident that the entire passage is a kind of "insertion" before the more direct answer in verses 14ff. to the question of verse 4 concerning when "all these things" are to transpire. With verses 14ff. we leave the initial woes period. The question of verse 4 is thus first answered in terms of when the end will *not* come. It is fairly obvious that verses 5–13, and in particular the key verses examined, are intended to weaken expectation.

Conclusion

We have observed the dialectic of near-expectation and "not yet" in Mark 13. We see eschatological expectation and distance expressed together.[10] The tension is heightened if we understand that events were occurring at that time that would have pointed to the apocalyptic expectation. This may be especially true of the universal gospel mission in verse 10. The apostle Paul saw the church's mission well underway (cf. Rom 1:8; 15:18f.; Col 1:6).

This tension in Mark 13 is finally present in verses 30–32, where near-expectation ("this generation will not pass away until . . . ," v. 30) is countered with "but about that day or hour no one knows . . . ," v. 32). The indefiniteness of the time of the Parousia expressed in verse 32 at least allows for accommodation to delay. The indefinite time conceivably could be interpreted within the time frame of "this generation" (v. 30)—however long a period this should be. On the other hand, it has been argued that "day" and "hour" as found here (and as well, "time," καιρός, v. 33) can reflect the complex "day of the LORD" in the OT (including use in the LXX tradition), and so "day" and "hour" in Mark 13:32 need not be

---

[10] Cf. Beasley-Murray, *Last Days,* 369. Geddert, *Watchwords,* 223–58, believes Mark is deliberately ambiguous. Disciples are to trust when there is no chronological answer to the relation of temple destruction to the end. I suspect that this comes too close to relieving the eschatological tension that Mark intends to convey.

intended strictly to qualify "generation" of verse 30.[11] This latter interpretation is feasible, assuming that verse 30 alludes to the signs of the end and not the Parousia itself. In this case, then, verse 32, speaking of the Parousia, would clearly be in tension with near-expectation that is signified in verse 30.

Our observation of Mark's eschatological outlook raises the question of its relevance for the community which Mark addresses. What was going on in the community which led the inspired author to give this word of exhortation and instruction? Earlier we observed that Mark 13 was primarily an exhortation, as seen especially in the βλέπετε (beware/be alert) structure of the discourse. If we recall the themes highlighted with βλέπετε, we have clues for discerning Mark's purpose. We saw the concern over messianic impostors and false parousia prophets. We also noted the prominence given to persecution of Jesus' disciples, while they carry forth the gospel message. And then we noted the call for alertness for the Parousia.

Seeking to discern an author's purpose calls for much caution. But given the clues in Mark 13, we may surmise that while Mark wishes to encourage expectation, at the same time a word of cool-headed wisdom is needed for a congregation living in an atmosphere prone to eschatological excitement and error. Compounding the situation is persecution. We can imagine that some Christians would be enticed with the "new theology" of the miracle-working fanatics, who offered a more accommodating message (vv. 6, 21f.). Possibly others would have needed the explanatory and encouraging word of the Marcan exhortation simply to enable them to live with apparent delay, while holding to expectation. Finally, allowing time for the world-mission of the gospel in verse 10 to be accomplished both gives eschatological significance to the mission and places eschatological delay in the most positive light.[12]

---

[11] Beasley-Murray, *Last Days,* 455–59.
[12] If Mark thinks of vv. 14ff. being fulfilled in the fall of Jerusalem, then a period in the 60s before the fall would better explain his eschatology that allows for delay, since the Parousia is to occur "in those days" (cf. v. 24). If Mark writes in the early 70s, then vv. 14ff. may refer to the arrival of antichrist sometime after the fall of Jerusalem, with the events of vv. 5–13 occurring first, cf. Gnilka, *Markus,* II, 195f.; Lambrecht, *Redaktion,* 151; Ford, *Abomination,* 78f. Marxsen, *Mark,* 166–89, includes both Jerusalem's impending destruction and the arrival of the antichrist, with the end very near and Christians admonished to flee Judea for Galilee, cf. Kelber, *Kingdom,* 1f., 139f. This approach does not sufficiently take into account the delay theme

In Mark 13 we find a parallel with 2 Thess 2 in that the respective Christian communities are faced with eschatological error and both are admonished to retain expectation, but moderated in light of events that must transpire first.

Matthew 24f.

Most of Matthew 24, from verses 3b to 36, parallels Mark 13 so closely that we ought to presuppose some kind of dependency, whether of one Gospel on another, or of both on a common tradition. Although I assume the priority of Mark, I shall attempt to develop our ideas here with only minimal reliance on any such hypothesis. On the other hand, I think that in any case such comparison with Mark at points will be useful in recognizing Matthean distinctives.

Near-expectation of the End

Matthew has the same indications essentially that we found in Mark 13: the disciples' question of the end in relation to temple destruction (v. 3); apocalyptic woes (vv. 6–8); the *logion* "this generation will not pass away until" (v. 34). Granted this, we must note a significant modification, as well as additions, in Matthew's expectation motif.

(1) The lead question from the disciples concerning the end in relation to temple destruction differs from that of Mark. In Matthew the two parts of the question allow for some separation of the temple destruction from the Parousia and the end of the age. In this way Matthew highlights the parousia and "the end."

> " 'Tell us: (A) when will this be and (B) what will be the sign [τὸ σημεῖον] of your coming and of the end of the age?' "

In contrast, Mark's version keeps "the sign" as a referent to the temple destruction, *as well as* the (other) end time events: " 'Tell us, when will this be, and what will be the sign (τὸ σημεῖον) that all these things are about to be accomplished?' " (13:4).

(2) There are other indications that Matthew highlights expectation of a future parousia of Jesus in ways not found in Mark. First,

---

of Mark 13, cf. Conzelmann, *Outline,* 144. Our discussion is argued in more detail in my "Eschatological Delay," 257–59, 263–65. On date and locale, cf. n. 1 above.

Matthew seemingly prepares for his emphasis on the Parousia in chapter 24 in that he closes the "woes" unit of chapter 23 with not only the pronouncement of judgment on Jerusalem in verses 37–39, but with the denial of Jesus' presence in the future until Jerusalem says: " 'Blessed is the one who comes in the name of the Lord.' " (We may contrast the location of the parallel passage in Luke 13:34f.) 24:30 corresponds to verse 3 in again linking "the sign" (τὸ σημεῖον) to the appearance of the Son of man. Second, 24:30 corresponds to verse 3 in that "the sign" (τὸ σημεῖον) is again linked with the appearance of the Son of man. Third, Matthew underscores watching for the parousia in his telling of Jesus' allusion to the days of Noah (24:37–39 = Luke 17:26f.). Fourth, at the conclusion of his version of the eschatological discourse, Matthew gives far more attention to the theme of watchfulness and final judgment with respect to the Parousia (24:45–25:46). There are three parables plus an apocalyptic judgment scene. The parables say essentially the same thing: Watch! Be ready for the Son of man! Fifth, in Matthew 13 two parables distinctive to Matthew speak of the Parousia of chapter 24. The parable of the "weeds" (vv. 24–30, 36–43) tells of the Son of man sending his angels "at the end of the age," (cf. 24:3, 31), which is "the harvest." A similar "harvest" is in verses 47–50, where the angels separate the evil from the righteous, again, "at the end of the age." These two parables not only resemble Matthew's Parousia stress for "the end of the age" in chapter 24, but they are the only two interpreted parables outside the four soils parable earlier in the same chapter. Sixth, Jesus promises to be with his disciples to the "end of the age," as they disciple the nations (28:19f.). The "end of the age" is again prominent in Christian expectation.

Thus Matthew differs from Mark in that he makes a greater distinction between the fall of Jerusalem and the Parousia of the Son of man, and he also points more frequently to the Parousia, while encouraging expectation of the end in the early Christian community that he addresses. We will want to consider why Matthew's approach differs to this extent, but first we shall explore the possibility of a "delay" motif in his apocalyptic eschatology.

Delay of the End

As in Mark 13, despite the ominous portent of war, "the end is not yet" (24:6); and the apocalyptic woes are but the "beginning of the birthpangs" (24:7). However, in Matthew the most interesting paragraph at this point is 24:9–14. Matthew's concern particularly comes through here.

The paragraph begins with "then" (τότε), an adverb to which Matthew is clearly partial and which we may take to indicate a temporal progression from the beginning of the apocalyptic signs in verses 4–8 to the events Matthew now sets forth in verses 9–14.[13] Persecution is at the hands of "all nations" (πάντων τῶν ἐθνῶν), verse 9, rather than by Jews (cf. 10:17 = Mark 13:9). The tribulation (θλῖψιν) coincides with the church's mission "throughout the world . . . to all the nations" (ἐν ὅλῃ τῇ οἰκουμένῃ . . . πᾶσιν τοῖς ἔθνεσιν), verse 14. The nations again are prominent in 25:31ff., where their treatment of Christ's family members decides their reward. The thrust of verses 9–14 is very universalistic. Time must be allowed for this to be accomplished.

The universal proclamation of the gospel is especially prominent in Matthew, in concluding this unit. The end cannot come until all the world has been evangelized. In Matthew's terms, this means making "disciples of all nations" (28:19). Time must be allowed for this. The fact that Matthew concludes his Gospel on

---

[13] Τότε occurs approximately ninety times in Matthew, only six times in Mark, and possibly fifteen times in Luke. Over half of the NT occurrences are in Matthew. Detailed analysis of Matthew's use of this connective shows that approximately seventy or more times sequence of action is indicated (e.g., 2:7; 3:13; 7:23; 11:20; 12:29; 15:1). The comparatively fewer times that simultaneous action is indicated speak of fulfilled prophecy (2:17; 27:9); or there are almost always other extenuating reasons for non-sequence of action that account for the rendering. An exception is 25:1. In Matthew 24f. out of sixteen occurrences of τότε, I find thirteen that definitely have or include the idea of consequence or subsequence. Excluding an unusual use in 25:1, the exceptions are in 24:23, 40, with each use of τότε clearly reflecting back to what precedes. Jeremias says use of τότε in Matthew as a particle of transition meaning "thereafter" is an Aramaism and a departure from the classical usage, *Parables,* 82, n. 52. Cf. Holman, "Eschatological Delay," 277f., for some further detailing of evidence for my rendering of τότε in 24:9. *Contra* Lambrecht, "Discourse," 319. Gundry sees 24:3–14 as "non-eschatological," *Matthew,* 475–81. This seems like an overstatement in light of 24:8 ("beginning of the birthpangs"). It is quite unlikely that Matthew intends simply to indicate additional events for the beginning of the end-time period which he sets forth in vv. 4–8. He is carrying the action forward chronologically, but still within the overall period of distress. Verses 4–8 tell when the end is not to come. Verses 9–14 then set forth other calamities during the time before the end finally arrives. Thus the eschaton is lengthened. This contrasts with Mark, who gives no indication of temporal sequence in his parallel account in 13:5–8, 9–13.

this note probably indicates that the Christian community he addresses (and we might add, the church generally) was to get on with the job, though with an eye to "the end of the age" (v. 20). Apparent effects on the church in the crisis times of which Matthew writes are in verses 10–12. Following his announcement of tortuous persecution to come in verse 9, τότε (then) starts verse 10. What follows is a consequence of this persecution. At this point themes prominent elsewhere in Matthew are present. We may surmise that this indicates Matthew's earnest involvement in what he records: apostasy, betrayal, the activity of false prophets leading many astray, and lawlessness.[14]

We now turn to the "watchfulness" theme of Matt 24:36–25:30. As indicated above, there is an implicit near-expectation standpoint in that the early disciples were to take the "watch" exhortation seriously. On the other hand, within these pericopae a delay motif is at least implied.

Ignorance of the "day" and/or "hour" concludes the instructional units (usually parables) within 24:36–25:13. Following the introductory *logion* in 24:36 (" 'But about that day and hour no one knows, neither the angels of heaven, nor the Son, but only the Father' "), we find the exhortation to "keep awake" or "be ready" for

---

[14] Key verbs include σκανδαλίζω (cause to sin or fall into sin), v. 10. This is found fourteen times in Matthew, with at least nine other references expressing religious or moral failure within the professing community. Ψευδοπροφήτης (false prophet), while only in 7:15; 24:11, 24, is more prominent in Matthew than in any other NT book. Concern for false prophets shows itself in 7:15ff. (without synoptic parallel) and is similar to the reference in 24:11 in the danger of deception from many such persons. Πλανάω (v. 11) is used eight times in Matthew, including directives regarding wayward community members in 18:10–14. This concern should be paired with the stress on false prophets in Matthew. Ἀνομία in v. 12 occurs only in Matthew (four times) among the Gospels. It is linked with false prophets and with sinning. What appears to me to reflect particular Matthean interest is discussed in more detail in Holman, "Eschatological Delay," 280–84; also cf. Holman, "A Lesson," esp. 50–54. D. Wenham has argued plausibly for Matthew's use of tradition in vv. 10–12, *Rediscovery*, 256–59. This interests us because of the apostasy motif here, as in the book of Daniel. And Wenham's position does not necessarily conflict with seeing special Matthean interest in themes introduced in these verses. Matthew intends to describe intense eschatological calamity within the Christian community. These problems for Matthew were most likely already in existence to some extent. We shall return to this possibility when attempting to identify the life situation that his Gospel addresses.

the day/hour in 24:42, 44; 25:13. The admonition is implicit in the similar statement of 24:50.

The parable of the ten bridesmaids is distinctly Matthean in the Synoptic tradition (25:1–13), and it is in this pericope that delay of the leading character is featured most prominently. Jesus plainly says: "the bridegroom was delayed" (v. 5).[15] Half of the bridesmaids were caught off guard because they did not reckon with delay! But of particular note is the comparison at points with this parable and Jesus' words to the miracle-working false prophets in another distinctive Matthean passage, 7:21–23. Specifically, in 25:11f., the foolish bridesmaids say " 'Lord, lord, open to us.' " He replies: " 'Truly I tell you, I do not know you' "(οὐκ οἶδα ὑμᾶς). According to Matthew 7:21 many will seek entrance to the kingdom on the day of judgment by saying: " 'Lord, Lord. . . .' " Jesus will respond: " 'I never knew you' " (οὐδέποτε ἔγνων ὑμᾶς), v. 23).[16]

The Matthean Community

Matthew's distinctive stress on watchfulness for the Parousia and his preference for language which speaks of moral and spiritual deviation may be clues of a community problem which explains his eschatological distinctives. (In particular we noted terms that are brought together in the distinctively Matthean passage of 24:9–14, a passage in which he expects the eschatological period to include problems of apostasy, false prophets, and lawlessness within the Christian community.)[17] In short, has disillusionment over nearness of the parousia been responsible (at least in part) for a tendency toward lawlessness (ἀνομία) in the community? Is this why he stresses watchfulness the way he does?

---

[15] Not to be overlooked is that χρονίζοντος (delaying) opens v. 5. Also, as Bornkamm has observed, delay is seen as an illusion of the wicked servant in 24:48; but in 25:1ff., the illusion of the five foolish bridesmaids is that they counted on the nearness of the bridegroom's arrival, "End-Expectation," 23. For a different emphasis, Beasley-Murray, who minimizes the significance of "delay" in the parable, *Jesus and the Kingdom,* 212–15.

[16] The closest elsewhere in the NT we come to such language is Luke 13:25, 27 (= Matt 7:22f.). The only other instance of "Lord, Lord" (κύριε, κύριε) in the NT is Luke 6:46 within a passage that parallels Matt 7:21, 24–27. Matthew appears to have expanded a Q passage in 7:21–23. This leads us to consider the possible life situation in the community addressed by Matthew that calls forth his version of the synoptic apocalypse.

[17] See p. 121 with n. 14.

Looking at this Gospel more generally, I am pointed in the above direction. There is a strong ethical emphasis in Matthew, especially in chapters 5–7 and 18. In 7:15–23 there is warning against false prophets. It is likely that for those whom Matthew addresses, the teaching of the earthly Jesus is being threatened, as certain prophets, claiming inspiration from the risen Lord, point away from careful attention to the Jesus tradition (cf. 7:22f.). This not only contributes toward explanation of the large blocks of Jesus' teaching in Matthew's Gospel, but it also provides an attractive rationale for his christological thrust. This may also help account for the Matthean OT citations to authenticate the mission of the earthly Jesus (2:5, 23; 4:14–16; 8:17; 12:17–21; 13:35; 21:5; 27:9f.) and the well-known confession of Peter in 16:16. Of course if Matthew's congregation was Jewish, he would have additional reason to stress an OT basis for the mission of Jesus.[18] Furthermore, only in Matthew does the earthly Jesus promise his spiritual presence when two or three are gathered in his name (18:20) and promise his presence to last until the end of the age (28:20). It appears that Matthew would have his readers/listeners recognize the continuity between the earthly Jesus (whose teachings fulfill the law and prophets, 5:17–20 with 5:21ff.) and the risen Christ who inspires true prophecy and other charismatic manifestations.

Even if the above brief explanation for the life situation behind Matthew's Gospel is far from reckoning with all factors involved, the following does seem fairly clear:

(1) There was a problem with false prophecy and it affected true Christian discipleship based on the Jesus tradition. Thus those affected would be unprepared for the Parousia.

(2) An apocalyptic Parousia is part of the Jesus tradition and expectation is to be maintained. But at the same time expectation must make room for delay, at least from a human perspective. The false prophets may well have been capitalizing on the non-occurrence of the *apocalyptic* Parousia of Matthew 24. This could be the case especially if the Gospel was published in the 80s or 90s, as scholars often hold. This would also explain Matthew's separation of the fall of Jerusalem from the Parousia, as we have discussed.[19]

---

[18] For discussion concerning Jewish composition of Matthew's congregation see Kümmel, *Introd.*, 112–19.

[19] Concerning separation of the "fall" from the Parousia, R. T. France holds that vv. 4–35 address the time when the temple will be destroyed, but that vv. 36ff. indicate the time of the Parousia, *Matthew*, 333–52. This is

(3) The continued delay of the Parousia would help to account for the laxity within the community addressed by Matthew, especially as a question mark was placed over the Jesus tradition by false prophets parading as followers of Jesus. We may thus see Matthew interpreting the synoptic apocalyptic tradition to meet the needs of the Christian community of his own time.

Finally we must ask whether there was a delay problem for Matthew himself. There is no evidence of this kind of "how long" concern, as we found it in the contemporary Jewish apocalyptic literature. We cannot even say that for Matthew's community *generally* that there was a delay problem. Rather, Matthew, like Mark, seeks to maintain a balance between a further waiting period of unknown duration, on one hand, and near-expectation of the Parousia, whose signs are already in evidence, on the other hand. Matthew uses the synoptic apocalypse tradition to combat error affecting his community, as Mark has done. In so doing he seems to be tapping an underlying delay problem that has affected at least some in the community.[20] It is possible that there was a similar delay crisis for some whom Mark addressed, but this is not so evident. Besides the additional crucial passages in Matthew (24:9–14; 25:1–13), his temporal structure of eschatological events (based on Mark 13?) is significantly extended in comparison with that of Mark.[21] Mark appears to have given a decisive character to the delay idea while retaining a greater cohesion between the fall of Jerusalem and the Parousia. In light of community needs, Matthew has accommodated eschatological delay by emphasizing the role of the future for events which must yet transpire before the end comes. But it is a future in dynamic tension with the present situation.

Luke 21:5–36

Luke's version of the synoptic apocalypse is found primarily in chapter 21, although there is material in 17:20–27 which parallels

---

theologically attractive in avoiding the problem of the "this generation" *logion* in v. 34, but it is exegetically unconvincing.

[20] Cf. Strecker, *Der Weg,* 185f. and Bornkamm, *"Verzögerung,"* 124. Trilling, *Israel,* 43–45 has somewhat less place for delay in Matthew, it seems. Cf. discussion of Strecker and Trilling in Rohde, *Rediscovering,* 74–99.

[21] Grässer apparently fails to recognize this when he says that Matthew essentially reproduces Mark without updating the apocalyptic prophecies, *Problem,* 170, 217f.

part of Matthew 24. As in Mark 13 and Matthew 24, destruction of the temple and the time of the end are linked (Luke 21:5f. with what follows). Likewise, again there are *logia* which encourage expectation of the Parousia. However an intervening period is even more prominent in Luke than in either Mark or Matthew. Luke clearly shows distance between the destruction of Jerusalem and the end (vv. 20–24a with vv. 24bff.). We shall see that this coincides with other marks of "delay" in Luke's version of the synoptic apocalypse.

Expectation of the End

Luke makes clear that foreboding signs of the Parousia are to be observed (vv. 25–27). Jesus indicates to those whom he addresses that when these signs begin to occur (ἀρχομένων δὲ τούτων γίνεσθαι), redemption is near, verse 28. A parable is then given to illustrate expectation (vv. 29–31). The crux text of "this generation will not pass away until all things have taken place" (v. 32) follows. Surely this would serve all the more as an exhortation for Luke's audience to anticipate the Parousia if the *logia* were first given the contemporaries of Jesus.[22] But as if this were not enough, Luke follows with his version of an exhortation to watchfulness in verses 34–36 "to stand before the Son of Man." This is more pointed than the largely parabolic Marcan and Matthean concluding exhortations. For Luke preparedness means avoiding carousing, intoxication, and cares of life, along with engaging in prayer (vv. 34–36). This may point to a life-situation in the church addressed by Luke. We shall return to this. Thus Luke also has an emphasis on eschatological expectation, as do Mark and Matthew.

This orientation of expectation is not unique to chapter 21. The day of the Son of man, while not around the corner, is a day Jesus' disciples are to expect (17:22–37, esp. vv. 24, 30). Because that day will come unexpectedly, the disciples must give attention to being prepared (12:39f.).[23]

---

[22] Conzelmann, *Theology of St. Luke,* takes v. 32 to refer to "mankind in general," 105 with n. 2. (On Conzelmann, see n. 24 below.) This interpretation has been widely rejected, cf. Chance, *Jerusalem,* 94. Also see above n. 8 on "this generation."

[23] There are other expressions of eschatological imminence in Luke–Acts; e.g., Luke 9:27; 10:9, 11; 18:1–8; Acts 3:19–21, cf. Chance, *Jerusalem,* 91–95.

Delay of the End

What is striking about Luke is that given his expectation motif, the idea of delay is more overtly and systematically developed than in Mark or Matthew. Amidst a general similarity and pattern of ideas, there are important differences from Mark and Matthew.[24] We shall now identify several distinctives of Luke in chapter 21 which signal eschatological delay.

(1) The disciples' initiating question in verse 7 practically parallels that of Mark 13:4, except for one critical phrase:

> When will this be, and what will be the sign that this is about to take place [the temple destruction] (Luke 21:7);

> When will this be, and what will be the sign that all these things are about to be accomplished (Mark 13:4).

In the Greek text Luke has γίνεσθαι ("to take place") instead of Mark's συντελεῖσθαι πάντα ("all . . . to be accomplished"). Luke veers from both Mark and Matthew in that the eschatological import of the question is downplayed as Luke focuses more narrowly on the temple destruction.

(2) In verse 8 Luke's version of the discourse has the warning against messianic deceivers (cf. Mark 13:6 = Matt 24:5), but Luke includes a further word (absent in Mark and Matt) from the mouth of the deceivers: "The time is near!" (ὁ καιρὸς ἤγγικεν). ("The end" in v. 9 makes preferable the view that an apocalyptic event is the subject.) In Luke this expression of imminence is from impostors. (Contrast Mark 1:14f. = Matt 4:17).

(3) Verse 9 contains four single-word "alterations," where otherwise verbal parallels with Mark 13:7 and Matt 24:6 are quite closely maintained. (a) Instead of "rumors of wars" Luke has "insur-

---

[24] Conzelmann's *Theology of St. Luke,* originally published in German in the 1950s, created a new day for Lukan studies. However his position that Luke has recast eschatology with redemptive history, placing the Parousia in the far distant future in an effort to accommodate the church's awareness of delay, has been properly contested or at least moderated by many other scholars; e.g., Kümmel, *Introd.*, 144f.; Talbert, "Quest"; Ellis, *Eschatology*. It has been common to see Luke editing in light of events past A.D. 70 where his version of the synoptic apocalypse differs from Mark. However, we ought not to rule out Luke's possible use of other sources, cf. Marshall, *Luke,* 754–77. In either case, Luke's distinctives stand.

rections" (ἀκαταστασίας), which would fit the Jewish War more precisely. (b) "Do not be terrified" (aorist passive of πτοέω seems stronger than "do not be alarmed" (present passive of θροέω in Mark 13:7 = Matt 24:6. This would fit Luke's more realistic statement of the fall of Jerusalem (cf. esp. vv. 20–24). (c) Having referred to wars and insurrections in verse 9, Luke sharpens the thought that "this must take place" (δεῖ . . . γενέσθαι) before the end (cf. Mark 13:7 and Matt 24:6) by saying that "these things must take place *first*" (Luke adds πρῶτον to what Mark and Matthew have, emphasis mine) before the end. Though the difference is little, the preliminary role of the distresses is highlighted. (d) In verse 9 Luke has "the end will not follow *immediately*"(εὐθέως), whereas Mark 13:7 and Matthew 24:6 have "the end is still to come/the end is not yet"(οὔπω). Again the difference is small, but it shows particular sensitivity to the temporal issue. It is significant in light of the other Lucan distinctives. (Later we shall say more about the life-situation that Luke apparently addresses.)

(4) A major difference in Luke's structuring of the discourse occurs in verses 12–19. With his opening "but before all these things" (NASB; πρὸ δὲ τούτων πάντων), Luke places disciple persecution and suffering *before* most of the calamities that are eschatological in the Synoptic parallels (cf. Mark 13:8 and Matt 24:7f. with Luke 21:10–12). We have a clear de-emphasis of the eschatological significance of Christian suffering, somewhat similar to what we find in the placing of the Matthew 10:17–22 parallel in the context of Jesus' ministry, rather than with the kind of eschatological suffering in the Mark 13:9–13 and Matthew 24:9–13 parallels. It is also noteworthy that Luke does not include the promise of reward for the one enduring to the end (εἰς τέλος, cf. Mark 13:13b; Matt 24:13). Rather he has: "By your endurance you will gain your souls" (v. 19). Thus eschatological overtones are avoided. Of course Luke's description of the era of suffering is expanded in Acts (e.g., 4:5–22; 5:40f.; 7:54–8:1; 16:19–24). Furthermore in Luke 21:12–19 the ongoing gospel witness as eschatological (in the context of suffering) is not found (contrast Mark 13:10; Matt 24:14).[25]

---

[25] Chance, *Jerusalem*, 95, finds support in E. Schweizer and Hiers in saying that Luke did not include this missionary *logion* because Luke conceived of the Christian mission as already accomplished (cf. Acts). Since the end had not come, it would make Jesus look wrong. This seems to be saying too much for Luke. We could just as well argue that Acts 1:8 and chapter 28 were intended to encourage the church of Luke's day to complete the

(5) The most consequential of Luke's distinctive interpretations of the synoptic apocalypse tradition thus far, and that to
which preceding observations have pointed, is Luke's pericope of
the Jerusalem crisis (vv. 20–24; cf. Mark 13:14–20 and Matt
24:15–22). Apart from the first three words in the Greek text and
verses 21a and 23a, there is very little verbal similarity with Mark
and Matthew. Luke (or his tradition) historicizes what the other
Synoptics present in more distinct apocalyptic language (cf. esp.
Mark 13:19f. and Matt 24:21f.). In Mark and Matthew this eschatological crisis is followed by cosmic signs and the Parousia
(Mark 13:24–27; Matt 24:29–31). Luke instead first refers to the
captivity of Jerusalem and a worldwide dispersion of Jews (εἰς τὰ
ἔθνη πάντα) for an undetermined length of time, but "until the
times of the Gentiles are fulfilled" (v. 24). He then refers to the
cosmic signs and the Parousia. Even more clearly than Matthew,
Luke has shown that the arrival of the Parousia is to extend
beyond the era of Jerusalem's destruction, which traditionally had
been regarded as the end-time. Or we might say that for Luke the
end-time is a longer period than was otherwise held in Jewish-
Christian tradition. But all is within God's sovereign control
(21:24c).

A somewhat wider look at Luke–Acts will support the foregoing
"delay" motif and also help in locating a plausible life-situation
which called forth Luke's synoptic apocalypse.

Luke 17:20–18:8

This passage anticipates themes that appear in chapter 21. Expectation is highlighted, as Jesus' disciples are told of the sudden-
ness of the Parousia (vv. 22–24). Seduction, normal secular pursuits,
and crisis circumstances are outlined, presumably to enable the
disciples to be prepared "on the day that the Son of Man is
revealed" (vv. 23–37). This reminds us of the admonition to watchfulness in 21:34–36.

On the other hand, contending with delay is inferred in the
warning that the disciples will unsuccessfully long to see "one of
the days of the Son of Man."[26] Also, the fact that Jesus must first

---

missionary proclamation. The lack of an eschatologically oriented missionary mandate in Acts 1:6–8 can be explained otherwise, as we shall see.

[26] "One of the days of the Son of man" (v. 22) is a very unusual phrase
and has been interpreted in various ways. The important point is that it most

(πρῶτον) endure much suffering before the days of the Son of man is stated in verse 25. In light of Luke's emphasis on disciples' suffering before the eschaton period (21:12, see above), the overtone here is probably that of suffering in the messianic community as well (cf. 17:22).

One more observation should be made. Three of the motifs in chapter 21 that contribute to Luke's imminence-delay tension are here: concern for suffering, deception regarding the eschaton, and spiritual preparation for the Parousia. Note that the passage is introduced with the Pharisees' question of when the kingdom was to come (v. 20f.). This fits well with what we have seen in Luke's rather unique synoptic eschatological teaching.

The unrighteous judge parable in 18:1–8 illuminates ideas introduced in 17:20–37. The parable (unique to Luke) encourages continual prayer by those who are tempted to "lose heart" (v. 1). The answer to straitened circumstances is such prayer, even as the godly in 21:36 are to pray always, while anticipating the Parousia. Prompt (ἐν τάχει) justice is promised those suffering from persecutors, even as the widow found justice, but it is to those who "cry to him day and night" (vv. 7f.). Thus the timing of the Parousia is linked to earnest prayer for that day (cf. Luke 11:2 = Matt 6:9f.). However the pericope concludes on a negative note (beginning with πλήν, "yet"), questioning whether there will be faith on the earth in the day of the Parousia (v. 8). With this expectation-delay tension, there is evidently before us a difficult pastoral situation which Luke desires to address, and we would add, the Spirit of God through Luke.

The Lucan Community

We cannot tell how widespread or provincial the community is which Luke addresses; but even from our brief survey of his version of the synoptic apocalypse and related texts, it has become likely that he does have a particular community situation in view.[27]

---

probably reflects longing for the Parousia (cf. vv. 23–24), which fits well with Luke's delay motif.

[27] There is much more to be said in a full discussion of the Lucan community situation, which we cannot here explore. The broader authorial purpose is given by Luke himself in Luke 1:1–4 (cf. Acts 1:1) in which he states his intent is to confirm the instruction that has been given to Theophilus, to whom he dedicates his work. (I take Luke–Acts to have a wider original audience than Theophilus, though he alone is mentioned after Hellenistic custom wherein a work would be dedicated to a particular

We wish to attempt an explanation of why events before the end in the synoptic apocalypse are de-eschatologized by Luke, while encouragement is nevertheless given to anticipate the Parousia. In the way he presents the Jesus tradition we have observed Luke's particular interest in warning against eschatological deception, including the nearness of the final time, his warning against adopting a "this-worldly" lifestyle, and his warning of persecution and suffering. Also, in the way he presents the Jesus tradition, he urges watchfulness and prayerfulness.

Given the above data, we may see that the Jerusalem-temple crisis, uniquely set forth by Luke, appears integral toward a solution. (His interest in this calamitous event is also seen in 19:41–44 and 23:28–31, both distinctive to Luke.) Regardless of whether 21:20–24 is a redaction of Mark or essentially another form of the Jesus-tradition, Luke's employment of the passage in the context of eschatological delay leads me to think that he is writing in light of the A.D. 70 crisis.[28] Luke's frequent detailing of Jewish rejection of the gospel in Luke–Acts, along with success of the Gentile mission,

---

individual, cf. Haenchen, *Acts,* 136, n. 3; Aune, *Literary Environment,* 120f.) Many scholars properly understand Luke as a "salvation-history" theologian. What we have explored would be a subset of this larger picture. For significant research from 1950–83, one may consult Bovon, *Luke the Theologian.*

There are other passages in Luke–Acts that bear on the expectation-delay tension. Luke consistently tones down eschatological language, apparently seeking to moderate expectation. We see this first in a comparison of Luke with other synoptic passages: 4:14–20 (cf. with Mark 1:14f. = Matt 4:12, 17); 9:27 (with Mark 9:1 = Matt 16:28); 22:69 (with Mark 14:62 = Matt 26:64). Note also Luke 19:11 as introductory to the parable of vv. 12–27. In Acts 1:6–11 the issue of when the kingdom would be restored to Israel is sidestepped in favor of the missionary endeavor. In Acts 3:19–21 the time of the Parousia depends on Israel's repentance. There are glimpses of the final judgment and/or final resurrection (Acts 10:42; 17:30f.; 24:15, 25), but whether Luke intends to indicate an imminent denouement is debatable.

[28] In this case Luke could be writing in the "times of the Gentiles" (Luke 21:24). (A composition date after the Jerusalem crisis need not discount a valid prediction by the earthly Jesus.) It is very difficult to suggest a more precise date, although a date not far removed from A.D. 70 might make the "this generation" *logion* (Luke 21:32) more understandable within Luke's delay schema. Scholars often date Luke somewhere between 70 and 90. Ellis, *Luke,* 57f. and Marshall, *Luke,* 771, both date Luke just after the year 70, but also suggest the possibility of a date just before the fall of Jerusalem. The abrupt ending of Acts may be at least partially explained in terms of a desire by Luke to conclude on a note of the gospel's advancement amidst suffering, which would be consonant with the outlook of Luke–Acts.

provides a divine reason for Jerusalem's destruction. But at the same time it would raise eschatological problems in light of familiar apocalyptic tradition of the end as associated with the Jerusalem crisis (esp. Dan 9:26f.; cf. Mark 13:1–4). Luke exhorts Christians not to lose heart while they live in an environment characterized not only by worldliness and opposition, but also by apocalyptic fever.[29] The same eschatological outlook which would lead some to disillusionment would spawn undue apocalyptic excitement in others. Luke's message would be an antidote to both.

Luke's message provides the community with an interpretation of the Jesus tradition which allows for (further) eschatological delay, while not abandoning a meaningful hope of the Parousia. In fact, with the wedding in Luke of watchfulness with delay, it is probably better to speak of a "vigilance-delay" tension even more than of "imminence-delay." In the meantime believers are to be involved in the gospel mission (cf. esp. Acts).

Luke's highlighting of an interim period before the Parousia, and consequently a lessened emphasis on an imminent parousia, is consonant with his stress on a present salvation throughout his Gospel and the Acts. The time of fulfillment has arrived (e.g., Luke 3:4–6; 4:17–21; 7:27; 24:44–47; Acts 2:16–21, 25–36; 3:18–26; 8:32–35; 13:32–39, 47; 15:15–18).[30]

A Conclusion Regarding the Synoptic Apocalypse

As in 2 Thessalonians, the motifs of Jewish apocalyptic continue to be expressed in the three variations of eschatological teaching that stem from the Jesus tradition. However, in the synoptic apocalypse we have even more echoes of Jewish apocalyptic than in 2 Thess 2, and with a broader inclusion of messianic woes that are to precede the end.[31]

---

[29] On apocalyptic fever note Ellis, *Eschatology,* 19.

[30] On present salvation in Luke see Marshall, *Luke: Historian,* 94–215; cf. Grässer, *Problem,* 144. The theme is recurrent in the birth narratives, 1:46–55, 67–79; 2:11; 2:25–32; Luke uses σώζω when Mark and/or Matthew have a parallel statement without Luke's σώζω idea, 8:12 = Mark 4:15 = Matt 13:19 (present experience?); Luke 8:36 = Mark 5:16; Luke 8:50 = Mark 5:36. Two other significant passages found only in Luke are 19:9f. and 23:43. But the final kingdom remains outstanding. Luke has an agenda for believers who live in between these times.

[31] This is not to overlook the heavenly Son of man motif which is consonant with later Jewish apocalyptic that is more transcendentally

Tension between expectation and delay is always present, though significantly modified. It is apparent that the varying community situations influence the way that this tension is expressed. In fact we have observed a progression between the three Gospels.

(1) In Mark the idea of delay is quite distinctively added to the traditional Jewish themes of various woes, end-time tribulation, and the denouement. The gospel mission is linked to the delay theme as well.

(2) In Matthew the eschaton is described in such a way as to suggest a more lengthy period. Matthew's parables regarding the Parousia make more of an issue of the delay. Reckoning with delay is seemingly tied to the moral and spiritual laxity of community members. The gospel mission is stressed more than in Mark's Gospel.

(3) Luke goes further than Mark or Matthew in separating the eschaton from preceding world events which are otherwise found in the synoptic apocalypse tradition. A corresponding expectation theme, while certainly present, appears to be slackened even more than in Matthew.

In light of the foregoing observations of the three Gospels, we conclude that a progression in adjustment to what appeared, or what was beginning to appear, to be a later Parousia is quite likely reflected in the synoptic apocalypse. The apocalypse tradition is obviously flexible to accommodate the somewhat varying needs of the early church.[32]

---

oriented (Mark 8:38; 13:26; 14:62, all with parallels), cf. Kümmel, *Promise,* 88, who attributes all to Jesus.

[32] The trajectory of the Synoptic tradition clearly runs into the early second century with the Apocalypse of Peter. As found in Maurer, "Apocalypse of Peter," 664, the following part of this apocalypse (part 1) is instructive for us (italicized portions are from Maurer and indicate the Synoptic text):

And when he was seated on the Mount of Olives, his own *came unto him* and we entreated and implored him severally and besought him, saying unto him, "Make known unto us what are the *signs of thy Parousia and of the end of the world,* that we may perceive and mark the time of thy Parousia and instruct those who come after us . . . in order that they . . . may take heed to themselves that they mark the time of thy coming." And our Lord answered and said unto us, *"Take heed that men deceive you not* and that ye do not become doubters and serve other gods. *Many will come in my name saying, 'I am Christ.' Believe them not and draw not near unto them. For the coming of the Son of God will not be manifest, but like the lightning which shineth from the east to the west,* so shall I *come on the clouds of heaven with a great host in* my *glory.* . . ."

The prophetic hope of a culminating act of God in history has continued to be reinterpreted. First, through traditional Jewish apocalyptic themes, especially those found in Daniel. Now, in light of the Jesus tradition and the anticipating of his parousia, we witness a further interpretation of the hope of the arrival of the day of the Lord.

This part of the apocalypse is preserved in Ethiopic. Concerning date, cf. James, "Recovery," 22; Bauckham, "Martyrdom," 450. Obvious redaction of the Synoptic tradition betrays the fact the "delay" was a problem for the second-century community. Doubt and apostasy are evident issues. On the other hand, the author apparently holds to near-expectation. The themes of religious deception, apostasy, and persecution with martyrdom are underscored (parts 3–13) and these belong to the end-time (parts 1f.).

EXCURSUS: IMPLICATIONS FOR THE "HISTORICAL JESUS"[1]

OUR FOCUS HAS BEEN ON THE NT DOCUMENTS AS WE HAVE them, rather than on a critical reconstruction of Jesus' teaching prior to the rise of the early church. However it is appropriate to make a few observations on the Jesus tradition in light of our foregoing investigation.

We earlier surveyed expectation in Jewish apocalyptic eschatology and noted that it extended into the era of Jesus and his followers. Such expectation is similar to what we see in pronouncements ascribed to Jesus in the Gospels. Perhaps the most striking are the following:[2]

> Truly I tell you, there are some standing here who will not taste death until they see that the kingdom of God has come with power (Mark 9:1 and parallels).

> Truly I tell you, this generation will not pass away until all these things have taken place (Mark 13:30 and parallels).

> When they persecute you in one town, flee to the next; for truly I tell you, you will not have gone through all the towns of Israel before the Son of Man comes (Matt 10:23).

Even if we assume that at an early date the church created such sayings in light of Easter faith, the retention of the sayings in

---

[1] For a somewhat moderate and up-to-date assessment of the issue, cf. Sanders, *Jesus and Judaism,* esp. 3–58; Meier, *Marginal Jew,* esp. ch. 4.

[2] I have developed my understanding of these Synoptic texts in Holman, "Imminent Parousia," 20–31.

the Synoptic accounts when non-fulfillment would be an embarrassment testifies in favor of their authenticity.[3] They amount to a near-expectation eschatology that had already characterized at least a significant part of Judaism, though with more specificity in the Jesus sayings. What is especially new is that Jesus sees himself in the center of anticipation. How we handle this will depend on our prior view of Jesus. But that Jesus' outlook was in some sense one of near-expectation has been widely held by scholars.[4] If we understand the early church to have attributed such personalization of apocalyptic hope to Jesus, independent of his own teachings, then we have to explain what lay behind that attribution to Jesus. From my perspective, it is much more likely that such sayings originated with the earthly Jesus (at least in some form) and then became meaningful to the early church in light of its Easter faith. An alternative viewpoint that the early church mistakenly attributed such sayings to Jesus because of its Easter faith is based on assumptions which clearly lie outside the perspective of the Synoptic Gospels and which lead to other challenges of explaining a radical transformation of the original dominical sayings.[5] Of course the way one handles such matters depends in

---

[3] On the criterion of embarrassment generally, cf. Meier, *Marginal Jew,* 168–71, who also warns against using this criterion in isolation from other criteria.

[4] Cf. Marshall, *Luke: Historian,* 129, who has claimed (though at least now overstated) "there is complete agreement among scholars" that Jesus regarded the end and the kingdom as imminent, with even C. H. Dodd having moved in this direction, cf. ibid., n. 3. Bultmann has said that the "certainty" with which Jesus proclaimed the end to have arrived was unique to Jesus, *Theology* 1.6. More recently, Sanders has said that 1 Thess 4:15–17; Matt 16:27f.; 24:30f. "quite possibly go back to Jesus" and that "it would be rash to deny to Jesus this complex of ideas," *Jesus and Judaism,* 145f. *Contra* Borg, "Temperate Case," 81–101.

Concerning Jesus' relation generally to his (Jewish) followers, Charlesworth, *Jesus within Judaism,* 3: "The dreams, ideas, symbols, and terms of his earliest followers were inherited directly from Jesus. Thanks to fundamentally important discoveries and publications, these are now seen to be anchored deep within the world and thought of Early Judaism (c. 250 B.C.E. to 200 C.E.)." This statement seems significant, even though Charlesworth hardly deals with apocalypticism and Jesus.

[5] From a source critical standpoint, the apocalyptic ideas of a transcendent new world in which Jesus (the Son of man) occupies center stage, and an imminent arrival of this new age have multiple attestation in the Synoptic tradition. These themes are either explicit or presupposed in the: (1) triple tradition of Matthew, Mark, and Luke (Matt 16:27f. = Mark 8:38 = Luke

large part on the view adopted regarding Jesus' own messianic consciousness. And if Jesus *was* the risen Lord of early church belief, then there is little reason why Jesus would not have previously seen himself as vitally involved in the fulfillment of the prophetic new age.

With Jesus' knowledge of the Scriptures, along with his prediction of the destruction of Jerusalem (deeply rooted in the Jesus tradition, cf. above, p. 113), he would have acknowledged the relevance of the Daniel prophecies, as did his contemporaries. Hence, eschatological expectation with attending woes, with background in Daniel 9 and 11 for example, are easily attributed to Jesus' own teaching.

Granting the place of an indefinite time for the end in Jewish apocalyptic, we can also allow for ignorance of the "day" and "hour" (Mark 13:32 and parallels) to have belonged to Jesus' perspective.[6] (The delay theme is more pervasive in Jewish literature than scholars usually have recognized.) The warnings to "watch" need not be considered later additions by the early church due to a delayed parousia. Rather the indefiniteness of the actual end helps explain why much of Jesus' teaching about the kingdom seems to allow for ongoing community life that is not always preoccupied with when the end is going to occur.[7]

We have grounds for concluding that the biblical perspective of a dialectical tension between expectation and delay was part of Jesus' own outlook, however much the early church adapted his teachings for the contemporary circumstances and needs that early congregations later faced.

9:26f.; Matt 19:28f. = Mark 10:29f. = Luke 18:38–30; Matt 24:29–36 = Mark 13:24–37; Luke 21:25–33; Matt 26:64 = Mark 14:62 = Luke 22:69); (2) Q (Matt 24:37–41 = Luke 17:26–37); (3) Matthew alone (10:23; 13:37–43; 25:1–13; 25:31–46); (4) Luke alone (17:22–24; 18:8). In addition the same perspective is in John 5:25–29. Crossan, *Historical Jesus,* 238–59, among others, argues that "Son of man" as titular was not original with Jesus. Even should we grant this, an apocalyptic expectation in Jesus is not of necessity tied to such use of the term. Cf. the apocalypticism of 1 Thess 4–5; 2 Thess 2, which evidently has roots in the same tradition as the synoptic apocalypse; e.g., Wenham, "Paul."

   [6]Cf. Strobel, *Kerygma,* 85. Meier, *Marginal Jew,* 168f. argues for authenticity of this from the "criterion of embarrassment," that is it limits the knowledge of Jesus.

   [7]Cf. Borg, "Temperate Case," 89–92, though I am arguing against Borg's fundamental thesis of a non-eschatological Jesus.

Finally, to say that Jesus shared certain eschatological ideas with some of his contemporaries need in no way marginalize his prophetic voice which stood out among his contemporaries. No other person saw himself at the center of the great event to come as did Jesus.

10

REVELATION

FROM THE STANDPOINT OF LITERARY GENRE, WE COME TO
the one apocalypse in the NT. Actually the book of Revelation
consists mostly of epistle (chs. 2–3) and (especially) apocalypse
proper (chs. 4–22). At the same time it is identified as a "prophecy"
and its author is a prophet (1:3; 22: 6f., 9f., 18f.). Observation of
how themes introduced in the epistolary section are drawn out in
the apocalypse proper will be important in our considerations of
eschatological expectation in the communities addressed by John of
the Apocalypse.[1]

Date

The most important single historical development for establishing an authorship date is conflict which the early Christians of
Asia (chs. 2f.) and of Rome (cf. chs. 13; 17) had with the secular
authorities of their day. (Concerning Rome, practically all scholars
recognize at least an allusion in Revelation to Rome as the political
force in the first century.) The likely time is either the later period

---

[1] Bauckham helpfully sees Revelation as an apocalyptic prophecy in the
form of a circular letter to seven churches; the seven messages are introductions to the rest of the book, *Revelation,* 2. Similarly, Roloff: "Revelation is a
prophetic writing that contains numerous apocalyptic motifs and elements
of style, but whose form is chiefly characterized by the purpose of epistolary
communication," *Revelation,* 8.

For our purposes it is unnecessary to attempt to identify "John" (1:1, 4,
9; 22:8). The traditional position has been that he was John the apostle.
Difficulties with this view and discussion of alternative approaches may be
found in the NT introductions and commentaries.

of Nero (emperor 54–68) or the last years of Domitian (emperor 81–96). By far most scholars now hold to the Domitian date, which is supported by the external witness of Irenaeus in the second century along with internal data.[2]

For understanding eschatological expectation in Revelation, it will be important to keep in mind that neither the Nero nor Domitian dates coincide with the portrayal of Christian persecution in the book as a whole. The Neronic persecution was essentially limited to Rome and far from the universal suffering seen in the Apocalypse, especially in chapters 7, 13. On the other hand there is hardly evidence that the *mass* persecution of Revelation 7, 13 existed under Domitian.[3] Eusebius speaks of pagan authors who wrote of Christian persecution and martyrdoms (*Hist. eccl.* 3.18). But evidence is lacking that the persecution was on a mass basis. Neither is there evidence that the suffering of Christians in Asia (cf. Rev. 2f.) can be traced to the Domitian persecution of Christians. In fact Jewish persecution seems to be as much of a concern as that from pagans (cf. 2:9; 3:9). A kind of unofficial "cooperation" between the two groups may be implied in 2:9f.[4] Furthermore in Ignatius' letter to the church at Rome about 107 there is no trace of a pogrom against Christians in Rome a few years earlier. This would seem strange in view of Ignatius' own anticipation of martyrdom in Rome.

It is quite possible that we ought to think of the persecution under Nero being present in the mind of John when he wrote later in the time of Domitian. We ought to conclude that the worldwide persecution so graphically described in Revelation had not transpired, but there were signs on the horizon of its coming. Later we shall return to implications that the dating of the Apocalypse in

---

[2] Cf. e.g., Prévost, *How to Read,* 17. For arguments for the Domitian date, see e.g., Kümmel, *Introd.,* 466–69 and Collins, *Crisis,* 54–83. Schüssler Fiorenza, *Revelation,* 126, n. 3, identifies seventeen commentators who hold to this date. For a Neronic date, cf. Robinson, *Redating,* ch. 8. Robinson actually holds to six months after Nero's death.

[3] Cf. Frend, "Persecutions," 150f.; Sherwin-White, "Early Persecutions," 200f.; Boring, *Revelation,* 15–18; Thompson, *Revelation,* ch. 6, p. 116. Persecution that did exist in Asia was probably fostered by emperor worship, for which Pergamum was conspicuous (note "Satan's throne" in 2:13), e.g., Ramsay, *Letters,* 293f.; Charles, *Revelation,* 1.60f.; Beckwith, *Apocalypse,* 457f.; Kraft, *Offenbarung,* 64, Hemer, *Letters,* 82–87. For Revelation 13 and archeological evidence of the emperor cult at Ephesus, S. Friesen, "Ephesus," 24–37.

[4] Cf. Ramsay, *Letters,* 271; Collins, *Apocalypse,* 92.

relation to Christian persecution have on our understanding of
expectation of the Parousia in the Apocalypse.

Near-expectation of the Parousia

As already discussed in earlier chapters, anticipation of the
eschatological age characterizes documents of godly communities
from the time of the OT prophets. Following our survey of an end to
the present world in Jewish and early Christian apocalyptic, we are
ready to see how eschatological expectation reaches a high point in
the Apocalypse in the anticipated "coming" of Jesus Christ.

Besides specific short texts (6:10; 10:6; 12:12), anticipation and
portrayal of final salvation and judgment is almost continually before us in the apocalyptic visions of chapters 4–22. This creates a
literary atmosphere of expectancy. The least we can say is that the
underlying mood of much of the Apocalypse pulsates with imminent expectation on the part of John. But this theme is explicitly
highlighted in an *inclusio* format which begins and concludes the
Apocalypse. It starts and ends with reference to the imminence of a
(second) coming.

Thus, in the prologue the revelation of Jesus Christ (meaning
from Jesus Christ?) which is for Christ's "servants" and mediated to
Christ's "servant" (δοῦλος) John through the angel, concerns "what
must soon take place" (ἃ δεῖ γενέσθαι ἐν τάχει), 1:1.[5]

Similarly in the epilogue, the message for God's "servants"
(δοῦλοι) though the angel concerns "what must soon take place"(ἃ
δεῖ γενέσθαι ἐν τάχει), 22:6. Then the one who is speaking
immediately adds: "See, I am coming soon!"(καὶ ἰδοὺ ἔρχομαι
ταχύ), verse 7. As in the prologue, this statement of imminence is
followed by "for the time is near" (ὁ καιρὸς γὰρ ἐγγύς ἐστιν).
This explains why the scroll is to remain unsealed (contrast Dan
12:4). With this return in the epilogue to the prologue statement of
expectation, it is clear that the entire contents of the Apocalypse are
to be read and heard with earnest expectancy that the coming of the

---

[5] According to BAGD the adjective ταχύς can mean: (1) quickly or
rapidly, (2) without delay, at once, (3) in a short time, soon. In light of the
synonym ἐγγύς (near) in the ἐν ταχεῖ/ταχύ passages discussed in this part
of our study, the third is preferable, though the second is possible. Then in
v. 3, just before his salutation, John gives a reason for the blessing to those
who read and hear the message: "for the time is near" (ὁ γὰρ καιρὸς ἐγγύς).

Lord Jesus is near. In fact the final prophetic word is: "Surely I am coming soon" (ναί, ἔρχομαι ταχύ). The "servant" response is: "Amen, Come Lord Jesus!" (22:20).

The "I am coming soon" (ταχύ) promise recurs in 22:12. Only this time the word is linked to a reward according to the work (ἔργον) of each community person. There are notable parallels with the letters of chapters 2–3, where we find interrelationship between: (1) Jesus' assessment of the "works" (ἔργα) of the various churches (2:2, 5, 6, 19, 22, 23, 26; 3:1, 2, 8, 15), (2) the promise of recompense (negative or positive) (2:5, 7, 22f., 26–28; 3:3–5, 9f., 12, 16, 21), and (3) expectation of the Lord's coming (2:5, 25, 3:3, 11, 20; cf. 2:16). In this manner the "coming" of the Lord in the Apocalypse proper is bonded with the several messages to the churches in chapters 2–3. This leads us to consider the meaning of the "coming" of Christ as it first occurs in the letters, before being played out in the Apocalypse proper.

The letters of chapters 2–3 are introduced in chapter 1 with the blessing of God "who is and who was and who is to come" (vv. 4f., cf. v. 8.) and with the announcement that Jesus Christ is "coming" (v. 7). This sets the stage for the glorious risen one of verses 12–16 to addresses the Asian communities in chapters 2–3 in light of his coming.

The letters themselves seem to distinguish between conditional restricted "comings" and the unconditional and final coming. But similarities of vocabulary probably indicate some kind of continuity between the two kinds of "comings."

Conditional and apparently more restricted "comings" are described in: "If not I will come to you and remove your lampstand" (2:5) and "If not I will come to you soon (ταχύ) and make war against them with the sword of my mouth" (2:16).

More unconditional and conceivably universal "comings" are found in: "Only hold fast to what you have until I come" (2:25) and "I am coming soon (ταχύ); hold fast to what you have" (3:11).

Two other "coming" words are expressed in conditional terms, but nevertheless of probable universal application in light of later texts in the Apocalypse: "If you do not wake up, I will come like a thief, and you will not know at what hour I will come to you" (3:3, cf. 16:15); "If you hear my voice and open the door, I will come in to you and eat with you" (3:20, cf. 19:9).

In light of the prologue and epilogue texts already examined, the Apocalypse evidently conceives of a final universal parousia. On the other hand, there is obvious correspondence between this and a coming or comings of the Lord that have more restricted and localized significance and which are expressed in conditional terms. In light of the fluidity of anticipated "comings" that we have set forth, we can recognize an eschatological tension between "comings" of a more local significance and the final grand parousia. This in turn would likely contribute to imminent eschatological expectation. In addition we should be careful about reading too much apocalyptic literalism into the final coming, since there is clearly continuity in the manner in which this and the preliminary comings are described.[6]

The dominant theme of the Apocalypse is clearly one of eschatological anticipation which seeks to encourage a lively expectation of the soon coming of Christ among those who must endure in an unfriendly world unto that time.

Delay of the Parousia

It may seem strange that in a document so intensely anticipatory that we should also find a counter theme of any consequence. But from another standpoint, we have observed this dialectic in both prophetic and apocalyptic writings from earlier times.

We have already laid the foundation for a modified "imminence" motif in Revelation in our discussion above on the dating of Revelation. We have noted that the heightened *world* conflict leading to mass Christian martyrdom was not present in John's day (cf. 3:10). Observe in particular the limited persecution in 2:10, 13. (We could compare the attempted genocide of Jews in Western Europe in recent history to the projected mass martyrdom later in the Apocalypse.) Even granting the surrealistic black and white portrayals that characterize apocalyptic genre, with its sometimes grotesque imagery, the message of the Apocalypse proper is clearly that wherever in the world that the church exists (every tribe, people, language, and nation), extreme suffering is

---

[6]G. B. Caird goes too far in making the apocalypse proper refer to the local visitations without expectation of an imminent final parousia, *Revelation*, 32. However he further explains his position when he says that John "expected the final coming of Christ to be anticipated in more limited but no less decisive visitations," ibid., 49. Those favoring the possibility of preliminary comings include: Beckwith, *Apocalypse*, 450, 460, 474; Schüssler Fiorenza, *Revelation*, 49; Mounce, *Revelation*, 88f., 98f., 111f. Also, Charles, *Revelation*, 1.44, n. 1, though his view that the letters were composed during the reign of Vespasian and later re-edited in the time of Domitian (ibid. lxxxix, xciv, 43–48) is infrequently held today by scholars, cf. Schüssler Fiorenza, "Revelation," 744.

the order of the day (cf. 7:9–14; 13:5–18, esp. vv. 7f.). The same local issues in chapters 2–3, that is of persecution (cf. 2:9f., 13) and false seductive religion (cf. 2:2, 14–16, 20–23; 3:4)—probably a form of incipient gnosticism—are immensely magnified in their geographical proportions and intensity in the balance of the book.[7]

That the Apocalypse is concerned with the whole of human-kind is evident. Phrases such as "every nation, from all tribes and peoples and languages" (7:9) abound (cf. 5:9; 7:9; 10:11; 11:9; 13:7; 14:6; 17:15). The "nations" (ἔθνη) are otherwise designated as the scene of activity for persecution, false religion, and divine interven-tion (cf. 11:2, 18; 12:5; 14:8; 15:3f.; 16:19; 18:3, 23; 19:15; 20:3, 8; 21:24, 26; 22:2). These themes are introduced in the letters within the local Asian parameters and then envisioned for much larger actualization in times ahead, in the rest of the Apocalypse. It is interesting that although the Apocalypse does not explicitly make worldwide evangelism a prerequisite for the Parousia (cf. Mark 13:10 = Matt. 24:14), this is nevertheless presupposed in the uni-versal Christian persecution (ch. 13).

It is these various factors in locality versus universality, in a way separating the letters in chapters 2–3 from the Apocalypse proper, which provide grounds for our consideration of a complementing "delay" factor in eschatological expectation of the Apocalypse.

Granting the basis for a moderated imminent expectation in the interface of the epistolary/apocalyptic structure of Revelation, we may observe the "delay" idea most sharply focused in chapter 6 and in particular in the fifth seal, verses 9–11. Here is probably a reflection of community concern with respect to delay.

> When he opened the fifth seal, I saw under the altar the souls of those who had been slaughtered for the word of God and for the testimony they had given; they cried out with a loud voice, "Sover-eign Lord, holy and true, *how long will it be* before you judge and avenge our blood on the inhabitants of the earth?" They were each given a white robe and *told to rest a little longer, until the number would be*

---

[7]On incipient gnosticism in Asian churches, cf. Swete, *Apocalypse*, 37; Schüssler Fiorenza, *Revelation*, ch. 4. Roloff, *Revelation*, 51f., who simply says "gnostic heretics." Hemer, in commenting on Rev 2:14f., posits a practical Gnostic element in Nicolaitanism, but not Gnosticism as such, *Letters*, 94. Gnosticism became full-blown in the second century. Justin Martyr speaks of professing Christians who eat things offered to idols (cf. Rev 2:14, 20) and says that their teaching is demonic. He associates them with Gnostics (*Dialogue with Trypho* 35). According to Eusebius, *Hist. eccl.* 4.18, the back-ground for the *Dialogue* is Ephesus.

complete both of their fellow servants and of their brothers and sisters, who were soon to be killed as they themselves had been killed [emphases are mine].

In response to the "how long?" (ἕως πότε) cry from the martyred souls, they are told that they must rest a little longer (ἔτι χρόνον μικρόν) before their deaths are avenged on the "earth-dwellers," verses 10f. (The "earthdwellers," οἱ κατοικοῦντες, in Revelation are those destined to suffer the eschatological judgment of God, 3:10; 8:13; cf. 13:8, 12, 14; 17:2, 8.) That which holds back the day of reckoning is the necessity of the future martyrdom (v. 11). This corresponds to the mass martyrdom in chapters 7 and 13.[8] Note the indefiniteness of the divine reply: "a little longer." This contrasts with the more definite answer to the similar question in Dan 8:13 at the time of heathen oppression. The indefinite period of waiting until further martyrdom has occurred makes for "delay," thus counter balancing imminent expectation.

The martyrdom motif surfaces in two important parenthetical sections that follow: 7:9–17 and 11:1–13. Both are part of interruptions that occur after the sixth member of a sevenfold series: 7:1–17 follows the sixth opened seal and 10:1–11:13 follows the sixth blown trumpet. In both cases one would expect the Parousia to follow with a seventh seal/trumpet blast. But instead there is an interruption with depiction of martyrdom. Consequently the delay theme in the fifth seal of 6:9–11 is reinforced. As a matter of fact, before the seventh trumpet sounds, the delay is explicit in 10:5f. with the angelic oath that the waiting period is about to end ("no more delay," ὅτι χρόνος οὐκέτι ἔσται). This is best understood as a reflection back on "a little longer," ἔτι χρόνον μικρόν, of 6:11.[9] The angelic oath seems to answer to the similar oath in Dan 12:7, where two and a half "times" had to transpire first. Here is "imminence," but in the service of answering to delay.

Confirmation of the significance of the fifth ("delay") seal is found in the observation that this seal is unique among the individual events portrayed in the seven-fold series of the seals, trumpets, and bowls (cf. also 16:1–21). All other events (usually woes, depending on how one interprets the first seal of 6:1f.)

---

[8]The desperate "how long" addressed to God resembles that found in Zech 1:12 and (apocalyptic) Dan 8:12; 12:6 (cf. 4 Ezra 4:33, 35; 6:59; *2 Bar.* 21:19; *Apoc. Ab.* 28:2). The cry is found in the psalmists' prayers: 6:3; 74:10; 80:4; 90:13; 94:3.

[9]Cf. Caird, *Revelation,* 128; Ritt, *Offenbarung,* 59.

affect the earth and/or the "earth-dwellers," but the fifth seal
concerns Christians. This fact in itself might not be too sur-
prising, since the contents of the seals derive quite obviously from
the Synoptic apocalypse or (more likely) the tradition behind it,
which includes the persecution theme (Mark 13:9–13 = Matt
24:9f. = Luke 21:12–19).[10] But even there the persecution motif
is devoid of the key "how long?" The persecution issue differs
radically in the fifth seal where the overt concern is over delay of
the final judgment rather than a warning of coming persecution
with encouragement to endure. Of course the implication for
John's communities is that they must be prepared to endure. And
ought we not to see the patience of these communities tested
further in the reply which promises additional delay of an undetermined length? At this point there is eschatological delay, not
met with the assurance of "imminence," but with further delay! In
Rev 6 John has made quite explicit the delay motif, which in the
Synoptic tradition is more inferred.

Not to be overlooked in the fifth seal is the positive significance
that delay assumes, due to the necessity of further suffering for the
"word of God." It is participation in the witness and victory of Jesus
Christ (cf. 1:5; 12:11; 15:2; also Mark 8:34–38; Phil 3:10f.).[11]

Finally, we need to remember that the delay theme in the fifth
seal is within the context of apocalyptic signs (the other opened
seals in ch. 6) which were understood to be part of the end-time
period. We clearly see such messianic woes in Jewish apocalyptic
(surveyed earlier). For this reason the Synoptists were led to qualify
expectation with "the end is not yet" when presenting such signs.
Likewise, in Rev 6 we have a clear instance of the dialectic between
eschatological expectation and delay.[12]

---

[10] Charles, *Revelation,* 1.158– 60, charts parallel ideas between the Synoptics and Revelation; cf. Lohmeyer, *Offenbarung,* 58f.; Vos, *Synoptic Traditions,*
181–92; Court, *Myth,* 50, 75. Court believes that the "how long" of Rev 6:10
derives from Zech 1:12, even as the horses in the first four seals are taken
from Zech 6:1ff., ibid., 58.

[11] I owe the insight to Bauckham, "Delay," 31, 36.

[12] In seeking to understand the "delay" motif in Revelation, we need to
ask at what chronological point within the sequence of visions does John
stand when he addresses the communities. If he is at the point of the sixth
trumpet and sixth bowl (9:13–21 and 16:12–16) and the announcement of
"no more delay" in 10:6, then the "delay" must be essentially in the past and
the time left very short, apparently Vielhauer, "Apocalyptic," 624, who has
Domitian as the eighth king in 17:11 and the beast of 11:7 and 17:8, cf.

The Asian Community Situation

The communities are threatened with persecution from without and heterodoxy from within. This is similar to what we discovered in examining the community situations addressed by the Evangelists. If John wrote toward the end of the first century, by that time the problem of a delayed parousia would likely have compounded the threat, if not partially explained it (cf. 2 Pet 3:3–13). Sixty or more years would have passed from the time of the earthly Jesus. Certainly a near-expectation is understandable from the prophetic voice of John. John's prophecy from the risen Lord was intended to meet the particular needs of the congregations in Asia

---

Bauckham, "Delay," 35f. I believe it is correct to place the reign of the beast in the time of the sixth trumpet/bowl. But is this *Sitz im Leben* for the Apocalypse? For the following reasons this is questionable.

(1) John devotes much attention to events leading up to the Parousia and final judgment. The eschaton is underway (cf. "the time is near," e.g., 22:10), but to place John at the point of anticipating the seventh trumpet puts strain on his statement that the "prophecy" pertains to "what you have seen, what is, and what is to take place after this" (1:19). The directness of the prologue, letters, and epilogue does not lend itself to chapters 4–22 being a prophecy after the event.

(2) Similarly, the most natural way to understand 17:10f. is for the "present" (6th) king to be reigning when John writes. This would mean that a short reigning king (the 7th) is yet to come, before the beast takes over. In this case John foresees the great tribulation ahead in the not-too-distant future, but the length of time in between is indefinite. Identifying the seven kings is a problem with varied answers having been proposed, cf. Caird, *Revelation,* 217–19, who takes seven here to be symbolical; Ladd, *Revelation,* 228–31, takes the seven to represent seven kingdoms.

(3) Although we have good reason for recognizing a partial first-century fulfillment of the seals series of ch. 6 (discussed earlier with the synoptic apocalypse), we have much less reason to say the same for the effects of the trumpet and bowl woes. Much of the earth's surface is destroyed (8:7), a fair portion of humankind suffers disease and death (9:5f., 10, 15, 19; 16:2, 10f., cf. 8). Even allowing for the hyperbole of apocalyptic language, it is questionable whether such magnitude of calamities was occurring in Asia Minor or elsewhere.

(4) The severity of persecution in Asia seems to have been what the church more or less had always expected. Certainly the mass suffering described in the Apocalypse was not on the scene.

Returning to the fifth (delay) seal of 6:9–11, I conclude that it is to be understood as reflecting a genuine "delay" concern on the part of the church. I judge it is from this standpoint that John writes, cf. Court, *Myth,* 77. The woes of wrath are to be anticipated, but the time is indefinite.

at that time. To accomplish this he appropriately reckons with the challenge of eschatological delay.[13]

When we remember that the development of "delay" in the Pauline and synoptic apocalypses was prompted (at least in part) by a false eschatological enthusiasm (2 Thess 2:1–3a; Mark 13:5f., 21 and parallels), the presence of a "delay" motif in Revelation becomes all the more interesting, since there is apparently no comparable problem that John is addressing. (This could partially account for the more direct expressions of "imminence" than we have found elsewhere.) John seems to desire to rekindle expectation. To do so he must reckon with delay. Particularly revealing is the Sardis community which has need of an awakened parousia hope (3:1–3). But John knows that worse days lie ahead. A temporal gap of unknown duration lies between the situation wherein Satan has a foothold and the godly are enduring, on one hand, and where Satan's forces of the beast and false prophet are defeated, on the other (cf. 19:17–21). In his prophetic ministry John thus also provides a theological framework for understanding delay that is yet ahead.

As we have found elsewhere in the Apocalypse, near-expectation and delay are held in dynamic tension. If anything, the tension has been heightened in the Apocalypse.[14]

---

[13] Cf. Kealy, *Apocalypse,* 156.

[14] "Delay" may possibly be recognized in various other ways in the Apocalypse. For example in 7:1 the afflicting winds are held in restraint until the 144,000 are sealed (cf. v. 4). Also, following the arresting announcement of "no more delay" (10:5f.) between the sixth and seventh trumpets, there apparently *is* more delay, since the seventh trumpet is reserved for a later time period ("in the days," 10:7; cf. 11:14f.), cf. Bauckham, "Delay," 35f., who sees John adding the mission of the church in 11:1–13 to accent the "imminence-delay" tension within which the church must live.

Part Four: Conclusion
and Challenge for Today

11

REVIEW AND CONCLUSIONS

IN THIS STUDY WE HAVE SURVEYED MANY DOCUMENTS WHICH reflect eschatological expectation of various groups or communities from possibly before the monarchical era in ancient Israel to at least the end of the first century A.D. We have moved from focusing on the prophetic literature of the OT, to literature incorporating apocalyptic ideas in early and later Judaism, to apocalyptic eschatology in the NT. Consequently our approach thus far has been mainly historical and literary in exploring backgrounds of NT apocalyptic expectation. It now remains for us to ask the question, "So what?" Might our conclusions inform us for a meaningful hope at the close of the twentieth century?

We will first summarize conclusions from the foregoing discussion and draw inferences. Then we will consider implications for a contemporary biblical hope. The latter is of course a much more subjective matter. Conclusions here will depend to a great extent upon one's philosophical and theological orientation.

Review of Critical Eras

In my opinion the most striking features of the biblical hope are its unique origin in ancient Israel and then its persistent development throughout the centuries of biblical history. Despite national subjugation and a failure of expectation to be wholly realized, Israel's faith abides and reaches its final expression (from a Christian viewpoint) in both fulfillment and expectation of the hope in the NT.

(1) The Davidic-Solomonic era was decisive in forming Israel's "golden age" hope (cf. 2 Sam 7; 1 Kgs 4:20f.). Despite failures, this model of a successful monarchy, national prosperity, and triumph over enemy nations was to become definitive for Israel's hope in

later generations. This is especially evident in the hope message of the prophets, which included blessing for other nations as well.

(2) Following the Jerusalem crisis of the sixth century, details of a predicted national and spiritual restoration after exile come more into focus. At the same time fulfillment of the prophetic hope is seen as "near" in some sense, particularly in Jeremiah, Ezekiel, and Isaiah 40ff. Jeremiah's seventy-year prophecy (29:10-14; cf. 25:11-14) evidently had great impact on Israel's imminent expectation/delayed hope in later times. In Ezekiel the eschatological temple is uniquely featured as part of the messianic era, and in visionary form that anticipates apocalyptic eschatology.

(3) In the so-called post-exilic era, the tension between imminent expectation and a reckoning with a delayed fulfillment of the prophetic hope becomes more prominent (Hag, Zech, Mal and possibly Isa 56-66). Partial fulfillment of the prophetic hope is realized in the return of a remnant from captivity. The eschatological temple is anticipated. The surrounding nations are to be both subservient to Israel and sharing in the blessings of the messianic era. Especially in Zech 1-6 there is further expression of the visionary character of the apocalyptic genre.

(4) At least by the second century B.C. apocalyptic eschatology clearly comes into vogue, as the prophetic tradition is seen to have taken a radical turn (e.g., 1 Enoch's ten-week apocalypse). The Maccabean crisis becomes pivotal in affecting Israel's eschatological expectation in the second century and apparently afterward (cf. Dan 7-12). From a canonical viewpoint, in Daniel there is a partial fulfillment of predicted end time events in the Maccabean crisis. The result for future generations is expectation, but also of necessity a reckoning with delay, given the consummate character of the Danielic expectation. At times expectation in documents includes an earthly messianic era and the eschatological temple. Israel's enemies and/or the ungodly are often seen as judged by God, preceded by woes of the end-time period.

(5) For the early church, with the coming of Christ, his resurrection, and the gift of the Spirit, there is fulfillment of the prophetic hope, but "the end is not yet" (cf. Mark 13:7 = Matt 24:6; cf. Luke 21:9). Near-expectation is balanced with an implicit theology of delay. The nations receive the gospel and the enemies of God and his people are judged.

(6) For Christian communities later in the first century, "delay" appears alongside fervent apocalyptic expectation (Revelation) and helps to explain the manner in which expectation is encouraged

(Matt 24f.; Luke 21). The destruction of Jerusalem in 70 A.D. no doubt contributed to expectation but eventually to the quandary of delay (clearly in 4 Ezra and *2 Bar.*). The enemies of God and his people will eventually be judged. In the contemporary Jewish literature examined there is the dialectic of expectation and accommodation to delay from the standpoint of the apocalyptists. However in the NT documents fulfillment has occurred in Christ, and so hope for the consummation seems more fervent than in Jewish apocalyptic. This makes the delay motif all the more significant for us to consider.

Throughout the literature reviewed in our study, there is the tension between near-expectation and accommodation to delay in fulfillment of the hope. This hope progresses from an earthly hope at first, centered in a redeemed Israel, to a hope that eventually gives place to a heavenly, otherworldly fulfillment in the new age. However at times an earthly and heavenly future life are seen in the same documents (e.g., *1 Enoch* 90:20–39 with 91:15–17; 4 Ezra 7:26–31 with vv. 31–35; *2 Bar.* 29:1–8 with 44:9–15). Rev 2:26–28 and 20:1–6 with 21:1–22:15 might be pondered in this connection. At other times there seems to be an earth-centered hope, but within the incorruptibility of the new age (e.g., *T. Mos.* 10; *2 Bar.* 74:1–3; cf. Matt 19:27–30).

The hope progresses from a focus on: 1) Israel, to 2) a redeemed Israel and the nations, to 3), what may called a new Israel that *includes* the redeemed of the nations (e.g., Rev 7:9–12; cf. Gal 3:28f.). It is noteworthy that the eschatological temple becomes Christ and the people of God in the NT (John 2:19–22; 1 Cor 3:16f.; Eph 2:20–22), and in Rev 21:22 the Almighty and the Lamb are the temple. The enemies of God are not so much those against ethnic Israel, but those contrary to and against God's people in terms of the new Israel. It is these who are to be judged in the end. (This understanding is foreshadowed in the remnant or "true" Israel idea in Isaiah especially.) Thus progression in development of the eschatological hope is evident.

A Comparison of Expectation in Jewish and Early Christian Apocalyptic

This topic is very important as we tackle the question of the apocalyptic origins of early Christianity.[1] Similarities which we have

---

[1] For Käsemann's famous assertion of apocalyptic being the mother of Christianity, see above, ch. 2, n. 1.

already observed between these two literatures in eschatological expectation call for a summary analysis. Helpfully, both literatures point to a fairly wide geographical and/or ideological representation of thought as follows:

First, in Jewish apocalyptic we have a variety of ideas ranging over approximately three hundred years in what is probably Palestinian, and for the most part Hasidic, Judaism. But Hellenistic (Egyptian?) Judaism is also a locus of thought in the Sibylline Oracles.

Second, it is true that the eschatology of early Christian (NT) apocalyptic surveyed seems less diverse, and the authorship is more restricted chronologically. But the probable geographical spread of communities addressed is great: Palestine-Syria for Matthew; Greece for 2 Thessalonians (assuming Pauline authorship); Rome probably for Mark; Asia for Revelation. (Luke is more problematic.)

Thus in different ways the respective literatures appear to be associated with a substantial part of Judaism and of early Christianity.

(1) Similarities between Jewish and early Christian apocalyptic include the following:

(a) A near-expectation/delay tension. This is commonly related to divine sovereignty over human affairs. In Jewish apocalyptic, near-expectation as an answer to delay is apparently seen in the periodization of history in the guise of prophecy. Divine sovereignty is commonly seen in other ways in Christian apocalyptic.

(b) Human contingency in determining the arrival of the anticipated kingdom. In Jewish literature this at times is seen in the call to repentance that the days of blessing may come. Though not aired earlier in our study, this likely has some relation to the call to repentance in the Baptist's mission and of course the mission of Jesus (Matt 3:2; 4:17 and parallels). At least on the individual level, if not nationally, repentance becomes a condition for experience of kingdom blessings. Likewise the human factor is pertinent in Peter's repentance exhortation in his Acts 3 sermon (vv. 19–21) and also in the explanation of delay in 2 Pet 3:9, cf. vv. 3–8).[2] In the synoptic apocalypse there is the preaching of the gospel in all the world (esp. Matt 24:14), which must imply faithfulness to the commission to proclaim the good news throughout the world (cf. 28:18–20). A human contingency is then apparent here as well.

---

[2] The repentance motif for delay of judgment is found also in Jesus' teaching in Luke 13:6–9, as Jeremias, *Theology*, 140f., points out. Jeremias relates this to the possibility of God repenting in Jer 18:7–10.

(c) Belief that the arrival of the new age will be preceded by a time of eschatological woes: apostasy, tribulation of the godly, and natural, physical, and social calamities.

(d) Reinterpretation of earlier sources to meet community needs. This is to be observed in the salvation motifs of Isa 40ff. when compared to the earlier expression of them in chapters 1–39. We clearly see such use of sources in Dan 9, which is a reinterpretation of the Jer 29 prediction. The latter chapters of Daniel are (most likely) updated in the *Testament of Moses;* in Revelation (esp. chs. 13; 17); in 2 Thess 2; and even more explicitly in the synoptic apocalypse and 4 Ezra 12:10–25. As indicated at several points earlier in our study, Daniel was important and widely used in the formulation of eschatological events in both Jewish and early Christian apocalyptic. But given the Maccabean setting of Daniel, it is the re-use of Daniel that is significant. Our research has exposed the likely fresh interpretation and adaptation of texts to new historical situations within Jewish apocalyptic. We have seen this for example in our earlier discussion of the ten-week apocalypse in *1 Enoch* (93:1–10; 91:12–17), in a first century use of second century texts in Book 3 of the *Sibylline Oracles,* and in Qumran's use of the OT—we especially noted the Habakkuk Commentary. The same updating of texts occurs in both extra-biblical Jewish apocalyptic and in canonical Scripture, notably Daniel's use of Jeremiah.[3] It is also noteworthy that in both the pseudepigraphical and canonical literatures the canonical Daniel is more prominent than any other single document as a source for explaining eschatological expectation. Daniel relays the prophetic hope of Jeremiah in midrashic form; and then Daniel (or possibly at times the tradition behind Daniel) becomes

---

[3] Even though for doctrinal purposes a distinction is made between canonical and non-canonical literatures, it is important to keep in mind that early Christianity was born in a religious environment that was informed by Jewish apocalyptic generally, not only immediately by Daniel. Direct witness to this is seen in Jude 14, which refers to *1 Enoch* 1:9. Also, Jude 9 may refer to a lost ending of the *Testament of Moses,* cf. Bauckham, *Jude,* 67–76. Further evidence comes from the preservation of Jewish apocalyptic writings in Christian circles, as seen in early Patristic references, cf. Russell, *Method,* 33–35, 66–69. Extant versions of various Jewish apocalyptic documents in Greek, Latin, Syriac, Ethiopic, Coptic, Armenian, Arabic, and Slavonic also testify to early Christian interest in Jewish apocalyptic. Apocalyptic ideas such as the two ages, the messianic woes, and the messianic kingdom are developed and provided a background for NT Christianity, notwithstanding significant differences in Christian apocalyptic.

the basis more than any other document for the renewal of expectation in subsequent literature.

(2) We now look at differences between Jewish and early Christian apocalyptic.

Naturally the most obvious and fundamental difference is that in Christian apocalyptic eschatological hope has been and is yet to be realized in Jesus Christ. Beyond this there are at least four telling differences, the first of which we shall explore in some detail.

(a) The near-expectation of early Christian apocalyptic corresponds to a more real and urgent expectation than is generally found in Jewish apocalyptic. The expectation has a ring that leads us to believe it is more than simply an author's way of coping with delay. We see this in a variety of ways.

The "delay" motif in 2 Thessalonians and the synoptic apocalypse serves to diminish over-expectation in the face of an enthusiastic false near-expectation. There is no evidence of a similar situation in Jewish apocalyptic.

There is less stress on divine determinism in Christian apocalyptic, than in Jewish writings. In the latter it is seemingly to answer the delay question. This suggests somewhat less need to sustain expectation in the face of delay with Christian expectation.

The prominence of a "vigilance" motif in Christian apocalyptic, including Revelation, and its complete absence in extant Jewish works, as far as I can see, speaks rather strongly for a more strident expectation in early Christianity. (Absence of the theme in 2 Thessalonians is understandable, given the circumstances that necessitated the letter.) Judging from Revelation, we find expectation very keen at the end of the first century on the part of John and possibly one or two communities. This is significant, since we have found reason to believe that non-fulfillment of the new age/parousia hope after 70 A.D. affected not only Judaism, but to some extent early Christianity as well.

(b) Instead of stressing that "signs" belong to the end, as in Jewish apocalyptic (e.g., *1 Enoch* 91:6–19; 99:4–10; *Sib. Or.* 3:61–92; 4 Ezra 4:50–5:13; 6:17–28; *2 Bar.* 25:1–4; 72:1f.), the Synoptic apocalypse at times more overtly minimizes the eschatological import of signs. This is part of the attempt to moderate expectation. In Jewish apocalyptic the aim was more to keep expectation alive.[4]

---

[4]In not finding eschatological signs elsewhere in Jesus' message, Kümmel concludes they are from apocalyptic tradition and not from Jesus, *Promise*, 102–4. However, Kümmel appears to overlook that here Jesus to a great extent revamps the common *apocalyptic* use of such signs.

(c) While early Christianity employs explanations of eschatological delay similar to those found in Judaism (see comparisons above), such delay assumes a *positive* role in Christian apocalyptic, beyond anything in Jewish documents. This is evident in the gospel mission, clearly in the Synoptic apocalypse and at least implicit in Revelation, in that all tribes, tongues, and peoples hear the gospel before the end (cf. 2 Pet 3:9). Similarly, as we also saw earlier in Revelation, Christian suffering in the "delay" period of 6:10 may be understood to take on a positive significance in that it is participation in the witness and victory of Jesus Christ. It is noteworthy that in the Synoptic apocalypse and perhaps in Rev 11 suffering and martyrdom is the result of the gospel mission. This difference from Jewish apocalyptic of delay having a positive purpose is anchored in the christological character of NT apocalyptic, as is our next observation.

(d) The NT church was conscious of a realized eschatology in addition to its hope for the Parousia. In Luke–Acts the sense of a delayed parousia is especially before us, but it is here that we most fully see a *present* kingdom/salvation theology developed. It is because the kingdom *has* come that the Christian community is to be active in mission during the interim before the Parousia. Thus Luke says much about the gift of the Spirit, who energizes the church to fulfill Christ's mission before the Parousia. This NT distinctive of a realized eschatology (cf. Matt 12:28; Rom 8:23; 2 Cor 1:21f.; Eph 1:13f.; Col 1:13) is the best explanation of the imminent expectation that existed in the early church. It is also manifestly the best explanation of the positive role which eschatological delay could and did assume in early Christian expectation. Perhaps the closest we come in Jewish documents is the Teacher of Righteousness and the "new covenant" community at Qumran. But early Christianity goes far beyond Qumran in awareness of a Christ who has come, who has been raised, and who is presently active in the world through his people who have his Spirit. He would "soon" complete his redemptive work in the age to come. "The last event has already begun, precipitated by the life, death and resurrection of Jesus."[5]

Given the above data from our primary sources, we have to say that apocalypticism was certainly a useful vehicle through which to express eschatological expectation, and distinctive themes in

---

[5] Quote is from Barrett, "Eschatology," 150; cf. Dunn, *Jesus,* 317. Ladd, *Presence,* 99–101, observes generally an ethical passivity and loss of the prophetic tension between history and eschatology in Jewish apocalyptic, in contrast to biblical apocalyptic.

apocalypticism were at times found to be congruous with an end-time scenario. But it was the transforming Christ event, including especially his resurrection, as well as the subsequent experience of the Spirit, which must more fundamentally explain the apocalyptic hope as expressed by the earliest Christians. Therefore it is going too far to say that apocalyptic was the "mother" of Christianity.[6] Crucial distinctives inherent within early Christianity make a "mother/ child" relationship between Jewish apocalyptic and early Christian hope untenable.

A Historical-Critical Conclusion

With the continuing non-fulfillment of the Parousia, did early Christianity, as seen in the NT, experience such a crisis of faith that its theological direction in the ensuing centuries was profoundly affected? This has been one explanation for the development of Christian doctrine in the post-apostolic period.[7]

We have already seen that Judaism consistently accommodated itself to the problem of eschatological delay. In fact the expectation motif at times appears to be one way of coping with delay. Expectation was encouraged in that at particular critical times in the history of Israel there was partial fulfillment, notably in the return of the remnant in the sixth century and again in the successes of the Maccabean era.[8] At Qumran expectation was heightened with the "new covenant" community and the Teacher of Righteousness.

---

[6]Cf. p. 153, n. 1 above.

[7]Cf. Werner, *Formation*, e.g., 44, 46; Grässer, *Problem*, 178, 219. Note discussion in Berkouwer, *Return*, 66–76, of "consistent eschatology," a position that holds Jesus only taught a near-expectation and that the church subsequently had to modify this. Bauckham, "Delay," 3, n. 1, says the "hypothesis of a *crisis* [emphasis his] of delay in early Christianity" is now "generally abandoned." However, Grässer's book was reissued in 1977.

[8]The Maccabean era included a high point under the rule of Simon (142–134), when eschatological expectation within Judaism was probably heightened. According to 1 Macc 14:4–15 "the land had rest all the days of Simon," v. 4; "he extended the borders of his nation, and gained full control of the country," v. 6; "he established peace in the land and Israel rejoiced with great joy," v. 11; "he made the sanctuary glorious," v. 15. But especially telling is v. 12: "All the people sat under their own vines and fig trees, and there was none to make them afraid." This corresponds exactly with Mic 4:4 in describing the messianic era (cf. Zech 3:10). On such successes of the Maccabean era, cf. Russell, *Jews*, 60– 62, 69f.

Thus, given the Jewish background of early Christianity, the non-fulfillment of the Parousia in one sense was not a new problem. If Judaism could hold to an "imminence-delay" tension, so could this new messianic Judaism. Our examination of pertinent NT documents reveals that just such a tension was held by the NT authors and doubtless reflected teaching within the leadership of early Christianity. From another angle, if Judaism could reinterpret traditional texts in the face of new challenge, so could Christianity continue to make sense of the teaching of Jesus in later times. And this is in fact what we see happening, as the NT authors accommodate the message of Jesus to their communities, while maintaining expectation of the Parousia.

Furthermore, there was a fulfillment of eschatological hope beyond what had been experienced in Judaism—the dynamism of the Christ event and gift of the Spirit.[9] Therefore delay as a theological concern might be expected to be more entrenched in Judaism. The Jewish documents show more concern for consoling and reassuring than does the NT. If at least a part of Judaism managed to maintain an apocalyptic hope during the first century A.D., it is much more likely that Christianity generally would have survived without serious crisis. This does not mean that delay was of no concern within Christian communities, especially after the destruction of Jerusalem by the Romans. But it was hardly a situation that would have precipitated a radical reformulation of theology because of crisis.[10]

---

[9] Schillebeeckx, *Jesus,* 543, says that although the delay of the Parousia "did result in a crisis of a sort, fundamentally what Jesus' resurrection supplied was the irrevocable guarantee of the coming Parousia; so that for the Christians nothing essential was altered by this circumstance; it simply made plainer and more obvious the tension between 'already' and 'not yet,' between a presential and a futurist eschatology." Schillebeeckx believes that initially "Christians interpreted Jesus' resurrection as the start of his immediately subsequent Parousia," ibid., 542f.; cf. Pannenberg, *Jesus,* 106, 108.

[10] The presence of Jewish apocalyptic ideas as a background for early Christian eschatology was more significant than is often recognized.

12

SOME CONCLUSIONS FOR
FAITH AND PRACTICE

Hermeneutical Implications

We come now to consider what difference our findings make for the Christian church today.

The most obvious but also the most difficult task is to determine the contemporary relevance of biblical eschatological imminence. For Paul (as for other NT authors) the time had grown "short" (e.g., 1 Cor 7:29), but for us it has grown "very long."[1] After 2000 years how can we hold to "imminent expectation"? If so, do we have sufficient grounds for doing so, apart from or in addition to reasons for which the first-century church held to imminent expectation? Ought we to be characterized by an imminent expectation as was the early church?

These are questions that have elicited a variety of responses.[2] It seems to me that three approaches have been prominent in contemporary reflection.

(1) Surrender of a parousia hope in any literal sense, since it did not occur as predicted by Jesus and/or the early church. Such hope may be transposed into a present existential reality.[3] Or it may simply be abandoned altogether.

---

[1] The aphorism is from Beker, *Apocalyptic,* 115.

[2] For a variety of scholarly contemporary responses, cf. Willis, *Kingdom of God.*

[3] Notably Bultmann, *History,* esp. ch. 10. He concludes the book with: "Always in your present lies the meaning in history. . . . In every moment slumbers the possibility of being the eschatological moment. You must awaken it." Perrin has slightly modified Bultmann's approach in speaking of

(2) Retention of a parousia hope, but granting that Jesus and/ or the early church were wrong in their near-expectation, or at best, subject to an incomplete understanding of the chronological issue.[4]

(3) Holding to a parousia hope, including imminent expectation, but simply not reckoning very seriously with the NT data that point to imminent expectation in the early church. Rather, many of those with this position think of imminence almost solely in light of current events today. This might be dubbed "pop theology" and is a common viewpoint among many earnest Christians.

Another option emerges from our study, a variation of the second option above. There is an indefiniteness that is part of the "delay" motif in biblical expectation and which exists in tension with eschatological anticipation. This allows the mystery of God's sovereignty to have the final say. In this case we are speaking of "anticipation," a nuanced or low-keyed form of "imminence." In one sense the Parousia has always been "imminent" in that within any generation it *could* come.[5] On the other hand, the NT data seem to present early Christian imminent expectation as believing the end *would* come in the near future. But it is precisely this expectation which exists in polarity with indefiniteness and delay. In various ways in biblical eschatology (as well as extracanonical Jewish apocalyptic) there is an interplay between the human factors that make for indefiniteness/delay, on one hand, and near-expectation on the other (cf. esp. Jer 18:5–11; Acts 3:19–21). If we are to apply a biblical eschatology to today's church, we need to include this dialectic in our present day application of biblical futuristic eschatology.[6]

---

the kingdom of God as that which every man experiences "in his own time," *Jesus,* especially 197–99; quote is 198f.

[4]Many scholars who take the near-expectation statements as from Jesus assume him to have been mistaken at this point. Cf. Beasley-Murray, *Last Days,* 448, but who recently has altered his personal view of this interpretation of Mark 13:30 in light of further critical consideration, 448f., 456.

[5]Ladd, *Presence,* 338f. calls for a "dynamic sense of imminence" in the present day church in order to preserve its true character. Speaking of Paul's apocalyptic hope, Beker, *Apocalyptic,* 114f., observes that Paul's imminent hope cannot be duplicated by us in the twentieth century *in the same manner.* The passage of time prevents us from doing so (emphasis mine.) However he believes that Paul's hope has a "catalytic" meaning for us, which includes a *"concrete occurrence* of God's final incursion into history" (emphasis his). He also helpfully says that "the delay of the parousia" motivates us "to discern God's radical transcendence over all our wishes and expectations," 120.

[6]Contrary to this, there is a revival of post-millennial eschatology which understands the apocalyptic end-time ideas to have been fulfilled in the first

In holding to the integrity of a biblical hope that has yet to reach finality, it may be helpful to remember that fulfillment of earlier prophecies was experienced at critical points: the "post-exilic" return; the Maccabean success (in light of a canonical Daniel's predictions); the advent of Jesus, his resurrection, and gift of the Spirit; "messianic woes" and the destruction of Jerusalem; and preliminary "comings" in Rev 2.[7] Beyond the canon we can point to the eschatological signs in history since the NT era. The other side of this is that it has been the ongoing delay in a consummate fulfillment of the hope in any given age that has led to an ongoing contemporizing of relevant biblical texts and further expectation. This was true in the biblical eras and has understandably been the case in the church since.

There are other hermeneutical implications that are related to the above primary consideration.

(1) The re-use of eschatological texts by biblical authors in the face of a lack of consummate fulfillment can be a model for us. We would not wish to claim the same divine authority as we attribute to the inspired authors of Scripture. But at the same time relevant texts can point to what we might yet expect. For example, fulfillment of the mandate for universal preaching of the gospel can yet be viewed as a preliminary to the second coming of Christ, though I doubt that Christians will be in a position to say authoritatively just when such fulfillment will have occurred. Nor are we in a position to say exactly how soon after the fulfillment of that mandate that Christ will return. In the same way, we have justification for expecting evil

---

century, except for the return of Christ; e.g., "dominion theology" in Chilton, *Paradise Restored,* esp. chs. 10–23. Proponents apparently seek to relieve the imminence/delay tension, which I see as biblical. I believe that a more authentic handling of the overall biblical data makes this approach untenable. However, to its credit it otherwise does reckon with NT apocalyptic in its historical context. Dominion eschatology fits hand in glove with Reconstructionism, which envisions a return to OT civil law and government in the millennium, cf. Bahnson, *Theonomy*; for a critique, Barron, *Heaven on Earth?* In view of the progressive nature of biblical eschatology, this also is hermeneutically suspect.

[7]Cf. Williams, *Renewal,* 3.309–12. However for an interpretation that does not see Matt. 10:23; 16:28; 24:30 and 26:63 (the last three with parallels) exhausted within the first century, especially with the destruction of Jerusalem in A.D. 70, cf. Holman, "Imminent Parousia," esp. 20–31; Ladd, *Presence,* 320–25, who speaks of the tension in the prophetic perspective between "the imminent historical" and "the indeterminate eschatological event." On coalescing of the near and the distant in the NT, Berkouwer, *Return,* 82–95.

to permeate the existing order, and at last, consummate evil. We may well say that such is yet to be expressed in ways that have been foreshadowed in the anti-god superman of Daniel's Maccabean scenario and in the "beast" of Revelation, which is seen there in an ancient Roman context.[8] In this case current "apocalyptic" events thus become signs of the times and point to the finale that is still ahead.[9]

(2) Biblical reinterpretation of texts in new historical contexts warns us against envisioning a reconstructed ancient geographical, ethnic, or cultural context for end-time events.[10] Even as the anti-god figure of Daniel and later the "beast" in Revelation moves from being Greek to Roman, so a final cultural manifestation of the evil personage could be different yet. There is no need for a revival of the Roman empire in any sense for the apocalyptic event of Rev 17 to transpire. For the same reason there is no need for a Jewish temple to be reconstructed to fulfill what 2 Thess 2 essentially anticipates in the ultimate blasphemy against God before the Parousia of verse 8.

(3) In view of the progressive character of biblical theology, those eschatological texts that are most explicitly related to Christ's redemptive activity are our most appropriate guide in applying the ancient text to the contemporary scene. Since fulfillment of the OT hope is climaxed in the redemptive work of Jesus Christ, it is retrograde to anticipate a nationalistic literal fulfillment of that hope, with earthly limitations of death (e.g., Isa 65:20), on the basis of OT texts.[11] The NT usually interprets that hope in more universal and transcendental dimensions.[12]

---

[8] For apt words on the typological relationship of such Danielic eschatological themes, see Goldingay's comment on Daniel 9 in our ch. 2, n. 20.

[9] Cf. Cullmann, *Salvation,* 292–313, esp. 301f. "Everything happening in our time, which is already the end time, is an omen of the end," ibid., 309; Ladd, *Presence,* 326f. For our discernment of the times, the Holy Spirit "helps us in the interpretation of Scripture which is performed in the context of the Church and with the means of scholarship given to us by God," Cullmann, *Salvation,* 301.

[10] Cf. Beker, who speaks of preserving the "abiding center" of Paul's apocalyptic gospel, while differentiating from what is contingent and time-conditioned, *Apocalyptic,* 105f.

[11] A "progressive dispensationalism" appears to allow more room for a progressive reinterpretation of prophetic and apocalyptic texts than has been usual within dispensational eschatology, cf. Blaising, *Progressive Dispensationalism,* 293f.

[12] Luke comes closest to retaining a more nationalistic garb for the OT hope, particularly in the birth narratives (Luke 1:31–33, 67–79; cf. 21:24;

(4) This brings us to the question of apocalyptic language to express the Christian hope. All language in a given age is of necessity tempered by categories and terms that grow out of the life and culture of those speaking and those addressed. In our case we have timeless theological concepts that must be presented in specific time-bound cultural contexts within biblical history. (For example a first-century cosmology more easily would allow for stars falling to earth, cf. Rev 6:13.) The inspired conveyors of divine truth must receive the message and then speak it in a language that is suited to their times. Beyond this is the problem anyway of conveying heavenly realities of the age to come to those of us whose lives are circumscribed by the present age. Therefore, given the great gap between heavenly and earthly realities, we must reckon with metaphor in religious language. The extent to which religious language is metaphorical is a matter of debate among theologians. This is the challenge for properly interpreting the apocalyptic categories and language of the ancient biblical documents.[13] We must allow breadth for the manner in which biblical prophecies may yet be fulfilled. It is not too much to say that all language, including that of apocalyptic, undoubtedly falls short of describing the ultimate realization of God's triumph and glory.

On the other hand we ought not to evacuate the biblical hope of its essential meaning that God will eventually triumph in human history in a climactic way through Jesus Christ. The fact that the eschaton has already arrived in the resurrection of Jesus Christ lays the cornerstone of an apocalyptic realism that we can expect to be consummated in terms of the biblical hope of a final parousia of Christ.[14]

Challenge for Praxis

Finally, we come to very practical implications of NT hope. The message of the NT is that the people of God are to live out their lives

---

22:29–30). This may be because his purpose is to show the continuity of the true (new) Judaism with the OT hope (e.g., 3:17–21, 25f.). His language at certain points approximates closely the terms of the OT hope. Elsewhere in Luke–Acts he assumes a more universal and transcendental eschatology (cf. Luke 18:29f.; 21:34f.; Acts 17:30f.).

[13] On language of biblical apocalyptic, Williams, *Renewal*, 3.312f. For broader discussion of the issue cf. Caird, *Language*, ch. 14; Dunn, "Demythologizing," 300f.

[14] Cf. Pannenberg, *Jesus*, 106–8.

in light of this hope (e.g., 2 Pet 3:11–13). Thus Christians ought to ask themselves whether or not their lives are different because of this hope. There is no room for ethical or spiritual passivity. Christians ought to be modeling the new thing God will do and for which they live in hope.

By their involvement in the very real needs of humankind today, Christians represent in the world the Christ who makes all things new. So far from being a reason to ignore the social concerns and struggles that belong to this world's alienations and sorrows, Christian hope should lead believers to display the concern of a God who saves and recreates.

Through the ministry of spiritual gifts Christians reflect the powers of the age to come (cf. Heb 6:4f.). Through a mission that includes "signs and wonders" toward the needy without, powers of the future kingdom are made manifest (cf. Rom 15:18f.).[15] Through the variety of Spirit manifestations within communities of faith, assurance of final redemption is made all the more sure (Rom 8:23; 2 Cor 1:21; 5:5). But first a contemporary awareness of the church's location in the line of redemptive history from the resurrection of Christ to the Parousia may help to revive the workings of the Spirit in congregations where these have been marginalized.[16]

Because world evangelization is linked to the arrival of final victory in the coming of Jesus Christ, world mission in the present time takes on eschatological significance.[17] In particular the coming to faith in Jesus as the Christ on the part of the Jewish people is a sign of the last times, according to Romans 11, especially verses 25–27. While the time of the end always remains in the sovereign and inscrutable counsels of God, present day believers have the mysterious and amazing challenge to participate in the arrival of God's triumph in the world through proclamation of the gospel throughout the world. In a way known only to God, the time of the

---

[15] Cf. Moltmann, *Spirit,* 188–92: "If, in the light of Easter, God's Spirit is experienced as the Spirit of the resurrection of the dead, then the healings experienced should be understood as foretokens of that resurrection and of eternal life," 189.

[16] Cullmann, *Christ,* 144, cf. 155; Dunn, *Jesus,* 310–12; Williams, *Renewal,* 3.298, helpfully observes that active participation in the charismata encourages eschatological expectation.

[17] Cullmann, *Christ,* 157, calls this the "unique character of the present," in that *"this missionary proclamation of the Church . . . gives to the period between Christ's resurrection and Parousia its meaning for redemptive history; and it has this meaning through its connection with Christ's present Lordship"* (emphasis his).

grand triumph of God in history is both within his sovereign ordering of history and within the contingency of human obedience to the commission.

There is the challenge of maintaining expectation after twenty centuries of non-fulfillment of the Parousia. The problem of the delayed Parousia has been critical in NT studies. Various approaches have been taken to solve the problem.[18] Whatever the answer, and perhaps only God finally knows, we have seen that delay assumes a positive character in NT expectation. It is the church's time for mission. It is the time for participation in the sufferings of Christ, that we might share in his resurrection victory also.[19] For the many who suffer physically for their Christian witness, even unto death, in various nations of the world today, such suffering speaks of living for a cause that is greater than ourselves.

We conclude with where we began in our Introduction. Eschatological expectation is at the core of NT faith. If twentieth- and twenty-first-century Christians are to be "Christian" in the true sense of that word, they too must be motivated and guided by the end of all things—that which gives significance to everyday life while living between the times, between Christ's resurrection and his coming again.[20] The time of the end is known only to God. In the meantime let us who are Christians be awake and pray: "Thy kingdom come!"

---

[18] Cf. Moltmann, *Future,* 36–40.

[19] Cf. ibid., 39: "We ought to solve the problem through a theology of the cross." Moltmann speaks extensively of the theology of the cross in his *The Crucified God;* note esp. 65–81, 187–99.

[20] Cf. Moltmann, *Hope,* 327: "Only when a meaningful horizon of expectation can be given articulate expression does man acquire the possibility and the freedom to expend himself, to objectify himself and to expose himself to the aim of the negative, without bewailing the accompanying risk and surrender of his free subjectivity. Only when the realization of life is, so to speak, caught up and held by a horizon of expectation, is realization . . . the gaining of life."

INDEX OF MODERN AUTHORS

INDEX OF ANCIENT SOURCES